YOUNG, TRIUMPHANT, AND BLACK

YOUNG, TRIUMPHANT, AND BLACK

OVERCOMING THE TYRANNY OF SEGREGATED MINDS IN DESEGREGATED SCHOOLS

EDITED BY

TAREK C. GRANTHAM, PH.D.,
MICHELLE FRAZIER TROTMAN SCOTT, PH.D.,
AND DEBORAH A. HARMON, PH.D.

PRUFROCK PRESS INC.
WACO, TEXAS

Library of Congress Cataloging-in-Publication Data

Young, triumphant, and Black : overcoming the tyranny of segregated minds in desegregated schools /
edited by Tarek C. Grantham, Michelle Frazier Trotman Scott, and Deborah A. Harmon.
    pages cm
  ISBN 978-1-61821-029-6 (pbk.)
  1. Gifted children--Education--United States. 2. African American students. 3. African Americans--
Education. 4. Segregation in education--United States. 5. Discrimination in education--United States.
6. Academic achievement--United States. I. Grantham, Tarek C.
  LC3993.9.Y693 2013
  371.829'96073--dc23
                                2013000763

Edited by Lacy Compton

Cover and layout design by Raquel Trevino

ISBN-13: 978-1-61821-029-6

Prufrock Press Inc.
P.O. Box 8813
Waco, TX 76714-8813
Phone: (800) 998-2208
Fax: (800) 240-0333
http://www.prufrock.com

TABLE OF CONTENTS

FOREWORD

I signed my first teaching contract in 1977, packed my compact car with my worldly possessions, and said a tearful goodbye to my family in Maine. I was to begin my career as a high school history teacher in a rural community in southeast Georgia, and I saw this opportunity as an exciting adventure. Though my new community with its tobacco fields, majestic pine trees, friendly people, and sweet tea was a much different place for me, I enjoyed my immersion in a culture that was so far removed from my New England background.

My new high school incorporated grades 9–12 with African American students representing one third of the student body. From the opening day of school, I began to learn so much from the young people in my classroom. I was eager to take on the challenge of delivering curriculum suited to the needs of my students. My teaching assignment included three different sections of U.S. history: remedial classes, classes for students on grade level, and one Advanced Placement course.

On that first day, I met my students in the classes designated for teenagers who struggled academically. I had been informed by my department chair to essentially plan on teaching reading skills in the context of history curriculum. As I introduced myself, I looked out at an overwhelming majority of Black students. Later that morning, I met the on-grade-level group and noticed an equal balance of Black and White students. I finished my day with the Advanced Placement group, and I left school that afternoon feeling troubled. I reflected on Tremayne, the only African American student in the Advanced Placement class. I could only wonder what he was thinking on that first day, and throughout the year, I often reflected on how he must be feeling as the only Black student in that setting.

Tremayne was an intellectual who viewed the world through logic. He excelled in mathematics. His penmanship appeared like calligraphy, and his paintings won art contests. He led the school's football team to a championship season and was elected student body president. Tremayne was a gifted student with true multipotentiality. I remain grateful for my experience working with this young man who had such a profound influence on me as a beginning teacher and my later decision to pursue a career in gifted education. My work with Tremayne and others like him also inspired me to pursue research studies examining the lived experiences of gifted young people from diverse backgrounds.

More than 30 years have passed since I looked out at those Black and White faces in my classroom and asked, "What's wrong with this picture?" As a beginning teacher, I realized there was a serious problem with the racial distribution of students in my classes, and I was convinced that there were other students like Tremayne who needed to be enrolled in AP history. Having grown up in Maine, I had virtually no exposure to African Americans. Both my high school and college experience had been devoid of Black students and courses in multicultural education were nonexistent during my undergraduate years. Regardless of my lack of exposure and experience with African Americans, I believed that what I saw happening in my high school was immoral.

I learned some important lessons as a beginning teacher working with Tremayne and many other Black students. I am forever indebted to these young people who taught me so much. Not having been formally trained in issues of diversity, I discovered success teaching Black students by treating them with respect, maintaining high expectations for all students, and listening to what they had to say. These three rather obvious components to my teaching approach translated as authenticity to my Black students. They realized that our backgrounds were worlds apart, yet they saw that I valued them, appreciated their remarkable potential, was sincerely interested in understanding their culture, and wanted to comprehend the challenges they faced in their school and community.

I continue to question the inequity occurring in racially divisive schools in this country; however, I am hopeful that the plight of gifted Black students will change because of dedicated scholars, educators, parents, and community leaders such as the authors featured in this text. As a novice teacher, I would have greatly benefitted from this significant anthology. Many teachers today are unable to address the needs of gifted Black students because they lack an understanding of their home and school experiences. They remain unmindful and often fail to question why students like Tremayne are not in gifted programs. Such thinking only perpetuates inequity.

To address this challenge, Tarek Grantham, Michelle Frazier Trotman Scott, and Deborah Harmon have brought together authors who share their thoughtful perspectives and highlight their own life experiences to assist readers in examining the challenges of gifted Black students in school. As you examine their contributions, you will appreciate that the authors honestly reveal the profound reality of the often complex lives that gifted Black students face. Moreover, the authors do so with respect for how these students persevered with support from their families and friends. As you delve into the chapters, you will naturally empathize with the compelling life stories of the young people featured. You will develop a better understanding of the significant factors that influence Black students' academic performance, as well as acquire an appreciation for how extended Black families foster resilience in their children. Moreover, you will be challenged and inspired to become proactive in your efforts to understand and address the needs of gifted Black students, their families, and their community. *Young, Triumphant, and Black: Overcoming the Tyranny of Segregated Minds in Desegregated Schools* will play a significant role in bringing about positive change in the school experiences of gifted and high-achieving Black students. Teachers and parents will benefit from this narrative collection, and university educators who include this text in their course readings can certainly plan on thought-provoking class discussions. As a result, gifted Black students whose lives follow that of Tremayne and mirror the experiences of those found within these pages will remain indebted to Tarek Grantham, Michelle Frazier Trotman Scott, and Deborah Harmon for their life-altering contribution.

Thomas P. Hébert, Ph.D.
Professor, Gifted and Talented Education
University of South Carolina

CHAPTER 1

INTRODUCTION

*by Tarek C. Grantham, Michelle Frazier Trotman Scott,
and Deborah A. Harmon*

There is no magic, either in mixed schools or in segregated
schools. A mixed school with poor and unsympathetic teachers,
with hostile public opinion, and no teaching of truth concerning black folk, is bad. A segregated school with ignorant place-
holders, inadequate equipment, poor salaries, and wretched
housing, is equally bad. Other things being equal, the mixed
school is the broader, more natural basis for the education of all
youth. It gives wider contacts; it inspires greater self-confidence;
and suppresses the inferiority complex. But other things seldom are equal. The Negro needs neither segregated schools nor
mixed schools. What he needs is *education.* —W. E. B. DuBois

Almost 80 years later, we see evidence of what DuBois predicted
in the educational experiences of Black students today. When Black
students enter into the classroom, they want and expect to be provided
with a meaningful education that is reflective of and responsive to their
interests, abilities, and culture. However, more often than not, gifted
and talented Black students' needs are not met because many educators do not know how to reach them and, as a result, overlook them
for consideration in advanced programs. Educators who maintain a
deficit mindset and fail to acknowledge and to nurture behaviors asso-

ciated with giftedness in Black students accept their absence in gifted and advanced programs. Inaction perpetuates inequity. Whether this is done deliberately or not, deficit thinking represents, in essence, segregated thinking, and having a segregated mind can be detrimental to all children.

What are the experiences of gifted Blacks in desegregated, predominantly White schools with teachers who do not look like them or understand who they are? How do gifted Black students survive and thrive in de facto segregated Black schools? What are the barriers faced by gifted Black students from predominantly Black neighborhoods that must be torn down? How do dedicated parents, culturally responsive teachers, and other culturally competent educators confront the racism and discrimination that impact gifted Black students? The stories presented in these chapters provide you with (a) windows and lenses to view the challenges of Black students in the classroom, (b) the opportunity to reflect on triumphant Black students' experiences, and (c) a guide for you to discuss and answer these important questions. By sharing the lived experiences of talented Blacks from different backgrounds, you are encouraged to think about your connections to Black students and their experiences. Compelling personal narratives and biographical accounts reveal the tyranny of segregated minds and the triumph of gifted Black students as they and their families confront desegregated racially divisive institutions. (Please note that some of the chapters use pseudonyms to protect the students' identities.)

The chapters within this book are intended to give you a glimpse into the lives of Black students who represent our children, sisters and brothers, fathers and mothers, cousins, aunts and uncles, nieces and nephews, and our friends. When reading these stories, we identified with many of the situations, circumstances, opportunities, and triumphs that these individuals faced, either because we have lived them or we have members in our family and network of friends and colleagues who have been there. The chapters are organized to allow you to think about an overarching issue or topic and to help you view the many different and complex dynamics that have occurred in the lives of the talented Black students featured. We purposefully have not included our commentary or research on the various topics discussed by the authors in our hopes that it will lead you, the reader, into thinking more deeply about what the individuals have faced and how their stories can be applied to others' struggles.

The chapters are divided into sections that include:

- ➤ **Section I: Access Delayed or Denied.** This section highlights three very different stories with one common theme: inequity. Many African American students who are gifted and talented remain unidentified or unnoticed in their schools because of inequitable attitudes, policies, or procedures and poor attempts to recruit or retain them in gifted and talented programs.
  - o In Chapter 2, you will meet Colby, a gifted dancer who entered a prestigious private school of performing arts and transformed from being denied access to major performance roles to becoming a school leader and advocate for Black students.
  - o In Chapter 3, you will connect with Jaimon Jones as he traces his educational journey and how being denied an official label in school did not dim his shine.
  - o Starting with her experiences as a student not identified for her school's gifted program, you will hear from Valija Rose in Chapter 4, who became a teacher and teacher-educator. Her K–12 experiences provided the foundation for the equity-based teaching practices she engaged to minimize Black students who were delayed access to gifted and advanced classes.

- ➤ **Section II: Black Males Overcoming.** Black males in gifted and advanced programs in predominantly White settings are an anomaly. These chapters offer insight into the dramatic ebb and flow of survival when you are one of a few Black males in advanced classes.
  - o A mentoring relationship with Malcolm to keep him motivated to stay in school is the focus of Chapter 5. By motivating Malcolm through e-mail, Skype, and other elec-

tronic forms of communication, Gilman Whiting helped him navigate real-life issues. Whiting reveals an intervening method with gifted Black males that proves useful when close proximity is not possible.

- In Chapter 6, the story of Alex, a smart young man who experiences tragedy and a slow recovery, highlights how a substantial amount of attention is critical to support Black males' transition between school levels and to help them cope with emotional challenges.

- In Chapter 7, Samuel Maddox highlights how he (and his mentee) navigated the fourth-grade failure syndrome, conceptualized as a phenomenon indicative of an education system that disenfranchises students by suppressing their critical thinking.

- In Chapter 8, Christopher Johnson shares his personal experience throughout his academic life to show that no matter the circumstances in private or public school, residence in Michigan or Florida, or matriculation in a 2-year or 4-year college, if you want something bad enough, you will make it happen.

- Counselors tell the story of Eric and David in Chapter 9. They give a glimpse into the nature of a sibling relationship that empowered two brothers to achieve academic success in spite of teachers who were resistant to help Eric and David's parents and in spite of an African American male teacher who struggled to maintain his professionalism.

➢ **Section III: Resilient Black Females.** These chapters bring forth the essence of the profound strength of gifted Black girls and Black women, many of whom face different social, emotional, and physical challenges that their male peers may not experience.

- Chapter 10 tells the story of a young, gifted Black girl who was grade-skipped. In this chapter, Ain A. Grooms talks about the lies she told and her struggle with being the

Black girl who came from the suburbs. Although lying was not a source of pride, it provided a personal hiding place for her to continue to excel against uninviting peers and classroom settings.

- Chapter 11 presents Tiffany, who lives in a predominantly Black community where the advanced classes include predominantly White students. Her struggles center around the outcomes of her sexual decision making. You will learn how she, her family, friends, and school personnel responded to help her move past disappointing herself and her family and toward meeting the academic demands in school.

- In Chapter 12, Shani Harmon, a Black girl who made it to the Ivy League, gives us a glimpse into her life from elementary school through college, and how she handled changes in her school setting along with interactions among her Black, minority, and White peers.

- In Chapter 13, counselors tell the story of Tianna, a gifted Black female who struggles with sibling and family responsibilities and has difficulty connecting with peers because of established cliques.

> **Section IV: Negotiating Multiple Identities: Ability, Race, Class, and Place.** Black people are not a monolithic group and not all students who are Black experience school in the same manner. This reality is discussed in these stories that encourage us to think of multiple layers of dynamics and challenges that can exist among Black students with differing abilities, racial and ethnic heritage, family income levels, and residence in America.

- Sheneka Williams, a product of small-town America, shows how she negotiated name-calling with the support of the "Goonies" in Chapter 14. Sheneka also tells of how she went on to become one out of six Black students in the "A" track in a rural southern school to earn a doctoral degree.

- In Chapter 15, Dawn, an excited young girl who loved school, shares how she faced a new reality in a school district's predominantly White magnet program that aided in its efforts to desegregate schools. As a result, Dawn, the little [Black] fish in the big [White] pond, struggled with her racial identity and experienced an emotionally dark period in middle school.
- In her home country of Ghana, Beryl excelled with confidence and was identified as a student to be grade-skipped. However, soon after matriculating in a predominantly White institution in rural Pennsylvania, her academic career began to take an unproductive turn. Chapter 16 tells the story of Beryl, an international student with limited experience in the American educational system, who struggled to find herself and good mentors to help her.
- In Chapter 17, Kiesa Harmon experiences the intersection of race, class, giftedness, and having a disability. Being twice-exceptional brings confusion from teachers who are unable to understand or accept its existence—especially in a Black student. Kiesa shares her struggles to form her own identity as she encounters discrimination from teachers, rejection from White peers, and colorism from Black females. With the support of her family, she successfully completed her journey.

- **Section V: Black Students in College.** Whether attending historically Black colleges and universities (HBCU) or predominantly White institutions (PWI), Black college students face unique experiences as they pursue their undergraduate and graduate degrees. The chapters in this section confront these issues as they tell the stories of six very different students.
  - In Chapter 18, Kordell, a college student who is enrolled in an elite honors program, shares his experiences being one of the only Black males in a predominantly White pro-

gram, defying a common perception about his hometown that "nobody gets out of Harper County."

- o Following the K–12 experiences of a Caribbean transfer student, we find in Chapter 19 that Karen's aspirations to pursue college are thwarted and misguided by unsupportive teachers and counselors. Although she questioned her ability, Karen was affirmed by her father's expectations that encouraged her to triumph in the face of self-doubt, poor academic advising experiences, and financial difficulty.
- o Chapter 20 follows four gifted Black male athletes as they face various stereotypes about their academic abilities in their collegiate experiences at predominantly White institutions.

- ➤ **Section VI: Village Perspectives on Gifted Black Children.** The six chapters in this section highlight the importance of family and the community of educators working together to support the achievement of Black students in gifted and advanced programs.
  - o In Chapter 21, Hezekiah's mother walks us through the highs and lows of schooling she experiences with a gifted, African American, high-energy son whose behavioral problems did not subside with multiple interventions. As conscientious parents who became comfortable with acknowledging their challenges with educating Hezekiah in school, his parents shared past behavioral information straightforwardly with school personnel in order to work more collaboratively with them and to achieve better outcomes for Hezekiah in school.
  - o In Chapter 22, Robin Vann Lynch, a mad mom, reflects on her mother's reaction to the ugliness that Robin experienced in school. A fired-up Mrs. Vann gave Robin the wisdom and courage to stand up for her own gifted daughter, Tracey, and other Black children in school. Armed with research and the resolve to advocate vigorously, this mad

mom helped Tracey eventually become identified for the gifted program and defied naysayers who were concerned about her ability to excel.

- In Chapter 23, an unwelcoming learning environment pushed a gifted 9-year-old to the brink of failure, compelling his mother to confront a Southern teacher's traditional ways of teaching. Deficit thinking created barriers for Brent and offended his mother, but a proactive mom helps us to understand what parents of gifted Black males may have to overcome to achieve social justice.

- In Chapter 24, Kristina Henry Collins, a teacher advocate, chronicles her encounters with Mrs. Langford and her son, a gifted Black male diagnosed with ADHD. In her account, the mother and son, Isaiah, must navigate a stakeholders meeting to decide on what to do about Isaiah's declining behavior. Through Mrs. Collins' lens, we are encouraged to understand that regardless of her background, Mrs. Langford is a parent who wants the best for her son and is trying her best at home.

- In Chapter 25, Sonja L. Fox recounts what it has been like being a parent of gifted siblings and the set of skills necessary for Black children to navigate educational systems and to survive in society from childhood to adulthood. This chapter includes snapshots of what it took to raise siblings with different academic, social, and emotional abilities and needs.

- In Chapter 26, Sabreen Jai reflects as a teacher on the knowledge she gained about characteristics of gifted children and how her increased awareness of giftedness influenced her ability to recognize it in her own child.

➤ **Section VII: Gifted Black Students' Perspectives on the Village.** The authors pay homage to key members of the village that inspired them to maximize their potential in school and to achieve academic and professional success.

- In Chapter 27, Shawn Adams, a musical phenomenon, talks about his experience growing up with music: singing, trumpeteering, and playing piano. His grandmother, mother, and a mentor surrounded Shawn, identifying and nurturing his gifts in music and helping him to excel.
- Living in Ark-La-Tex, TX, and being raised by educated Black parents who were teachers and preachers, Fred Bonner and his family were considered an upper middle class family. Chapter 28 reveals his success story and rejects stereotypes of unengaged Black families raising underachieving Black males. Solid relationships with his grandmother, mother, and father influenced Fred's positive attitude in school and his high academic self-esteem.
- In Chapter 29, Bantu Gross brings to light the significance of fatherhood in navigating school and life for a gifted Black male. Through Bantu's successes and failures in school, we see how his father's teachings and presence in his life helped to ground him and direct him toward a faith walk that would restore and renew his pursuit of academic achievement.
- In Chapter 30, Alonzo's story of growing up gifted in Iowa with his single mother is told by a counselor who followed him in school and home.

> **Section VIII: Pathways Uplifting Giftedness in Blacks.** The three chapters in the final section of the book look at how the authors utilized other pathways to success.
  - In Chapter 31, Cheryl Fields-Smith provides a biographical sketch of her daughter's journey as a gifted, Black student. Cherranda initiates a "test" of her White classmates and discovers something about herself. After this experience, Cherranda began to use poetry as a means of expressing herself and affirming her ideas. Samples of her poems are featured.

- In Chapter 32, J. Sean Callahan tells his story of how hip-hop provided the therapy he and his brother needed to exist among segregated minds in predominantly White schools. Hip-hop lyrics ministered to them by promoting individuality and self-awareness. This chapter sheds light on the power and promise for hip-hop and culturally responsive pedagogy to meet the needs of gifted Black male students.
- In Chapter 33, Eric M. Bridges gives a personal account of his experiences as a student in gifted and advanced programs during the 1970s. He attended public school in DeKalb County, GA, during the height of the desegregation program known as majority to minority student busing. At his predominantly African American high school, Eric had a progressively liberatory education that enabled him to achieve freedom and dignity.

SECTION I

ACCESS DELAYED OR DENIED

CHAPTER 2

EDUCATIONAL MALPRACTICE IN GIFTED AND FINE ARTS PROGRAMS

by Erinn Fears Floyd

BACKGROUND

Colby was born and raised in a small, rural southern town well known for its vital role as an important site in various stages of African American history. She was exposed to the rich history and culture of the town and the arts at an early age. By age 2, she was enrolled in formal, classical dance training. This is Colby's story.

LOOKING BACK

Privileged. That's what people say I am. I am a talented, intelligent, social butterfly, well liked by many. Schoolwork has always been a breeze for me. I was valedictorian of my eighth-grade Catholic school class. In elementary school, I often won community and school oral and writing competitions. I was asked to speak at programs for school, church, and special groups.

All of these accolades deemed me privileged, but someone must have forgotten to tell my Algebra I teacher. She must not know or care that I have something important to say or ask in this class of hers because she has ignored my hand. I have lost the feeling all the way down my arm because it has been in the air for what seems like an eternity! I have a question, but she will not recognize me . . . as privileged, as worthy, *at all*. And, I get the same disregard in dance class, although I am attending one of the top performing arts high schools in the nation, as a classical ballet major. My Black classmates and I are overlooked for major roles, get little to no attention in class, and are seldom praised for correct execution of choreography when compared to our White counterparts. If this is what privileged feels like, then I'd rather not be Black and privileged.

My name is Colby, and being accepted at this school made my family and elementary school teachers extremely proud of me. I went kicking and screaming because I was uprooted from the familiar (friends, hometown, family, and routine) to audition for the unknown. Attending this school meant moving to a strange city, living in a dormitory, and making new friends—some from foreign countries and others that were from places in the U.S. that were foreign to me. It also meant adjusting to a new schedule, school, teachers, and curriculum. It meant having to justify being there. It meant proving my worthiness to attend. It meant fitting in.

Of all of the observations I made during my initial time at this school, the one that stands out the most is that I am one of only a few African American students. Of those who auditioned with me in my specialty area (about 12), I am one of two students offered admission to the program. I later learned that the numbers aren't much better in the other departments (i.e., theater arts, creative writing, music, and visual arts). Getting admitted is next to impossible for students of color. Staying in is another story altogether.

I am one of countless African American students who feel trapped within their own identities; torn between being both proud and frustrated to be identified as gifted. For me, it seems that being gifted and talented is a double-edged sword that has been turned on me, threatening to slash my hopes and dreams of succeeding with the multitude of odds that I, and others like me, face.

ACADEMIC RIGOR

At my school, the typical day of instruction is, in fact, the equivalent of 2 days in one. Each student benefits from 6 hours or more of core academic instruction as required to earn a state high school diploma and at least 3 hours of performing arts instruction in a chosen specialty—creative writing, dance, mathematics and science, music, theatre arts, or visual arts. In my experience, it is often the academic rigor that halts matriculation of my fellow African American students as opposed to the rigor of the performing arts component.

PERFORMANCE RIGOR

At many performing arts high schools like mine, the traditional secondary curriculum is broken into segments where the academic courses and performance training within the performing arts specialty or "major" are offered during the regular course of a school day and the specialty courses are repeated after school. Like that of academics, the performance rigor is apparent, challenging, and expected. To this end, a typical school day may begin at 7:30 a.m. and not end until 7 p.m. Specialty area rehearsals last longer and are more demanding when a particular department hosts a concert or performance.

For my few friends and me, fitting into the "stereotypical" dancer's image and profile is not an easy task. Although not explicitly stated, this image is ingrained in the culture of traditional performing arts schools and the attention thereto or lack thereof causes teachers to single me out for some glaring "flaws" beyond my control such as physique (e.g., hips, thighs, legs) or some unconventional way of executing a classical ballet move.

The attention I receive is not kind, or flattering, but at least I am visible to the world-renowned instructors, who have performed on stages all over the globe in their day. I often leave dance class battered (pointe shoes are no friend of my toes) and emotionally bruised by my instructors. Imagine Debbie Allen's character from the television series *Fame* times 60. The difference between her character and me is that she knew that she had worked hard to excel and her efforts were not totally futile. But to me, if my algebra teacher paid me a fraction of the attention I received in dance class, I might just have a chance.

RACE RELATIONS

White privilege reared its ugly head early in my tenure at this wonderful school. While I was preparing to go into ballet class, a classmate called me the "N" word. I was mortified! But so was she when she realized what she'd done. That was the first and last time I was called that word to my face, and I'm not saying that my reaction was proper, but it solidified my stance on racial slurs and discrimination. It also let others know that racialized name-calling would not be tolerated. I made it clear that I was *not* having it! There have been several incidents like this, and my fellow students of color and I have been forced to deal with the attitudes of our White peers, whose behavior reeked of White privilege, elitism, and racism.

A warm and welcoming environment is often hard to come by for the Black students at my school. There are countless days when students of color are given the cold shoulder and treated as the "outsiders." But, because our survival is paramount, we often gather at mealtimes to provide a strong show of support for each other and to share the most recent events of the day or week. To us, we are all we have. Many of us attending the school are boarders living in the dormitory. We do not have the immediate presence and support of family, beyond a phone call. So these mealtimes empower us and help us face another day.

I often take note of the African American students who come to the school and remain only for a short time. I think how much it reminds me of a mill. They arrive, meet their fellow Black students, enter classes—academic and artistic—and before long, they are packing their suitcases or book bags because they have been expelled for failing grades or not "cutting it" within their department. There are so many tears and so little understanding about the "system." Students' lives are turned upside down, but it seems as if the school continues to look for its next cohort of tokens—not missing a beat.

RAISING AWARENESS

I feel compelled to make a difference—not just for me, but for my Black peers who are currently enrolled here, as well as those to come. One spring, when it became obvious that the needs and importance of the Black students took a backseat to those of the White students, I decided to speak up. It was clear that the traditional ballet performance was not choreographed for students of color, especially because it left us standing on the sidelines for long hours of rehearsal. I couldn't take it any more, so I finally spoke up! In response, the dance director allowed an assistant to choreograph a modern dance performance for the Black students. I used my voice again when the Black students were excluded from a program during one of the tours with the ballet company. Our costumes were not prepared in time for the show and in turn, our parents arranged meetings with school administrators to discuss the issues, including the issue of the annual ballet performance not including major roles for the Black students, even though they financially supported the gala. Needless to say, they now pay more attention to students of color, the costume fiasco has not reoccurred, and our concerns did not go unheard.

I continued to advocate for equity. When I shared the Black student dancers' disgust with the traditional practice of dancer selection for *The Nutcracker* ballet, a signature performance and significant fundraiser for the school, the dance director specially rechoreographed a famous scene in the ballet so the Black senior dancers could showcase their talent. This was extremely important because Black dancers were relegated to menial roles year after year because the selection as a premier or chorus dancer was rare for Black students. My stance set the precedent for changes within the department. The performance was a major success that elevated the esteem of the Black dancers and made a positive, lasting impression upon fellow White dancers and the audience at large. It was the first performance of its kind in the history of the school's ballet production.

Unrelated to the fine arts curriculum, when the students wanted to have a prom, like other "regular" high school students in the city, I spoke up. After speaking with school leaders, I was given permission, along with my classmates, to plan and sponsor a spring dance for the upperclassmen. Again, this set a precedent for my peers and me, and allowed us to make a change within the politics of the school that had a positive impact on our educational experiences.

Today, when I return to the school, I still look for signs of equity yet realized. The expectation of respect for individual and ethnic differences has now become a natural part of the curriculum and department protocol. I now see Black dancers taken into consideration, something that was long overdue. They are even being acknowledged and have the option of wearing flesh-colored tights and shoes.

I know my work is not yet complete and I will continue to fight against educational malpractice at my high school alma mater. I will still scan the halls, the photo walls, and the faculty for Black faces, and as long as there is such a place worthy of Black talent, I will continue to fight for Black students and encourage them to stand up for themselves, because they too, like me, finally realize that we are privileged and deserve to be there.

QUESTIONS FOR REFLECTION

1. What assumptions became apparent that many faculty at the performing arts school held regarding Black dancers?
2. How do you believe Colby handled herself at school? What might have been the reactions from her teachers, administrators, and friends?
3. Have you or minority students with gifts in performing arts experienced situations like Colby faced? In what ways was their experience similar to or different from Colby's?
4. How might Colby's situation appear in performing arts schools today in rural areas? Suburban areas? Urban areas?
5. What steps do special performing arts schools need to take to attract and retain talented Black artists?

THE OUTCOME

Colby has matured into a racially conscious educator who recognizes that the "fight" continues for today's students of color. Her adolescent wake-up call to issues of race ignited within her a zeal for empowering the voices and experiences of African American students. Colby's matriculation at the performing arts school made a significant impact on her personal and professional disposition regarding the intersection of race and place and created in her an unwavering conviction in the damage segregated minds pose to students. Today, as a wife and mother of young children, Colby struggles with overemphasizing race in discussions with them and fervently prays they grow up without replicating her powerfully painful introduction to its role in her life. She is thankful for her early life's lessons and for her mother, who was proactively conscious enough to ensure they were provided in an authentic setting.

CHAPTER 3

FINALLY GIFTED

by Jaimon Jones

BACKGROUND

I teach United States history in a rural high school. In our school, the student population is not very diverse, with 20% identified as African American, 70% as Caucasian, and 10% as Hispanic.

In my 6 years of teaching in this setting, I have worked with gifted students in my social studies classes. Teaching these students is a joyful experience; however, I have observed a critical problem. The underrepresentation of gifted Black males within my classes is overwhelming. In my years of teaching within this school district, I can count the number of Black males who have received gifted education services, totaling about three. Although the state of Georgia has adopted a multiple-criteria approach to identification in order to identify and serve more minority students, I have not seen an increase in the number of culturally diverse students receiving gifted education services at my high school. At the current time, there is not a single Black male enrolled in the gifted program. Ford and Grantham (2003) explored the issue of the underrepresentation of culturally diverse students in gifted programs. These scholars called for a change from deficit to dynamic thinking where negative views of culturally diverse students were replaced with high expectations for success. With this change in thinking, schools would expand their views on giftedness, use instruments that are culturally sensitive, identify and serve gifted underachievers, and develop stronger relationships with parents. These efforts would lead to more culturally diverse students being identified and served. As an African American educator of gifted students, I have a personal connection to this issue, and I share my story to help shed some light on the problems facing gifted Black males in schools.

My story takes place in Georgia public schools from 1992 to 2002. My father was in the military so my family moved often. Due to his assignments, we lived in Georgia before the change in Georgia's law for gifted identification took place and again, later, following the change in Georgia law. These are my experiences as a student.

MY STORY

SEPTEMBER 1992: SECOND GRADE

My family moved to Georgia in 1992 from Kansas. I was excited about my new school and I announced, "Mommy, you can make A's at this school. I am going to make all A's." Indeed, this new setting granted letter grades for students and not just a "satisfactory" or "unsatisfactory" report. When the first grading quarter ended, I proudly displayed my report card to my mother, "Look. I did it. I made all A's." I confidently tackled another grading period with the same results, "Wow. I can't believe I did this again!" I told my mother.

"Well, that's what happens when you want something and you try your best. Good job," she replied. Later that year, my teacher, Ms. Lott, announced that we were going to take a test. "Now this test is not like the normal tests we take. This is not for a grade but more to see how well you are learning. Make sure that you get a good night's sleep and just try your best."

That morning at breakfast, I told my mother, "We are going to take a test that tells us how smart we are. I am going to do great because I am really smart." We took the test and later received the scores. "Look, Mommy, I made a 99 on reading. And I made a 97 on verbal. What does that mean?"

"Well, son" she began to explain, "It means that you did a really good job and that I am proud of you." Though I performed well in the verbal sections of that state administered test, my math scores were not as high.

"Mrs. Jones, we need to meet with you about your son," a school official explained. "We are concerned about your son's math scores. The disparity between the verbal and math scores could indicate that he may have a learning disability. We would like to test him for special education."

Due to Georgia's law for gifted identification at that time, my high verbal scores did not warrant an investigation into my verbal abilities, and I was not identified. Under the old Georgia law for gifted identification, a single psychometric score determined gifted identification. Factors such as motivation, achievement, or creativity were not considered. With that being the rule, my strengths did not become the focus of the identification process.

DECEMBER 1994: FOURTH GRADE

Though I was not identified for the gifted or special education program, I continued to experience academic success. I finished second and third grade earning straight A's. In fourth grade, I was selected to be a peer tutor for a second-grade student. My teacher, Ms. Dasher, explained to me, "Jaimon, you are such a hard worker and make such good grades, we think that you would be an excellent choice to become a peer tutor." I was thrilled—I was finally recognized for my hard work in school, and I had the opportunity to help another student. That year, I also made a new best friend. John Bell was also a military kid who had just moved to Georgia from Texas. He moved in the house down the street, and we were in the same class, so we naturally played together on the weekends. Although we were friends, we also developed an academic rivalry. John was accustomed to being the smartest kid in his class and so was I. After all, I had been at the school for years making all A's. I had received the Principal's Award in both second and third grade, and now I was selected to be a peer tutor.

"They probably just picked me because I know the school," I tried to explain to my friend. "I'm sure that next year you'll get the same chance." Although I expressed words of sympathy, inside I was a little happy that I had one-upped my friend.

Later that year, I noticed that John was being pulled out of class. "Hey man, what's going on?" I asked.

"Just some test," he replied. A few weeks later, John returned from one of his visits and had the widest grin imaginable on his face.

"What are you so happy about?" I snorted.

"Well," he sheepishly replied, "I am now in the gifted program."

I couldn't believe it. How could this person who just moved into town and was not selected as a peer tutor be selected for this program? Filled with jealousy and anger, that night at the dinner table I blurted, "John can't possibly be smarter than me. I'm just as smart. Why am I not gifted too?" I could not understand. "You are just as smart and just as good," my mother remarked. Though she attempted to console me, inside I felt inadequate. My family had purchased a set of encyclopedias that I became determined to read. The set of encyclopedias came with an extra set about electricity. "How cool" I thought. "Now I'll be able to know about electricity too." I embarked on a mission to read more to learn more. "I just need to get smarter," I thought to myself. "Next time, I will be just as smart and then I can be gifted too," I thought as I turned the pages of the first volume.

OCTOBER 1999: FRESHMAN ALGEBRA CLASS

"Quiet down. This is a high school classroom," is what Mr. Mack would always say. But what can you expect when you have a class full of students playing Spades? Mr. Mack was in the later years of his teaching career and taught ninth-grade algebra and senior calculus. I was enrolled in his algebra class. Although he taught higher level math, he did not challenge us. Every day at the end of class, Mr. Mack would allow us to have free time. Some students slept, others gossiped, some used time efficiently, but I played Spades. "Come on around that corner and get your head bust!" was the lingo that I learned that year. New to the game of Spades, I needed a mentor, Alex Cash. "Play to win, play to win!" is what he would echo. My family had moved back to Georgia the previous year from Virginia. In eighth grade, gifted students were able to take algebra for high school credit, while others took prealgebra. "But he has already taken algebra at his old school," my mother told school officials.

"He needs to take this now so he can take geometry in ninth grade which will allow him to take the most difficult math courses. That is the gifted track," the school replied. Not fully knowing the placement tracks, my parents agreed with the school's decision. Not wanting to take a more difficult class, we all came to agree that the school knew what was best. As a result, I learned to play Spades, kept up with the latest school gossip, and knew I had a place to do last-minute homework. I was never strong in math, and this class did not help to build my confidence.

"Quiet down," Mr. Mack would bellow again. Uproar caused by funny jokes or winning hands would subside for a moment only to increase again as the king of spades was played over the queen.

"That's another win for us," I told Alex as it was time to move to second period. "See you tomorrow," he replied. "And bring your MP3 so we can have some tunes tomorrow."

FEBRUARY 2001: SOPHOMORE ENGLISH CLASS

A typical conversation overheard in my sophomore English class would sound like this:

Melissa: I bet Jaimon got an A *(she sarcastically whispered to Erin)*, you know that he's her favorite. Anytime we want extra time for an assignment or to work in groups, we get Jaimon to ask Ms. Bond.

Ms. Bond: *(A veteran English teacher with a reputation for being demanding who challenged our class to become better writers and more creative thinkers)* I want to push you to do more. I just know that you are more capable. I want you to take the literary elements from our story today and make a creative song or story.

Melissa: Here she goes again. Doesn't she know that we have lives outside of this class?

Although Ms. Bond did challenge us more than other teachers, it was fun. In that class, we often had the freedom to explore and express our ideas in ways that were different.

Ms. Bond: *(One day after class)* Jaimon, I think that you are one of the brightest students in the class. I would like to have you tested for gifted education services.

Jaimon: *(To myself)* You can't be gifted, you're just average, you'll only really let her know how much you don't know. *(My friends' comments resurfaced and made me feel bad, but I agreed.)* Well, what would I have to do?

Ms. Bond: *(Responding to my hesitation)* It will be fine. It will be you and me just talking about things.

That evening, I informed my parents about the conversation with Ms. Bond. "She says she wants to test me or something like that." To my surprise, my parents were already aware. "Ms. Bond called us yesterday to talk about it. She said that she was surprised that you have not been tested. She couldn't understand why you weren't in the program." Knowing that Ms. Bond had confidence in my abilities gave me reassurance. Over the next few days, she gave me a series of tests that seemed foreign. "Just do your best and put whatever comes to mind first." I did just that.

After about a month, Ms. Bond stopped me after class. "I have news to report. I took the results of your test to our school's gifted education coordinator and presented a case for you to enter the gifted program. I would like for you to take my gifted English class again next year." I was thrilled. I was finally in a gifted program, but what did that really mean? I began to think, "What would these new classes as a junior be like? Who would be in these classes? Would the work be too difficult? Would I still make A's?" Joy quickly turned to fear as I finished that school year.

MARCH 2002: SENIOR AP EUROPEAN HISTORY

"And as a Black person, Jaimon, how does that make you feel?" Seated in a classroom of 12 other students, I was thrown off guard by the question. As the only African American student in my Advanced Placement classes the past 2 years, this was the first time that I had been expected to give the Black perspective.

"I'm not quite sure," I quietly replied.

Once I was enrolled in the gifted program, things at school changed. My classmates changed from familiar faces to peers I had never had courses with before. Accustomed to being friends with my classmates, I found myself in isolation from class to class. The students in the gifted program had been together since middle school. I was new to their world, and few attempted to welcome me in. "So, how do you pronounce your name again?" was a common means to open a conversation. In class discussions, I would feel intimidated to speak in fear of being judged, a censor I had never experienced before. "I just don't know if I can do it," I would often express to my parents. "It's just too hard." Reminding me of the benefits of being in the program, my parents would offer reassurance as I closed my bedroom door for another long evening of studying.

QUESTIONS FOR REFLECTION

1. Are current measures to identify gifted students equitable?
2. What role can schools play in creating a more equitable environment for gifted education nominations to occur like in Jaimon's school experiences?
3. How can greater parental involvement impact policy and procedures in gifted education practice?

THE OUTCOME

Being identified as a gifted learner late in my school career had tremendous impacts. I was able to take multiple Advanced Placement courses and received college credit as a high school senior. Due to a rigorous high school schedule, I was able to enter the University of Georgia as a sophomore, which allowed me to take electives in political science, history, and social science education, where I found my passion for teaching. Although my experiences throughout elementary and middle school were not suited for the development of my gifts, I was still able to experience an enriched high school environment that has helped me pursue my goals today.

REFERENCE

Ford, D. Y., & Grantham, T. C. (2003). Providing access for gifted culturally diverse students. *Theory Into Practice, 42,* 216–225.

CHAPTER 4

"I KEEP ON KNOCKING, BUT THEY WON'T LET ME IN"

PERSONAL AND PROFESSIONAL INSIGHTS ON ACCESS TO ADVANCED PROGRAMS

by Valija C. Rose

BACKGROUND

I am the daughter of two academics. My mother holds a doctorate in social psychology, and my father holds a doctorate in American studies. Both of my parents are the product of segregated schools—graduating from high school before the *Brown v. Board of Education* decision. Education was at the core of my family's values and our very existence. Education was viewed as a vehicle for personal and community uplift. I was conscious, even at a young age, of my responsibility in that community uplift.

My early years were spent in Plainfield, NJ, a suburban community roughly equidistant from Newark and New Brunswick, where Rutgers University is located. In the summer of 1967, Plainfield, like Newark, had experienced race-based riots. Although Blacks comprised about one third of the Plainfield population, many Black residents felt economically and politically disenfranchised. A shifting economy, lack of political representation, and perceived police brutality against Black residents combined to create ripe conditions for uprising. I grew up in the wake of the Plainfield riots, during a period characterized by White flight and a decline in the quality of the public school system.

MY STORY

KNOCKING ON THE DOOR OF ACCESS: MY EXPERIENCE AS A STUDENT

After spending first grade in a parent cooperative school, my mother placed me in public school. Although I had just turned 7 years old, my mother argued that I was ready for third grade based on my IQ scores and performance in school. As a trained social psychologist and product of the segregated South, my mother was well aware of the low expectations many White teachers had for Black children. Her education and experience had produced a healthy bit of skepticism about the schooling her children would receive and the expectations her children's teachers would hold. My mother's response to that skepticism was to arm herself with undisputable information. Every few years my mother administered a Weschler Intelligence Scale for Children IQ test to my brother and me. That way, no schoolteacher or administrator could convince my mother that her children were average—our IQ scores showed otherwise. My mother was successful in her quest; I was placed in third grade.

The start of the school year moved along seemingly without a hitch until I came home one day to announce that I would be going to another teacher's class for reading. Of course my mother went to the school to question this decision. My teacher explained that because I was slightly below grade level in reading I should be placed in a top second-grade reading group. My mother maintained that if I could be placed in a top second-grade reading group, I could be placed in a bottom third-grade reading group. My mother was successful in her quest yet again. I was placed in the bottom third-grade reading group only to finish the school year in the top third-grade reading group and as the most improved reading student in the class.

Although my third-grade teacher was relatively benign and even supported my academic growth overall, her solution to my below-grade-level reading was to place me in a top second-grade reading group as opposed to a bottom third-grade reading group. Instead of pushing me to achieve beyond my current achievement level, she favored a lower track alternative. Had it not been for my mother's know-how and willingness to negotiate the educational system, who knows what the lasting impact would have been on my reading ability and my sense of self.

In fourth grade, I was tested for the school's gifted program. I specifically remember the art component of the test. I was an excellent mathematics student and a much-improved reading student, but I was a terrible artist. I was heartbroken when I was not selected to participate in the gifted program. Although my mother consoled me during my disappointment, she was much more concerned about me working hard, maintaining my performance in school, and my teachers treating me fairly than whether or not I participated in the gifted program.

I remained in public school through fourth grade, only to transfer back to the parent cooperative I previously attended sometime in the middle of fifth grade. For sixth through eighth grades, I attended an African liberation school in New Brunswick. Although I was never identified as gifted, I was fortunate to attend grassroots schools that subscribed to a philosophy of education that allowed students to move at their own pace. For me that meant taking math classes with my brother 4 years my senior. But more than the schools I attended, I was fortunate to have a mother who had the knowledge, fight, and resources to ensure that her children attended schools where we could be challenged and could excel. For high school, I tested and qualified for admission into a public math and science magnet school in Newark.

PROVIDING OPPORTUNITIES FOR STUDENTS LIKE ME: MY EXPERIENCE AS A TEACHER

The two early schooling experiences I have described are part of my personal story, but they are representative of the larger, collective story of many gifted and high-ability Black students. The first experience illustrates how a teacher's actions or inactions can either limit or enhance opportunities and outcomes for students. The second experience illustrates how a narrowly conceived school- or district-level gifted identification policy can serve as a barrier to access to gifted, honors, and advanced programs and coursework. These experiences shaped me as a teacher—they shaped my teaching philosophy and my interactions with and expectations for students.

Teacher expectations. Some of my most memorable teaching experiences occurred at Booker T. Washington High School, an urban, high-poverty, predominantly Black high school in Norfolk, VA, where the majority of students came from single-parent homes. When I first arrived at Booker T., Algebra II was the highest course offering I was scheduled to teach. I will never forget the principal's response when I asked why I was not scheduled to teach an honors or advanced course. He said, "Here, Algebra II is advanced." I came to Booker T. after having spent 5 years at a suburban high school in northern New Jersey. There I taught a range of courses, and I started the school's Advanced Placement Statistics program. So I was floored by the principal's statement, and I didn't know how to interpret it. Was it a matter of low expectations? Or was it something else?

Although Booker T. Washington High School offered advanced courses in math analysis and calculus, relatively few students enrolled. Algebra II was the highest-level mathematics course assessed annually on the statewide Standards of Learning (SOL) end-of-course test. At the end of my first year, approximately 40% of all Algebra II students passed the SOL test, an improvement over the previous year, but a pass rate some 35 percentage points below the school district's average. By the end of my second year, 83% of Booker T.'s Algebra II students passed the SOL, matching the district's average. That year, Algebra II teachers engaged in test blueprint analysis, team planning, shared best practices, common marking period assessments, and sustained after-school and Saturday help sessions.

The following year, I taught three sections of Algebra II—57 students—more than half of all Algebra II test-takers in the school. I set a personal goal that 100% of my Algebra II students would pass the SOL test. My department chair, colleagues, and students thought I was crazy! My Algebra II classes were heterogeneously mixed; they were not honors classes, although some of my students were identified gifted. I had ninth graders and 12th graders and students in between. My students wondered if they, individually and collectively, could meet my goal.

I knew my 100% goal was ambitious, but I felt my students could do it. I wanted my students to experience success beyond anything they had experienced before. I wanted them to believe that they were not defined by their life circumstances, because that is what I believed. The first part of my strategy that year was to arrange all of the classroom desks into groups of four, two desks facing two desks, but at an angle so all students could see the blackboard. My colleagues wondered whether my students could sit together in groups for an entire school year and remain focused and on task. The short answer was yes. The seating arrangement encouraged students to work collectively. Even though student-selected groups were very competitive, both within groups and between groups, I had established an expectation that students and groups would help each other. Students were accountable to and responsible for themselves *and* for each other.

In addition to students working collaboratively, other key components of my strategy that year included building on prior knowledge, making explicit connections from one concept to the next, daily practice/homework, and requiring that each student participate every day. Over the course of the school year, my students' confidence and belief in their abilities increased as performance increased. I convinced them that with hard work, persistence, and a team spirit, we could do it. My goal became my students' goal. My expectations became my students' expectations. When test day came, they were as excited as I was. My department chair commented, "You can always tell which students are Rosie's; they're as crazy as she is." Guess what? My classes had a 100% pass rate—every single student in my three classes passed the Algebra II SOL! The school's Algebra II SOL pass rate was 95% that year, some 8 percentage points above the district's average and 14 percentage points above the state's average. Many of my 12th graders went on to college the next year; many of my ninth through 11th graders went on to take advanced classes including math analysis, AP Calculus, and AP Statistics. As I reflect on my experience that year, I hope my students left my classroom with the sense that they could and should enroll in challenging and advanced courses—and that they could be successful there.

School- and district-level policy. Although Algebra II was the highest level course I taught when I started my tenure at Booker T. Washington High School, eventually I had the opportunity to teach AP Calculus and AP Statistics. At that time, AP Statistics was a relatively new course offering at the school with few students, and AP Calculus had been experiencing declining enrollments. Schoolwide, less than 10% of all students were enrolled in any AP course. Black students comprised 85% of the school population, but their representation in AP and honors courses was far less. Noting these low enrollments and underrepresentation among Black students, the school and district made concerted efforts to provide Black students greater access to honors, advanced, and AP courses.

Many of my AP students had never been exposed to a curriculum as demanding as Advanced Placement, and, in their previous experience, they had not been expected to work with as much precision and persistence as were required in those courses. As a result, the vast majority of my students struggled. Many students understood the big concepts of calculus but got lost when applying the algebra and geometry formulas necessary to arrive at the correct solution.

Some of my AP Calculus students met their struggle with frustration. On several occasions I had to encourage students to remain in the course, convincing them that the benefits of participating in Advancement Placement extended far beyond that school year.

Participating in AP reinforced the habits of mind and encouraged students to persist through complexity and ambiguity. In my opinion, AP was more than a passing grade on the AP exam and the potential college credit students could earn. In the 2 years I taught AP Calculus at Booker T., only one of my students received a passing grade of 3 on the AP exam, which did not qualify for college credit.

Despite what some might consider my failure and my school's and district's policy failure to create positive Advanced Placement outcomes for Black students, I viewed the experience as a success—and so did my students. Several students returned after enrolling in college to share how meaningful AP Calculus had been to them. Some students realized the benefit of AP Calculus in their college math courses; others realized the benefit in their college courses more generally. One student in particular, Steven (a pseudonym), enrolled in calculus his first semester of college. He explained how the concepts just "clicked" his second time around. I am not sure whether Steven would have experienced the same success in that first college calculus course had he not taken AP Calculus in high school. But more than just completing one semester of college calculus, Steven went on to major in engineering, earning a bachelor's degree from a reputable state institution. Today he is a practicing engineer.

QUESTIONS FOR REFLECTION

1. Specifically, in what ways can you serve as an advocate or resource for Black students as they attempt to gain access to advanced coursework and programs?

2. What is your local school or district policy on access to gifted, honors, and advanced programs and coursework? Is it equitable? Does it provide Black students an opportunity to participate? If not, how might the policy be changed to provide greater access?

THE OUTCOME

In 2005, I was named Booker T. Washington High School Teacher of the Year. That same year, I was also named Norfolk Public Schools High School Teacher of the Year. I went on to become a high school gifted resource teacher, providing curricular and instructional support to honors and Advanced Placement teachers at two Norfolk high schools. Although I now work in higher education, I have remained in contact with numerous students. My Algebra II students who had the 100% pass rate on the state assessment have had differential outcomes. Some never went to college, but are working locally. Several have completed their undergraduate degree. And some have completed their master's degree!

My mother continues to be a fighter. She recently celebrated 10 years as a heart transplant recipient! She runs a nonprofit women's organization she founded in 1983. She remains a major source of inspiration, support, and sanity.

RESOURCES

Borland, J. H. (2004). *Issues and practices in the identification and education of gifted students from under-represented groups* (RM04186). Storrs: The National Research Center on the Gifted and Talented, University of Connecticut. Retrieved from http://www.gifted.uconn.edu/nrcgt/reports/rm04186/rm04186.pdf

Costa, A. L., & Kallick, B. (n.d.) *Describing 16 habits of mind*. Retrieved from http://www.instituteforhabitsofmind.com/resources/pdf/16HOM.pdf

Ladson-Billings, G. (2009). *The dreamkeepers: Successful teachers of African American children*. San Francisco, CA: Jossey-Bass.

Lohman, D. F. (2005). *Identifying academically talented minority students* (RM05216). Storrs: The National Research Center on the Gifted and Talented, University of Connecticut. Retrieved from http://www.gifted.uconn.edu/nrcgt/reports/rm05216/rm05216.pdf

Morris, J. E. (2002). African American students and gifted education: The politics of race and culture. *Roeper Review, 24*, 59–62.

National Association for Gifted Children. (2010). *Redefining giftedness for a new century: Shifting the paradigm*. Retrieved from http://www.nagc.org/index.aspx?id=6404

SECTION II

BLACK MALES OVERCOMING

CHAPTER 5

E-MOTIVATING MALCOLM
ACADEMIC ACHIEVEMENT
VIA ELECTRONIC MEDIA

by Gilman W. Whiting

BACKGROUND

On many occasions, I have had the privilege and opportunity to meet highly intelligent and ambitious students. With certain ones, we hit it off immediately and my engagement appears to have an impact on the students. But over time, in the absence of in-person conversations and contact, the effect of a chance encounter wanes. Is it possible to have an ongoing impact on students' academic journeys over space and time? How do we aid them in making lifelong changes? How do we, as mentors and role models, make our presence felt over the obstacle of distance?

This chapter chronicles what has now become more than a year-long relationship. This relationship, due to distance, is one consisting primarily of e-mails and occasional telephone calls. Lately, we have engaged via Facebook and, beginning in 2012, we used Twitter. (Names, dates, and locations have been altered in this chapter to assure privacy.) Malcolm is a young Black male student-athlete who recently opted to attend a community college as a result of receiving grades below his potential.

Malcolm was tested as gifted in the second grade. School for him, using his words, was "not like work but fun . . . I believed anything was possible and nothing was impossible." For many reasons, several life factors, both at school and at home, would cause him to not only regress to the mean, but sink dangerously close to failing all together (Barton, 2003; Barton & Coley, 2009; Wilson, 2009). As a high school junior, he was demonstrating what teachers saw as unacceptable behavior: constant lateness, unpreparedness, talking too much, questioning authority figures—and he asked far too many "follow-up" questions. When asked what was meant by too many follow-up questions, he clarified,

> The teacher would explain something and I got it, really I got it, but almost daily friends around me did not. I would ask the teacher if what she meant was this or what she meant was that, you know, just so I wouldn't have to explain it all day or [be] ask[ed] to see my work on exams.

In effect, his repeated questions were his attempts to not become the unofficial conduit for the teacher and at the same time undercut academic dishonesty by other students while testing.

We met on October 20, 2010. I was speaking to a group of 30–40 predominantly Black, gifted high school students in the Northeast. A nationally recognized gifted and talented program had supported the lecture. During the presentation, there were a few students who asked appropriately thoughtful questions. I knew I had hit my mark when several of them wanted to talk to me one-on-one, and had even asked for my e-mail and cell number. One student clearly had a "Come to Jesus" moment, as the saying goes. He asked, "What is a successful man?" As a proponent of the Socratic method, I threw the question to the group to grapple with and provide what I like to call "an operational definition" (Bridgman, 1945). The discussion yielded several possible answers, but there was no consensus on a definition. I was then asked quite pointedly, "What do *you* think a successful man is?" I responded that each person has his or her own individual definition; we debated the terms of success for a professor, doctor, athlete, and even a drug dealer. We ran out of time. But I knew that this would not be the last time that I would hear from this young man. The following sections contain e-mails from Malcolm.

THE STORY

SENT: OCTOBER 21 20:41
SUBJECT: MOTIVATION AND SUCCESS

Hello Dr. Whiting. My name is Malcolm. I was a student that came to visit you at Gifted U. on Wednesday 10/20. I know you get a lot of e-mails and I don't want to waste too much time but I just had a few things I wanted to say, I was the student who asked you what you considered a successful man. Dr. Whiting I'm a senior at JP high school and my parents have already given up on me. The word potential has been thrown around me like a football for years. I have been in accelerated programs and advance placement classes all my life, and in my opinion the aptitude is there, I understand the work. Not once in my school career have I felt like that was the right path. With all the potential I was marked with came an overwhelming amount of pressure.

From the day in second grade when I finished my advance placement test first and was told to sit down because there is no way I would be done. I scored in the 98%. To my ninth-grade seminar class where I was told I could not be a CEO on average because of my race. To even a year later where my first month of a new school I was searched for drugs, when I have never touched an alcoholic bottle or a weed at that point in my life.

I'm now in lower level classes and getting very average to below average grades. I probably can get into a good college with my athletics and SAT (over 1300) scores and could even get through it. But to be honest I don't know why I would when I don't know what my goal is in life. I don't know what it means to be successful. So I ask again what do you feel a successful man is?

SENT: OCTOBER 22 6:23
SUBJECT: MOTIVATION AND SUCCESS

Dear Brother Malcolm,

I was not attempting to be creative when I gave you that answer. I was being quite honest. To be real, it does not matter what I think is successful, it's what each of us, as individuals, thinks about quantifies or qualifies as successful. Many would call me successful, and I would agree. But in my heart, I know I have not lived up to all that I could be or do. So I am not happy with the opportunities I let slide by, the time I let get away. I feel success is the internal motivational need to drive forward and not settle for being told you can't be the CEO of a Fortune 500 company. That drive needs to be internal, at this point in life it can't be to impress your friends, your girl, or even your parents, but you. Now back to the CEO thing—let's be real, you must acknowledge statistics and that may be what your teacher meant. It sounds very much like what another Malcolm was told by his teacher when he said he wanted to be a lawyer. His teacher told him that "being a lawyer was no job for a n***er, that he should consider being a carpenter, that Jesus was a carpenter." That of course was a racist attitude of the time. But after many trials and tribulations, Malcolm X would go on to be considered one of the most intelligent men in history. You see man many of us . . . do not reach our full potential.

So, the question is, what do you do to motivate yourself to become more successful? Because you see, to me you already have demonstrated potential for greater success by writing me. Yes I get a lot of e-mails and no you're not taking up my time. Know this—if I can travel a short distance with YOU on YOUR journey and help YOU decide YOUR best options, then YOU make ME more successful.

So, just because you wrote this e-mail I will try to get to see you again at your school next week, probably Thursday. Let me know if this works for you. I haven't given up on you and I never will, so keep your head high and rise above the BS. There are more folks out there that expect you to fail than succeed, don't let THEM be your advisers . . .

Peace

NEXT THURSDAY

While visiting JP High, I was escorted around the school by one of the greatest teachers I had met in a long time (Ms. C.). We discussed as much as possible—from the subtle to the obvious problems in education in general, her school building, the gifted and talented (GT) and Advanced Placement (AP) programs, as well as the individuals we were both there to guide and motivate that day. I was met by smiles, finger pointing, and daps (hand shakes) by those who had traveled to Gifted U. I asked one of the young men, Geoffrey, what the finger pointing was about. He replied,

> I was happy to see you. I told a few of my boys about you. I had a chance to think about what you said and realized that if I had a Black teacher like you up in here . . . I was just surprised to see you. How long you here for?

This is the tough part of the job—not being able to stay and help these young gifted students feel okay about being awkward as they try to figure out and tap into that internal motivation to succeed.

We found Malcolm in detention. He sat working at a computer cubicle with his back to me. I had already been briefed on *why* he was in detention. The room monitor was a Black woman, a computer science teacher, who had both praise and confusion about Malcolm. She informed me quite simply that he is a "smart kid, almost a genius," and that she could not understand why he was in detention so frequently. She joked that his presence in detention was like another subject for him, but that at very least, he could catch up on his work because he spent a lot of time with athletics.

When he heard the voices and laughter, Malcolm looked up from his computer and turned. He gave me a sheepish smile. It was a smile with which I was all too familiar. I had given it to my father on countless occasions, just before he was about to take me to task for something I should *not* have done. Malcolm and I took a walk and talked. He showed me around his school. He clearly had mixed but mostly positive emotions and thoughts about the school. What motivated him was knowing that his peers and the faculty recognized him for the trophies in the school display cases. I figured it was time to ask the hard questions about his detention; why had he come so close to suspension? If his grades and tardiness did not improve, I knew he would be kicked off the football team. And he was so looking forward to the big games and the colleges coming to see him.

After a few minutes of posturing about how easy the work was and the low expectations teachers had of him (all of which was contradictory to what I had seen in at least three teachers—a Black woman and two White women), I said matter-of-factly: "I was told you are in detention because you're often late 4 out of 5 days of the week. How do your teachers make you late every morning? They don't live with you, do they?"

He related that, for the past 3 years, he chose to travel from another part of the city to attend this high school. He chose to attend this school not because it had such an outstanding athletic program—in fact, the school he wanted to get away from held top honors in basketball, football, and track and field.

His parents had divorced, and he was not only mentally torn due to the split, but was also physically torn. He now lived between two, sometimes three homes. He had attended JP for a year prior to the divorce. His new residential address when living with his mother required him to attend another school in a different part of the city. He actually lived on the border between two districts, and was able to take part in his school of choice, but the school in closest proximity had a much poorer retention and graduation rate. At this same school, he immediately ran into issues of random and unwarranted drug searches; he was locked out of school because of tardiness and locked in school because of the surrounding neighborhood. Daily, he feared for his personal safety. He decided to return to JP by using his father's address as the home of record. Occasionally, he would sleep at a relative's home that lived closer to JP, but oftentimes Malcolm was traveling 8–10 miles each morning to get to school. One of the requirements of choosing his school was that his family had to provide transportation. However, consistent transportation was not available to Malcolm. Subsequently, there was only one day a week that he could arrive late with no chance of repercussion—the day he had study hall as his first period.

I asked why he didn't alert someone about his dilemma. He responded in earnest, "I don't know if I can truly trust telling anyone, because they may make me leave and go back to that other school, and I'd rather drop out than go there."

Malcolm, like many Black males, does not trust that the "system" would work in his favor, or on his behalf. There are too many reminders that reinforce this distrust. Images and messages daily communicated through mass media not only affect the way "others" see young Black males, but they also have an effect on the Black males' psyche and view of self.

After my visit, I received this message from Malcolm.

SENT: OCTOBER 30 11:58
SUBJECT: RE: YOUR FUTURE IS BRIGHT

Dr. Whiting

I appreciate so much that you came in and visited me at the school Thursday. I had not read your return e-mail so it was more than a shock. I am sorry you had to see me in there, but I think it was good because you gave me some good ideas on how to handle many things. Yesterday, my football team and I were handed our second loss of the season and pushed out of the playoffs. It hurt in so many ways, because I can honestly say I have never worked harder at anything than this craft and team. It made me just think of the definition of success again. Because I was motivated and I worked so hard is not obtaining the goal okay?

Also as you advised I talked to my football coach about my situation with the traveling, And he organized it so I have privileges first period both days so I can come in anytime before 9:10 and go to his room so I thank you again.

I do want to stay in contact with you too, there has been many Black strong male figures in my life and I have never once took the opportunity to learn from them. I don't plan on wasting this one. E-mail me anytime.

SENT: OCTOBER 30 7:34
SUBJECT: FUTURE ORIENTATION—WHAT IF?

Malcolm,

Thank you. Sometimes, even when we plan and prepare we don't get what we want. Like the football victory, like our parents staying together or even showing us what grown ups are suppose to act like. But the wise man learns from all situations, both victories and defeats. You need to continue to learn from those difficult defeats and still make the right choice. I would like you to imagine a life without sports. What would you do if this is your final year of football? What is your next step?

I am here.

Motivating a student to do something he or she does not want to do, or be better at, is difficult enough, but maintaining motivation, especially when that student is faced with difficult decisions and even fewer options, requires that the student be quite self-aware.

Malcolm disappeared for several weeks. No contact. I sensed something was wrong. As his e-mentor-at-a-distance, the adult responsible for providing some measure of external motivation, I felt it was incumbent upon me to check in regularly, even when confronted with his occasional nonresponsiveness. I set a date to call or write in my smartphone. I synced it with all of my computers because I remembered what he wrote:

> I do want to stay in contact with you too, there has been many Black strong male figures in my life and I have never once took the opportunity to learn from them. I don't plan on wasting this one. E-mail me anytime.

He had chosen those words. They were not to inflate my ego, but a call for help, a desire for change. He had asked me to assist with this change. From the day I met him, he wanted help in moving the proverbial needle in the right direction. Finally, I received a reply.

> Hey Dr. Whiting,
>
> I hope you had a great thanksgiving, i had a very nice day to reflect and be thankful sorry i took so long to respond i have been stress[ed] to my end with football and its coincidental you ask me about it being my last year. well today I looked at my GPA and SAT scores in my first real attempt to really look into college and it is a lot worse than i thought, I went from a 4.0 to presently i have a 1.7 GPA and all the state school i wanted to go to have a minimum of 2.0. my SATs may save

me. i also found out my girlfriend is pregnant and the magnitude of everything is just to much for me right now. I feel down and out, trapped, unsuccessful and most definitely no longer motivated. Any advice would be much appreciated.

Motivation and mentoring often does not arrive in a nicely wrapped package. Sometimes, there is no packaging at all—just the raw truth. A motivational mentor cannot choose the subject or situation for which they are called to address. This was a moment that could change many lives. What wisdoms do we impart at moments like these? What is best for me may not be best for him. I called Malcolm so we could talk. An e-mail was not appropriate on this occasion.

MALCOLM RISING, FALLING, AND RISING AGAIN

SENT: JANUARY 02 21:54

Me and my friend's choice was to abort the pregnancy . . . but lessons have been learned. i had a certain cockiness about all of this when i look back but it is gone. Unfortunately, my grades can not be fixed as easy. i talked to my guidance counselor about the possibilities. If i can maintain an accumulated "a" average for the next three quarters ill have a 2.3. which is now an obvious goal but sounds very hard. also several school I've looked into offer a summer program for kids who have 1000 on the SATs or better, so with my 1425 there is option which lets me breathe a little easier.

Another follow-up telephone conversation with Malcolm revealed that the once energetic, motivated, young male was now despondent, despairing, discouraged, and unmotivated. He had not only begun to doubt his future, but his self-efficacy, his sense of purposefulness and "stick-to-it-ness," seemed to be collapsing. But Malcolm graduated. He opted for a community college in order to test the academic waters before jumping in feet first at a 4-year institution. He clearly had the potential to pursue the latter option, but he was now treading water, unmoored from his early self-confidence. He had, though, taken the next steps toward reclaiming a more robust academic future. I reached out to Malcolm again when I began writing this essay.

SENT: OCTOBER 8 8:12

Dear Malcolm,

I hope this e-mail finds you in great health. I was just thinking about you because I am writing this article on gifted Black males in the K–12 system. I thought about meeting you and all the issues you were facing. I know how I had to deal with everything from popularity to pregnancy, but now I am writing about motivation. What motivates us to keep going? To get through the BS and keep focus, even when we slip up a bit or a lot we find a way. When people make us feel we are only there because we are fast, have good hands, and a nice jumper. What's your motivation? What's your story?

I don't want to have to find you again, we supposed to be boyz and what not. I need to know how you're doing. I told you I would be there, but it is a two-way street.

Peace GwW

SENT: SUNDAY, OCTOBER 9 14:01

Hi Dr. Whiting

It is good to hear from you.

To be honest, it still makes me chuckle, hearing that question, because it is such a new emotion in my life. "What's my motivation" is my curiosity of life questions through life's answers. I have always been good at introspection, asking myself questions trying to find answers. To be honest all I ever knew was that I wanted to be happy. I wanted to have a life that I enjoyed, a family I loved, and a house that was truly mine; a simple dream but always mine.

What may help motivate other kids is to have them ask themselves and others: "What motivates them?" Also don't allow them to be satisfied with the dream but with the reality of their dreams. I'm in the process of writing my thoughts down in hopes of finding my own answers that I crave.

I read a quote on Facebook that really changed my life. "True Freedom is not freedom from responsibility or effort"

It's always pleasure communicating with you.

We are boys, always will be.

Malcolm

QUESTIONS FOR REFLECTION

1. What role, if any can you, the reader, play in keeping gifted Black students like Malcolm engaged?
2. How can you establish rapport using electronic media or electronic systems of communication with students from racial, economic, and cultural backgrounds different from your own?
3. How can you provide assistance or create a cadre of mentors for students like Malcolm?

THE OUTCOME

This work we do is evolving and ongoing, and far from final. Therefore, the outcomes change from student to student, context to context, and year to year. Malcolm, as with many of those I mentor from a distance is grappling with the complex meanings of manhood and masculinity and how they impact his life. His struggles for independence often lead to choices that have negative rather than positive consequences. Until Malcolm truly takes to heart and recommits daily to the principles of the Scholar Identify Model, his trajectory will follow a "ready, fire, aim" scenario—that is, a life outlook that lacks "future orientation," prior planning, and consistent focus in achieving goals (Whiting, 2006).

He is still playing sports and has one semester to complete his associate's degree; we have been contemplating next steps—work or more school. Although I understand the need for Malcolm, as a young Black man to earn money, as well as the real fear of financial burden and long-term loans, I must still attempt to motivate him, even if only via tweets, Facebook, and texts, to continue on the same path he took as a high school junior and senior. Doing otherwise is not an option. In the end, the payoff, what he will be able to earn in the future, will be much greater.

Finally, and most importantly, in my work, I will be a part of many young students' lives; they will all reach various milestones on their journeys, hence I hesitate to call these markers outcomes, as if the journey is complete. As one young mentee says, "You have been a person I can call on and I feel responsible to but in a different way and that has made the difference ever since, Thanks . . ." Malcolm has expressed this same sentiment. The journey is over when one's life is over. We can then evaluate those life outcomes, milestones, or highlights in the traditional sense: graduations, college enrollment, academic performance, test scores, career choice(s), family situation, contributions to the lives of others, and so much more.

REFERENCES

Barton, P. (2003). *Parsing the achievement gap: Baseline for tracking progress.* Princeton, NJ: Educational Testing Service.

Barton, P., & Coley, R. J. (2009). *Parsing the achievement gap II.* Princeton, NJ: Educational Testing Service.

Bridgman, P. W. (1945). Some general principles of operational analysis. *Psychological Review, 53,* 246–249.

Whiting, G. (2006). Enhancing culturally diverse males' scholar identity: Suggestions for educators of gifted students. *Gifted Child Today, 29*(3), 46–50.

Wilson, W. J. (2009). *More than just race: Being Black and poor in the inner city.* New York, NY: W. W. Norton.

CHAPTER 6

SEGREGATED AT THE GATEWAY TO HIGHER EDUCATION

ALEX BEFORE AND AFTER HIGH SCHOOL

by Angie C. Roberts-Dixon

BACKGROUND

Alex is currently a 22-year-old African American male who lives and works in a small city in the Southern part of the United States. There is a wide discrepancy between various members of the community, some of whom live middle class and upper middle class lives. However, a third of the population suffers social and economic disadvantage. This sector is made up mostly of African American people who are only one or two generations removed from the experiences of segregation and continue to face lingering effects of that era.

I met and knew Alex well as a member of that community, as he was involved in one of the mentorship programs in which I participated as mentor. He always seemed to be a bit of a precocious child, slightly opinionated, and questioning established social mores. I acutely remember meeting him at a community center when he was 7 years old. After greeting his mother who stood nearby, I looked at him and said, "Hello. You're looking very handsome today. What's your name?" Without skipping a beat, he looked at me, and with a challenging tone, said, "What's *your* name?"

As time went by, and Alex and I developed a mentoring relationship, Alex became like a little brother to me. When I moved away from the area, I kept in touch with him, and felt privileged to drive more than 9 hours to attend his high school graduation. It was one of the proudest moments of my mentorship experience. I felt as if I had done very little to help him get to where he was, but I was deeply moved by his tenacity and the fact that he had defied the odds by graduating from high school and being accepted at a prestigious institution of higher education. Despite his acceptance, Alex ultimately decided not to attend college at that time. His last correspondence to me took place 2 years after he graduated from high school. In his letter he wrote, "Just in case you're wondering what's going on with me, I'm going to University in January. I had to sort out some things and start living life for me. I know now that you learn from every experience in life." I wrote back to him, but never received another letter or phone call.

As you read, you will find that things have not yet gone according to Alex's aspirations. Reasons for this continue to plague my mind and resurfaced when I considered writing this piece. I have tried to get in touch with Alex. I have called his home and cell phone. After initial contact and after sharing my desire to talk to him, I made several phone appointments with him, but to no avail. At each attempt, he was either unavailable or would not return any of my calls. Eventually, his mother, Ms. Dawes, became frustrated by Alex's disregard of my messages and took it upon herself to call me back and offer her assistance. Some of the information in this piece comes from a phone interview that was conducted with her. The rest of the information comes from my personal recollection of Alex's experiences during the years that I spent in our close mentoring relationship.

ALEX'S STORY

Alex was identified as a gifted student at the age of 8, when he was a student in the fourth grade. Although Alex was attending elementary school in one of the smaller cities in the South, his mother had been fighting for years to have him assessed for the gifted program. Ms. Dawes noticed that teachers were resistant to this suggestion. Perhaps because of her personal experiences in the system, Ms. Dawes felt that the teachers' resistance was because of their doubts that Alex would be successful in the program. She had noticed Alex's increasing boredom in school and the increasing number of teacher reports stating Alex was a bright student, but he seemed to be falling short of his potential because of behavioral issues.

HOME AND COMMUNITY REALITIES

Ms. Dawes was wary of the educational system in which her children were enrolled. She herself was a product of that system, growing up in the era in which blatant segregation made the unequal distribution of resources an obvious slight to Black students. Ms. Dawes completed high school, but had not gone on to pursue higher education. Shortly after graduating, she had her first child, followed by another within a few years; Alex was the last of the three children.

Because of her own experiences, Ms. Dawes was aware that there were some who would look at Alex as a poor, Black child growing up in the projects, and not as a child who was bright and possessed a curious nature. She also knew that people would be more likely to look at Alex's outspoken temperament and lack of resources and would doubt his potential. However, she was aware of Alex's love of books and learning, the inquisitive nature that he manifested when examining new material, and his relentless pursuit of the things that he considered to be important.

Alex grew up in a predominantly Black community in which the expectations for academic achievement were poor. Within the community, approximately 66% of students did not graduate with a high school diploma. A sizeable percentage of the students who attended their high school graduations received a "certificate of attendance" symbolizing that they had attended their high school classes but were not able to pass the required classes or exams to obtain a diploma. Unemployment in the community far surpassed the rates in the rest of the city, and there were very few role models who held jobs that required a high school or college diploma.

As a member of this community, Alex appeared to be very similar to the other children. He dressed as they did, talked as they did, played games and sports with boys in the community, and had many of the same interests. However, in some very important ways, he appeared to be different as well. He spent less time outside during his free time and spent a considerable amount of time reading books in order to find the answers to questions that were of interest to him. With great pride, Ms. Dawes reported that she had read to Alex while he was still in the womb, and that she believed that this was a key part of why he was so drawn to books. By the time Alex had begun kindergarten, he was reading independently.

Alex's older siblings, Judy and David, finished high school, but neither of them went on to college. Alex's eldest sibling, Judy, was 5 years older than he, and maintained high grades until she began high school. At that time, her choice of peers and complications with chronic childhood diabetes caused her to lose interest in her academic pursuits. Alex's brother, David, was older than Alex by 2 years and had behavioral and academic challenges. David often appeared angry and impulsive and tended to be aggressive toward his peers and his siblings.

SYSTEMS OF SUPPORT AND SYSTEMS OF DOUBT

Growing up, Alex experienced several protective factors. In addition to having a mother who believed in his abilities, he also had the benefit of belonging to a religious community that supported his academic and social growth through extracurricular church-sponsored activities.

He was mentored by young adults who had graduated from college and were engaged in various professions. In addition, older members of the church community helped to teach Alex important morals and values. Alex stood out and was considered successful especially because he followed the guidance that he was given.

As early as the age of 7, it became evident that Alex had interests that were different from his same-age peers. Because of the family's heavy involvement in church activities, people in the community labeled the family as "stuck up," and believed that Ms. Dawes was too strict and thought her children were better than other children. Such labels pushed Alex and his siblings to see themselves as different from others in the community and caused them to keep a low profile. However, resisting negative influences paid off and Alex eventually qualified for the gifted education program during his elementary school years.

At first, Alex enjoyed the challenge of the gifted education program. When asked, the assistant principal described him as an "above and beyond" student. Although he was only one of two Black students in the gifted program at his predominantly White elementary school, Alex felt that he was finally with peers who were also invested in their educational achievement and had similar long-term goals. Alex's enrollment in the gifted education program necessitated his move to a school outside his neighborhood. Because of this, he began to encounter negative interactions from his neighborhood peers. Alex had the gift of a gregarious and "down to earth" personality, which led to him being accepted by many of his peers. However, he was bullied by those who were not his close friends. He was often called "bookworm" and "punk" and was physically assaulted on two occasions. Alex ignored the comments and was amazingly resilient. However, when he began to receive what he perceived as discrimination from his teachers, he became overwhelmed.

GIFTED EDUCATION EXPERIENCES

By the end of his first year in the gifted education program, Alex told his mother and mentors that he no longer wanted to participate in the program. "It's just too hard," he shared. "Teachers ignore me and don't listen to what I have to say. I'm always getting into trouble for things that I did not do, and I'm just tired of it."

Ms. Dawes appeared to support her son's decision or at least did not resist Alex's desire to exit the program. However, Alex ultimately changed his mind when he realized that leaving would mean that he would have to return to classes where he was not going to be academically challenged. Unfortunately, the bullying pressure from his peers became more intense while he was in middle school. During this phase of his schooling, he missed a significant number of days at school as a means to avoid being bullied because of a perception of being different. His absences were met without resistance from his mother, who sympathized with the social pressures that Alex experienced.

During his high school years, Alex continued to do well in school and it was clear that his peers, despite their earlier jealousies, saw him as a leader. Alex's fine leadership skills led to his being elected as class vice president during his junior year. By his senior year, he had joined several clubs and was chosen to be president of the pre-med club. This kept him on target to reach his long-term goal of becoming a surgeon.

Being elected to such an important role as class vice president meant that not only would Alex be expected to represent the class at important events such as graduation, but he would also be responsible for being a liaison between class members and school administrators. In this position, Alex was respected, but he had experiences that suggested that his outspoken and articulate demeanor may have made it more difficult for him to be positively received by administrators and teachers. Throughout his life, Alex always had to defend himself both verbally and nonverbally. However, advocating for his classmates before professional adults presented him with new challenges.

An issue for which Alex fought most eagerly was one in which the school administration issued a ruling that restricted girls from wearing clothes that administrators perceived as accentuating their figures. However, this restriction was only given to Black girls and not to girls of other racial groups. When Alex approached the administration about this discrimination, the principal responded by curtailing Alex's responsibilities in the school and then later threatening to withhold his diploma in an effort to silence him.

For Alex, this was the last straw in a long chain of resistance to his academic and personal successes over the years. Although he continued to maintain his solid class standing, Alex lost a great deal of personal drive as he fought the battle to gain the respect of school officials. He continued filling out applications for college and for scholarships, but by the end of his senior year, he admitted that he was "tired."

On the day of his graduation, Alex delivered the class address, and was among the top 10 graduating students. The mistress of ceremonies announced that Alex would be attending a prestigious university in the South, to which he had received a scholarship. However, Alex was actually more inclined toward a less prestigious school where his close friends would also be enrolling. According to Alex, he just wanted to be with his friends and not where he would continue to feel isolated.

LIFE AFTER HIGH SCHOOL

An important aspect of maintaining the resilience of gifted students is their cultivation of friendships with those who have similar goals. Alex had a close friend by the name of Drew. He had also grown up in a similar community within their small city and had similarly high aspirations. Tragedy struck when, a month after graduation, Drew drowned while swimming with a group of his friends.

This tragic occurrence appeared to throw Alex into great confusion. He spent hours watching television, often late into the night. Long after everyone else had fallen asleep, Ms. Dawes would find Alex watching movies that he and Drew had enjoyed. As Alex struggled to cope with the loss of his friend, the fall semester came and went, and he forfeited enrolling in college. During the fall following his high school graduation, Alex continued to work at a local convenience store where he had been employed as a high student. After a year of working, Alex enrolled in the Navy. However, that experience was short lived.

While in basic training, Alex experienced a swimming accident in which he was pushed into a pool and hit his head on the bottom of the pool. Following this incident, Alex was admitted to the Navy medical facility and after several weeks of strong advocacy on Ms. Dawes' part, Alex was discharged and returned home to live with his mother in the community where he grew up. Alex later reported that he felt like he was treated like "state property" and that his treatment in the military was harsher than expected. He soon returned to working at the local convenience store, and more than 2 years after being discharged from the military, he is still an employee there. He has since bought his own car and although he still lives with his mother, he considers himself to be financially independent and helps with the financial needs of his nephew, who was born shortly after Alex was discharged from the military.

For a short time, Alex enrolled in a local nursing program, but found it dissatisfying, and quit within months of beginning. When asked what his goals are for the future, Alex candidly states that he is "trying to figure that out" and has been known to repeatedly say that he feels that he has "not done anything with [his] life."

QUESTIONS FOR REFLECTION

1. How do we increase or modify the protective factors around Black students during the critical transition between high school and college?

2. How can educators assist Black students in making the transition to higher education around issues of self-preservation and developing a college student identity?

3. In what ways might programs in higher education, faculty, and administrators connect with the home systems of support (e.g., family and churches) to increase retention of Black males in college?

4. Should there be university reclamation policies and strategies in place to attract gifted Black students to reenroll and complete their degrees? Elaborate.

THE OUTCOME

Currently, Alex is working in his home city, and is looking for avenues toward continued personal growth.

CHAPTER 7

AIN'T THAT PECULIAR

GIFTED, BLACK, AND MALE OVERCOMING THE FOURTH GRADE FAILURE SYNDROME

by Samuel J. Maddox

BACKGROUND

Jawanza Kunjufu's (1985) research brings to light a peculiar trend in which African American males begin to disconnect from school academically between the second- and fifth-grade years. This phenomena, sometimes referred to as fourth grade failure syndrome (FGFS), occurs due to negative interactions between teachers and their Black male students, possibly due to lack of cultural awareness or outright racial/gender bias. FGFS is argued to be a root cause to many of the disparities we see between Black male graduation rates and their White or female counterparts. In this chapter, I will detail personal experiences as an intended victim of fourth grade failure syndrome to illustrate how this process occurs.

MY STORY

I FEEL GOOD . . . 'CUZ I GOT YOU

I loved school! I loved learning. Where this love came from was not a mystery. Although my parents had different educational backgrounds (my mother had a high school diploma while my father did not), they both had the ambition for me to get an education. They wanted me not only to get a good job but also to uplift myself and contribute to the betterment of my community. My mother's goals for me were more customary: good grades and academic achievement. My father's goals were more practical: learn things to help me be successful in life and not just in the classroom. I remember the excitement I felt when learning new ideas and concepts, only to be surprised that my parents' excitement exceeded my own. As I learned my numbers, my alphabet, how to spell, and how to read, my parents provided constant reinforcement. My mom would always search for new things for me to learn while at home and my dad would always have me apply my learning in the real world. "So if you can read, tell me what that sign says," he would randomly ask. This was all so thrilling for me as a young learner.

PAPA DON'T TAKE NO MESS

Now to be fair, it wasn't always simple. There were times when I didn't learn things as quickly and didn't excel. I recall bringing home a C on one report card. I was perfectly content that I was passing, but was quickly told by my mother that C's were not acceptable. I spent the next few weeks studying so I wouldn't bring another one home. I also recall the time in second grade, when a simple afterschool errand with my father turned into a life lesson that impacts me until this day. While purchasing a simple snack and soda at a local store, I allowed the cashier to give me incorrect change. I didn't count my change. I just returned to the car and my dad drove us home. Upon realizing that I had been cheated, he sat me down for more than an hour, teaching me about coin values. Since that day, I have excelled at counting money.

From my experiences with my parents, both the reinforcing and the corrective, I have learned that I need to master the knowledge I am given and apply it to my everyday life. From this perspective, I ended up not being like other students who were content with merely memorizing enough to pass the test, but I often strived to see the practical relevance of the knowledge I was receiving in school. As a result, I would frequently ask questions and try to think about the material we were being taught in a critical fashion. My teachers' responses to my questioning varied. Some were very reinforcing ("Good question!") and others felt mildly annoyed ("Yes, Sam, what is it now?"). My third-grade year, however, stands out.

MERCY, MERCY ME

By third grade, I had several years of learning under my belt and was excited at the prospect of another year of the same. Unfortunately, it was during this year that I received the most hostile response yet to my inquiries. Despite some mild annoyance from other teachers at times in the past, I knew that they still cared about me and my learning. It became clear in third grade that not only did my teacher not care about me and my learning, but she actually was threatened by my questions. I remember phrases such as "If I thought that was important for the class to know I would have told them" or "I guess you think you're smarter than me." It had gotten to the point where she would outright refuse to acknowledge when I raised my hand and to answer my questions. I even remember a joke my friend and I pulled where he would ask my question for me, and she would respond to him.

I have to admit this situation really caught me off guard. Although I was well aware of racism and that some Whites just didn't like Blacks, I had not expected this from my teacher. The fact that I had had White teachers in second grade who weren't hostile caused me to be completely blindsided by this teacher's behavior. Over the course of the year, with repeated interactions like this, I began to disconnect from school. My learning was being stifled and I felt unwanted in a place for which I had just months before had such reverence. I had no idea what fourth grade failure syndrome was, but I was living it.

I'M SUPER BAD

A stellar student until this point, third grade marked a time period where I had more discipline referrals that year than I had received my entire K–12 school career. I decided that if my teacher didn't care about me or my learning, then I wouldn't care about her class or her rules. I admire my mother's tact in dealing with the situation—she gave me corrective feedback on my aberrant behavior but also supported me by having meetings with my teacher, the principal, and any other necessary school personnel to bring to light how I was being mistreated. By the end of the year, I hated school, I hated my teacher, and even though I maintained good grades (again this was not an option) and met criteria for being an honor student, my third-grade teacher refused to give me the certificate that I had earned. Looking back on this experience and even knowing what I know today about fourth grade failure syndrome, it is still hard for me to reconcile my behavior during third grade with the person I know myself to be. I was taught never to be disrespectful to adults. I was taught to always behave with integrity, but all it took was this hostile interaction to make me belligerent and rude. Luckily, the next year I had teachers (one White, one Black) who encouraged my inquisitiveness, and I immediately began to love school again. I always wonder in the back of my mind however, what would have happened if I didn't have a good fourth-grade teacher and also how many other boys who loved learning had their efforts thwarted due to cultural bias like I had for that year.

WHAT'S GOING ON!: I CAN'T TAKE ONE MORE HEARTACHE

Although these experiences were occurring for me around the same time Jawanza Kunjufu was conducting his research on fourth grade failure syndrome, it pains my heart when I hear that other gifted Black males are still experiencing the same phenomena decades later, sometimes even in schools designed to work with gifted youth. Take Jake, a fifth grader. He is a young man who I have mentored for the past

3 years, and I have always been impressed with his keen insight. Jake has always had a quest for knowledge, so much so that he actually requested in kindergarten to be tested for a gifted school that his older brother was trying to attend. Jake had good experiences at his first gifted school and remained there until his family had to move at the beginning of his fifth-grade year. After the move, Jake was accepted to a new gifted school in the city to which they had moved. The new school did not provide as positive an experience. His previous schooling placed him ahead of most of the other kids in his all-White class at his new school. Being ahead of the kids at his new school created experiences for Jake eerily similar to my third-grade year. Jake's fifth-grade teacher frequently ignored his questions and even told him to stop raising his hand because the other kids were not where he was in the curriculum. Jake's mother reports that she noticed a tremendous change in her son. His motivation for school decreased, and she was concerned that his previous enthusiasm for knowledge may be affected. She met numerous times with the teacher and school, finding resistance. She expressed her intention to transfer him to a school where his potential would be nourished, and he would be free to pursue knowledge as he did before. Jake's story corroborates with what I and many other Black males experience in the American educational system. Instead of empowerment to equalize our circumstances, we experienced marginalization.

QUESTIONS FOR REFLECTION

1. Is it possible for the American public education system to ever become an "equalizer" in which disenfranchised groups will gain empowerment through knowledge? If so, how? If not what is the alternative?

2. How can parents encourage and advocate for their Black sons to overcome the fourth grade failure syndrome?

3. As we move toward a more global society with increased ease of interaction with people from other nations, how should we educate our Black males to ensure they are not left behind but architects of their own destiny?

4. What other factors outside of the school system (the media, music, literature) must we address to ensure that Black males are not socialized to accept mediocrity and marginalized?

THE OUTCOME

"The best revenge is doing well" is a phrase that gives me comfort when I recollect on the experiences of Jake and myself. As a licensed psychologist and college professor, I am now in a position not only to help foster critical thinking in the students I teach, but I also have had an opportunity to serve as an advocate and mentor for K–12 students who are having negative school experiences. Although Jake is in still in the midst of his battle, he remains resilient, determined that they are not going to stop him from gaining knowledge. As I have persevered, I have no doubt so shall he. With a passion for knowledge and the support of the community, we have the weapons we need to win these battles. After these battles are won, we must place ourselves in a position to give back to our community so that we can equip the next generation to win the war.

This chapter is dedicated to my mother (rest in peace) and father whose love and support helped me to overcome what obstacles came my way so that I might reach my full potential. I also dedicate this to you, all the other mothers, fathers, brothers, sisters, and cousins, biological or cultural, who stand up for our children.

REFERENCES

Kunjufu, J. (1985). *Countering the conspiracy to destroy Black boys*. Chicago, IL: African American Images.

CHAPTER 8

FROM NOTHING TO SOMETHING

by Christopher Oliver Johnson

BACKGROUND

I am a Black male student at a predominantly White institution (PWI). I took the road less traveled to get to this point, and I would not recommend taking that route. I grew up in the Midwest and have spent the majority of my adult life in the Deep South with a few stops back in the Midwest. I grew up with a mother who never went to college, and education was not that important to her. We never had a good relationship because I looked and acted just like my father, a man she could not, and still cannot, stand. Between the ages of 5 and 7, my grandfather passed away, my parents got a divorce, and my father passed away. Despite this, I bounced back from these events and still managed to do pretty well in school.

My paternal grandmother took a vested interest in my education. During elementary school, my mother would send my older brother and me to Chicago to spend the summer with her. If you ask my grandmother, she would tell you that she is the reason I am getting a terminal degree. She took me to the zoo, the museum, the aquarium, and the science center, opening my eyes to various experiences I most likely would not have seen otherwise. During middle school, I moved to Florida, and I did not see my grandmother for years because my mother did not like her and she lived so far away. In high school, I focused on athletics more than I did education. It was more of the same in college until I transferred to a historically Black university (HBCU) to complete my undergraduate degree. My story begins during elementary school, and it will end where I am now, at a predominantly White institution working on my Ph.D.

MY STORY

DAZED AND CONFUSED

I was born on the eastside of Detroit, MI. I attended five different elementary schools all over the eastside of Detroit. I remember having the most trouble in second grade after my father passed away. I was very close to him, and I think my mother resented that because of how he treated her. I remember going to stay with my grandmother, and although I was not doing very well at reading, I could recite the back of baseball cards, name all of the players, and easily recite all of their stats. My grandmother did not think this made any sense. So, one day she bought me an issue of *Sports Illustrated for Kids* magazine and instantly, I was in love! Because I loved sports, I did not even realize I was reading. Later, Grandma would give me the sports section of the newspaper and eventually *Sports Illustrated* magazines. Although those were much more difficult to read, she would help me with the words that I could not understand.

I always attended schools where the population was overwhelmingly Black. I remember going to a Black doctor, a Black dentist, and even living in a city where the mayor was Black. All of those things meant a lot to me, especially because my teachers and the principal also looked like me. In third grade, my mother sent me to a Catholic school that was predominantly Black. I loved that school because it promoted a great learning environment. Excellence was expected, and they didn't accept any work that was not your best. The Catholic school was extremely different from public school. One notable difference is that it featured its very own curriculum. While attending Catholic school, I was also able to experience the advantage of smaller classroom sizes and more individualized attention. I attended Catholic school throughout the fourth grade and I loved it—even started doing very well academically. When I entered the fifth grade, my mother remarried, gave birth to my younger brother, and shortly thereafter, my little sister was on the way. From there, I went to a Lutheran school for one semester and then reenrolled in a public school. At this point, I had a tough time transitioning to the public school environment. I had already learned everything that was being presented, so I became bored and began to "act out." I even got suspended one time for fighting because another kid was teasing me about my parents being too poor to afford to send me back to private school. I was in gifted classes, but even they were not challenging enough to me. Nevertheless, I made it through.

THE WONDER YEARS

The first semester of my sixth-grade academic year began in Detroit. I remember being a part of the gifted classroom and bringing my report card home to my mother. I had four A's and two B's, and all she responded with was just "Okay." I was crushed. I had worked so hard to get those grades and, at the time, really needed her approval. I really wanted her to be proud of me. Her reinforcement would have helped with my self-esteem and identity issues. Her nonapproval became a pattern that only got worse. I completed the second semester of sixth grade in Tallahassee, FL, because, one day, my mother and stepfather decided that Detroit was no longer a safe place to live. They decided to move my three other siblings and me down to Florida. I was not happy to be in the Sunshine State. Moving away from all of my family and friends to a place where I had no family or friends did not seem ideal. I remember being in gifted classes and being one of the only Black faces in them. I remember participating in P.E. class and seeing other Black kids. However, I was shunned because I was from Detroit, and I was in gifted classes. Some people would say that the other kids were "hating" on me. When I was in gifted classes in Detroit, I did not have to deal with "hating." Everyone in my gifted classes looked just like me. Needless to say, my transition to the South encompassed everything but southern hospitality.

I remember being in prealgebra class and asking the teacher what grade I needed earn to *not* be in this class anymore. She shared that if I earned a grade of C or lower, I would be removed and placed into the general math courses. If only I had my mother's support in school—when I showed her my C in prealgebra, I got the same reaction I received as when I got an A in that class.

In seventh grade, I attended middle school in Longwood, which was about 4 hours away from Tallahassee. I remember starting over again, trying to make friends and trying my best to fit in because I was no longer in gifted classes. However, this was a predominantly White school, and there were not very many Black students. As a matter of fact, there were more Hispanic students than Black students. I made average grades, but nobody really cared. My teachers didn't push me to succeed academically, nor did they expect much out of me. In my opinion, I think they were just happy that I sat in my seat and was quiet. I believe my mother cared more about my behavior than my grades. If my teacher called and said I was misbehaving, then I got into a lot of trouble. But, if I failed a test, it was not as important, especially because she never did that well in school.

In eighth grade, I grew a couple of inches, and I started becoming really good at basketball. I think once I became a better basketball player, I started getting more "love" from the other Black boys who attended the school. It took a while for me to gain their trust because I was new, and I was from out of state. Before I completed eighth grade, we moved again. But luckily for me, I remained in the same school district.

VARSITY BLUES

My eighth-grade year set me up for an interesting 4 years at high school. My high school's population was approximately 60% White, 20% Hispanic, 10% Black, and 10% other. I was excited to be at the same school as my friends from middle school, and my older brother, who was a junior at the time, attended the school as well. I was able to hang out with his friends too.

Ninth grade wasn't anything too interesting. I took my regular classes and earned average grades and I went about my own way. Tenth grade, however, was a transition year for me. I wanted to do something different and make a name for myself. I tried out for the junior varsity football team, and I was terrible. I had never played organized football before, and it showed. My brother was on the track and field and weightlifting teams, so I decided to participate in those sports as well.

I was decent in the shot put, but I was no good at weightlifting. I was motivated to do well in sports, because I did not like how it felt to lose. That summer I worked out with the varsity football team, and I got bigger, faster, and stronger. I was also determined to do better in school because I wanted to be eligible to play football in college. By my 11th-grade year, I went from being a bench player on the junior varsity team to becoming a starter on the varsity team. I was about 6' 2", 235 pounds, and I did well in school. Nobody made fun of me like they did the other Black kids who did not play sports. I guess I got a pass because I played sports; the fact that I was also really good did not hurt.

During my junior year, I started taking classes in business and marketing. I joined DECA (Distributive Education Clubs of America) and FBLA (Future Business Leaders of America). I participated in competitions and was required to dress up every Wednesday. I was happy about the experiences I gained from the clubs and courses, but I knew I did not want to major in business in college. I started hanging out with a racially mixed group of people during my junior year. We were all football players, and we all had one goal—college. The group was made up of White, Hispanic, and Black students. I had to dress up a lot and so did my friends, so we were considered to be one of the preppy groups, but no one messed with us because we were football players. We talked about college, and we all took the SAT together. We also took the SAT again during our senior year so that we could get better scores.

My senior year was my best year of high school. I was All Conference and All Central Florida in football. I went to regionals in track and field in two different events—shot put and discus. I was second in the state in my weight class on the weightlifting team; however, I decided not to compete at the state tournament because it was the same night as my prom. Looking back, I think that was one of the dumbest decisions of my life. I competed on the district and state level in DECA and FBLA and almost made it to DECA Nationals. I competed in a male pageant and even though I lost, it was a lot of fun. I was also a participant in a fashion show, and I thought I was "America's Next Top Model" years before the show came about.

SCHOOL DAZE

I had planned to go to colleges out of state to play football, but some things fell through and I did not get a scholarship. I ended up not going to college. While all of my friends were going off to college, I moved out of my parents' apartment and I moved in with my older brother. I had a full-time job and enrolled in the local community college for a semester. The following semester, I dropped out of school and just worked.

One day, one of my old high school football coaches called me and asked if I wanted to talk to a football coach from a small school in Iowa. Once the coach from Iowa heard that I had not gone to college, he convinced me to attend his small college the following year to play football. It was a small, private university, with about 1,000 students—half the size of my high school. About 95% of the Black males who attended the school played sports. The thing that sold me on the school was the fact that it was only 3 hours away from Chicago, and I got a chance to reconnect with my grandmother. Even though she was not a big sports fan, she and my aunts would come to my games to show their support and that meant a lot to me. I remember looking in the stands for my mom during high school games, but she was never there even though we only lived 5 minutes away from my high school.

My grandmother believed in me even when I was struggling in college. She told me stories of my father who graduated from college, and I didn't know that he had even attended college. She would tell me stories of family members who started schools back in the day and how important education was to our family. You see, my grandmother was very smart; she went to boarding school, but never went to college because she got married right after high school and started a family soon after.

I remained a student in Iowa for 2 years and made decent grades before I transferred to a small Roman Catholic private university that was only 30 minutes away from Chicago. I decided to transfer because the coach who recruited me accepted a position at that particular university and, of course, it was closer to my grandmother.

I spent all of my school vacations with my grandmother, including summer, Thanksgiving, and Christmas. Those were the happiest times of my life. We ate dinner together at the dinner table, and I was made to sit there until she finished eating. It would usually take her 2 hours to finish eating because she was so busy telling me stories, but I loved every minute of it. At this new school I did well in sports and went to nationals in track, even though the school focused on academics and the coursework was rigorous. I still maintained around a 3.0 grade point average while trying to participate in two sports and take a rigorous course load.

After 4 years of college at two different schools, I returned to Florida without a college degree. My grandmother wept because she did not think I would go back to school. My sports eligibility was up. School cost almost $30,000 a year, and I could not afford to pay the tuition.

Once back in Florida, I was able to get my job back at the company where I was working 4 years prior. After going through the remedial training, I knew I had to get back into school. My best friend had left school as well, but we knew that we needed to obtain a degree. He had attended an HBCU and was planning to return in January. As it turned out, I was planning to go to that same school at the same time. I was happy to know that someone I knew would be there to show me how to navigate my new surroundings.

Upon enrolling, I realized that the majority of my college credits did not transfer, so it was like I was starting all over. I was a 23-year-old junior, but I loved it. Just seeing all of the Black people and having Black professors made me feel like I was back in the gifted classes in Detroit. I did well at the HBCU, and it made me love school and learning again. Even though I worked full-time for the clerk of the courts, I kept my grades up.

After graduating with honors, I moved to Georgia to become an elementary school teacher. I taught for a year and decided to go back to school for a master's degree in educational psychology. I applied and got accepted to The University of Georgia. It was a culture shock for me. Going from an HBCU to a PWI, I was back to being the only Black male in my classes again. During my first semester, I struggled. I talked to my grandmother about it, and she reminded me of how proud my father would be if he could see me now. She reminded me of whose shoulders I was standing on and my need to uphold the Johnson legacy.

I remember being in classes and not really raising my hand to participate. I felt like I never had to raise my hand because the class always wanted to know my opinion about whatever topic we were discussing. I felt like they wanted me to say something so they could hear the Black perspective on whatever we were talking about. I never understood that, because my opinion was just my opinion, which may not be shared by other Black people. Furthermore, I am still 6' 2" and 235 pounds. I often get asked by people, mostly White, if I play football for the university; even though I am 30 and do not have any hair on my head, it is still assumed that I am attending this university as an athlete and not as a graduate student.

I remember one conversation I had with an older White man that upset me. He asked me if I played football, and I told him I was a doctoral student. He told me that tryouts were the following week, and I should go because the team could use me. I felt this man was implying that I was wasting my body by getting an advanced education when I should be on the field—the cotton field or the football field, as it seemed as though either would suffice for him. I spoke to another Black male student who is built like me, and he told me that he goes through the same thing. He told me it is not a compliment when they ask if I play football when I do not even look like I am undergraduate student. The assumption is that I was not smart enough to get into this school on my own merit and that I must have been accepted because I am good at football or some other sport.

QUESTIONS FOR REFLECTION

1. What are some possible types of checks and balances that can be put in place to ensure retention of Black males like Chris in gifted classes?
2. How much does a parent's academic upbringing and experience affect the academic success of his or her child?
3. When parents are not involved or concerned with their child's academic development, what other areas are affected? Are there different methods of motivation under these circumstances?
4. What factors contribute to the lack of motivation for African American males? Are these factors the same/similar to that of African American female students or students of other races/demographics? Why or why not?
5. What strategies would work to combat the prevalence of lack of academic motivation in African American male students?

THE OUTCOME

As all of my experiences continue to go through my mind, I have to remember that my only goal is to graduate, not to be accepted by people who did not understand me. I started focusing on being the first person in my family to get an advanced degree and that helped me to finish my master's degree in less than 2 years. I am currently working on my doctoral degree, which comes with its own set of challenges. I feel as if I have had to change the way I dress and act to appear less athletic, or, if this is even possible, less Black. I have 20/10 vision, but I wear glasses to appear less aggressive and to look more intellectual. The intention is to keep football far from the minds of my professors and peers.

The further I progress, the fewer Black people I see. I am trying to stay grounded and stay true to myself while navigating through this doctoral process. I try to hang out with other Black doctoral students in various settings. It lets me know that I am not the only one and we are experiencing some of the same things. Being at a PWI certainly does not make it easy . . . you must learn to play the game but not lose yourself in the process.

CHAPTER 9

TWO GIFTED AFRICAN AMERICAN BROTHERS ACHIEVING IN SPITE OF THE ODDS

by Dwan V. Robinson, James L. Moore III, and Renae D. Mayes

In many K–12 school contexts, gifted African American boys are wrestling with their minority status and are confronted with school professionals (e.g., teachers, school counselors, and administrators) who often offer little, if any, support. In these schools, persistent stereotypes and ambiguous paradigms consistently inhibit many African American boys from advancing to higher level classes (e.g., gifted or honors). Nevertheless, there are still examples of intelligent, accomplished boys who are exemplars not only for African American males, but also for all students. This chapter includes a discussion of two very bright African American brothers from an inner city who attended a private school and the experiences of their parents in helping them navigate the academic terrain of their school.

GIFTED BROTHERS

Eric and David grew up in a two-parent household in an inner city community. Both boys were identified as gifted in various subjects, based on traditional and formal educational assessments. Throughout both brothers' K–12 journeys, the schools where the boys were enrolled offered many enriching educational and extracurricular opportunities for students. Both Eric and David chose to participate in numerous opportunities available to them at their school, such as music, theatre productions, clubs, and sports. These experiences were also supplemented with travel throughout the Western hemisphere, with their parents, grandparents, and classmates. Preparation and hard work by Eric and David were obvious. The boys stood out among their classmates, both Black and White. Eric preferred having conversations with one of his teachers, Mr. Hatcher, over his peers because he enjoyed engaging in intellectual discussions. During a past course in the arts, Mr. Hatcher indicated that "there must have been some formal training somewhere in David's background" because he was doing so well.

RESISTANT TO PROVIDE HELP AT HOME

Not all of their teachers saw what Mr. Hatcher observed. Some of Eric and David's teachers showed reservation about them being gifted. Eric and David had already been identified as gifted in certain subjects on formal, standardized assessments. Eric and David's parents once met with two faculty members seeking guidance for projects at home to support classroom learning. Mrs. Fiske shared that Eric and David were not gifted in her mind, while Mrs. Beckham looked on. Mrs. Beckham, although not in full agreement with Mrs. Fiske, sat silently and chose not to intervene. Mrs. Fiske was reluctant to assist Eric and David's parents and would not provide advanced activities to be completed at home. The situation between Mrs. Beckham and Mrs. Fiske caused great anxiety with Eric and David's parents. The fact that the teachers were not cooperative in facilitating additional activities to support the boys placed the responsibility on the parents to create activities that would connect their academic learning with supplemental activities at home. Eric and David's parents were concerned that, if the boys were not regularly stimulated, they might lose interest in their academic subjects.

TIGHT BROTHERS

David looked up to his brother and often spoke of wanting to "be like Eric." He engaged his mother to help him shop for clothes like Eric. Ultimately, each boy developed into an impressive young man and distinct individual, with his own separate interests and aspirations. Although Eric and David ran into various barriers as they progressed through their schooling, the boys were still able to realize numerous accomplishments by helping each other and building on their inner drive to persevere. In addition, with the support of their parents and other well-meaning adults, both boys were able to achieve great success.

HIGH ACHIEVERS

Part of the evolution of Eric and David's achievement was their effort and proclivity toward being the best. They both expressed zeal to be on top in numerous endeavors. David was selected for honors because he was in the top 2% of his class. The boys occasionally talked about their performance and the need to submit the best assignments. Eric noted:

> I always felt that I needed to work hard to not only be at the top of my class but to perform well in many activities . . . Sometimes, it seemed that I had to be perfect because my teachers were judging me, and I even felt I needed to have perfect penmanship.

SOCIAL INJUSTICES

For the boys, an understanding of the societal injustices came from conversations with their parents and from being exposed to literature on structural inequalities and viewing documentaries where the inequity in urban schools and society at large was apparent. Their experiences in a Black church and in a home where both parents were keenly aware of potential imbalances that might confront the boys provided a solid foundation for them. Eric and David's parents were shocked by an unexpected injustice that came from a teacher who was African American and male. Mr. Williams embarrassed Eric in class. Eric was academically at the top of his class, and, although most of the class was disruptive, Mr. Williams singled Eric out to make an example of him. In other words, he verbally assaulted Eric and pointed his finger in his face. Eric's parents were shocked that Mr. Williams would treat their child like this or even that he would allow himself to get to the point of anger where he would lose control and put his finger in a student's face. Eric, his father, and Mr. Williams subsequently had a meeting to discuss the incident. As a result, public displays of anger never occurred again.

Eric experienced other faculty members who, like Mr. Williams, acted unprofessionally. For example, Mr. Malone served as a gatekeeper and created roadblocks to Eric's academic success. During his transition from middle to high school, Mr. Malone, a math educator, tried to interrupt Eric's natural progression and advancement into higher level courses. Mr. Malone withheld Eric's referral to the higher level course even though he had given Eric stellar evaluations and grades in his class. Eric had performed well above the curve, approached the coursework with an inquisitive mind, and was a regular participant in class exercises. Mr. Malone either did not believe that Eric could compete in upper level courses or had some prejudicial feelings about his ability to succeed in advanced classes. The fact that Mr. Malone would not enable Eric to matriculate into advanced classes could have impacted Eric's progression in high school. In addition, not enrolling in advanced level math classes could have affected his competitiveness on college applications when compared with other students. Thankfully, Eric's parents and other educators who had confidence in him were able to ensure that he tested into upper level classes.

QUESTIONS FOR REFLECTION

1. Would Eric and David have been as successful if they did not have parents as advocates or well-meaning adults who supported them? Explain.
2. What would have happened if Eric and David retaliated or showed anger in the various scenarios presented throughout the chapter?
3. What approaches might educators share to help equip African American males with coping mechanisms, when facing situations like those presented by Mr. Williams and Mr. Malone?

THE OUTCOME

In spite of the many hurdles in the both boys' paths, the existence of a well-networked support system helped them overcome the various roadblocks to success. Eric and David completed high school with the opportunity to choose from many of the top institutions of higher learning as college options. The young men were able to matriculate to schools that provided the best fit for their academic and career aspirations and college environments that were key for their social, emotional, and cocurricular development. The opportunities available for them exceeded their expectations as well as those of their parents.

SECTION III
RESILIENT BLACK FEMALES

CHAPTER 10

AGE AIN'T NUTHIN' BUT A NUMBER

by Ain A. Grooms

BACKGROUND

Lily was born in a mid-Atlantic city and moved with her family to a northeastern city when she was 2 years old. The northeastern city, although fairly small by demographic standards, is very well-known around the country. They moved to a predominantly Black section of the city, and Lily attended a preschool at a small, community school, founded on Afrocentric principles. She learned to read by the time she was 3.

LILY'S STORY

ELEMENTARY SCHOOL

In the early 1980s, I attended a small, progressive, diverse, private elementary school in the heart of the city—almost like a charter school before charters existed. In fact, my school was located on one of the "richest" streets in the city where some of the most high-end boutique shops were. I actually have no idea how my parents even found out about this school. The building where was my school was has now been turned into a restaurant.

I went to school with Black kids and White kids. And I had both Black and White teachers. The school did what it could to meet the academic needs of the students, and in my case, this meant that I was promoted. I basically skipped the second and third grades. I remember being in third grade in one subject and in second grade in another. My school was so small, and I'm sure that other students overlapped in different grades and classes just like I did, so no one seemed to notice or mind or make a big deal about it. I thought it was normal.

ACADEMIC PERCEPTION

I'm not sure I ever considered myself "academically gifted," but in junior high school, I realized I wasn't like everyone else. I knew that I was different but I didn't exactly realize how. My parents divorced when I was 3 years old and were both remarried by the time I was 5. Throughout elementary school, my mother and stepfather lived in a different African American section of the city than my father and stepmother, but I was fortunate to be able to continue attending the same elementary school, regardless of which house I was staying in. Although my father had primary custody, I spent lots of time in each household, and my grades never suffered.

I eventually moved with my father and stepmother to a neighboring suburb, about 10 miles outside of the city. I began junior high school (seventh grade) at the age of 10. Not only had I moved to a suburb where I didn't know anyone, but I also had gone from a diverse school where I had friends of all races to a school with little to no diversity. Additionally, I was 2–3 years younger than everyone else. The question I most hated to be asked was, "How old are you?" By the end of the first week of school, I had mastered the art of lying about it. I knew I was supposed to be older than 10, and since I was new in school and in the suburb, no one could prove that I was wrong.

Most of the Black students who attended my junior high school lived in the city and were bused to the suburbs. Either way, I didn't fit in. I was younger, and I lived in the White suburbs. I figured that if I lied about my age, at least there would be one thing that I would have in common with my classmates, regardless of their race. I don't think I ever admitted to either set of parents that I was lying about my age—I don't even remember if they ever asked about it. I guess they figured that since I was making friends, my age couldn't have been much of an issue.

HIGH SCHOOL VERSUS JUNIOR HIGH

High school was no easier. In fact, I absolutely hated high school. Even though this was the pre-Facebook/Twitter/Internet age, I felt like I was forced to grow up overnight. To me, being young in junior high wasn't that important because everyone was young, especially in terms of maturity. But for some reason, being young in high school seemed momentous. I didn't want anyone to ever find out. I felt like if everyone knew that I was young, then I would be branded a "baby," but it also meant that people might think of me as a "smart baby," which is somehow worse. This was definitely before the generation when it was cool to be smart, especially if you were Black.

In 1988, at 12 years old in the ninth grade, I was pretending to have firsthand knowledge of all of the things my classmates (Black or White) would talk about. My parents let me be immersed academically, but not socially. Even something as simple as having a driver's permit was not something I could legally do until my senior year in high school. Worse, my father wouldn't let me date because I was so young.

During junior high and high school, my friends from school were White, but because my father and stepmother still attended church in the city, my friends from outside of school were Black. All of my friends from church were the same age as me, but were in different grades. A couple of the kids at church jokingly called me Doogie Howser (a reference to a popular television series at the time about a boy who had graduated from medical school at age 14), but for the most part, it wasn't an issue with my friends there. I would sometimes go into the city and hang out with them or spend the night at their houses on the weekends. It helped me keep one foot in both worlds—one world where I could just be me and where my friends looked like me, and the other world where I had to lie to fit in every day and still never looked like everyone else.

Beginning in the ninth grade, there were two other Black girls in my homeroom, but we didn't interact much. They lived in the city and made it clear to me that I wasn't "like them." I went through 4 years of seeing them every morning in homeroom, and we never became friends. A few years later, I dated a guy who graduated from high school 2 years after me (we are the same age). I once asked him why we never spoke during high school. He told me,

> We [all the Black students who were bused in from the city] knew who you were. You were that Black girl from [the suburb], and we all knew you were young. I just didn't think you wanted to talk to me.

Throughout high school, I felt like I was having an internal struggle with myself about my Blackness. I felt like I wasn't Black enough for the Black students from the city but I was too Black to blend in with my suburban classmates. I was usually the only Black person in my classes (outside of homeroom), so I never got a chance to interact with other Black students, even those who also lived in the suburb. It didn't help that I was also on the swim team for all 4 years of high school. I was the only Black girl on the swim team until my senior year when another girl joined. Because she was a freshman, we were much closer in age than she knew, and I eventually confided in her about it. We remain friends until this day.

I graduated from high school 9 days before my 16th birthday. During my senior year, my mother and father (rightfully) figured that I was not ready for college, and after some lengthy discussions, I finally agreed to do a postgraduate (PG) year of high school. I was admitted to one of the top boarding schools in the Northeast, and I believe it was one of the best decisions I could have made (even though, upon reflection, I probably didn't have much say in the matter). Regardless of which household I lived in while growing up, there was never a question that I was going to college. The decision to do a PG year just delayed it by one year. All four of my parents had received either a graduate or professional degree (my mother and stepfather had graduate degrees in fine arts and education, respectively, and my father and stepmother were both lawyers), and so I had four very strong academic role models. I don't remember specifically talking about college with my parents, but I somehow knew that it was the only option for me. In my mind, it was impossible to consider anything else.

One of the best things about doing my PG year at that specific school was that it was close to my mother. She and my stepfather (and by this time, my stepsisters and younger brother) had moved to the Western part of the state while I was in high school. During my PG year, I was only about 45 minutes away from them, whereas I was almost 2 hours away from my father and stepmother (and younger brother and sister). Doing the PG year gave me a taste of freedom because I was "on my own," yet still had high school rules, including study hall, male/female visitation guidelines, and dormitory chores.

Most importantly, I felt I was able to "reinvent" myself there, or rather, I could finally be myself. No one at boarding school knew my backstory, and there were quite a few other Black students doing a PG year. I didn't have to pretend to be anything I wasn't. Everyone assumed I was at least 17 because I was doing a PG year, so I just let them. I didn't necessarily lie about my age, but I certainly didn't clarify. I had come from a secondary school situation where I was one of a few, and felt like I never fit into either the White or the Black group, to a school where I was still in the minority, but very quickly created friendships with the Black students there. I was on the swim team again, and instead of making fun of me about it, my friends came to some of my swim meets. Although there weren't many Black students there, it was a welcoming community and I built some very strong friendships.

I think I was insecure about my Blackness when I began my PG year because throughout junior high and high school, I felt like the other Black students were always questioning it, either because of where I lived or my school friendships. It was rarely done to my face, but I always felt the stares in the hallways. But my Black friends from outside of school—whether from church or from my mother's neighborhood—never had an issue with me or who I was. Doing the PG year helped me become more secure with who I was. It was okay that I was on the swim team. It was okay that I had some White friends because we all did. I felt like I was just another Black kid—something that had eluded me for so long.

COLLEGE ACCEPTANCE

I applied to college with one of my close friends from boarding school—she was also Black and doing a PG year. We were both accepted, enrolled, and were roommates for our freshman year. We attended a private, predominantly White institution located in a suburb of a predominantly Black Southern city. There were also several historically Black colleges and universities in the area. Again, I found myself in an educational setting where the Black community wasn't strong in numbers, but provided a strong network in which both my roommate and I became involved.

I was much more secure with myself than I had been in high school, but at times, I was still questioned about my Blackness by Black students who went to other colleges. My freshman year in college, I met a group of people from one of the neighboring Black colleges (one of whom remains one of my closest friends). One person questioned my reasoning for wanting to attend a predominantly White institution. He challenged me, remarking that I thought I was "too good" to attend a Black college, and that if I wanted "the Black experience, I would have to attend a Black school." I responded that I had received more financial aid from the White institution, and that by attending a predominantly White institution, I was reminded about my Blackness every day. It then escalated into an argument. By the end, we agreed to disagree. Some years later, we ran into each other in an airport and had a good laugh about our immature disagreement.

I think college was the first time that I didn't feel different. I was in an elite academic community (at the time I applied, my university was ranked ninth in the nation), and we were all there to learn. And have some fun too. I was still young—I was 17 when I began my freshman year, and graduated from college one month before my 21st birthday—but didn't feel left out at all. It felt like the difference between 17 and 19 during freshman year in college was not as pronounced as the difference between 12 and 14 during freshman year in high school. My friends from college have gone on to become doctors, lawyers, entrepreneurs, professors, nurses, teachers—everything.

I did, however, have my first major academic shock. Even though doing a PG year gave me a taste of being away from home, the classes were still very small, and we had a 2-hour assigned study hall every night, except Friday and Saturday. Once in college, I wasn't prepared to be in a lecture hall with 300 other students at 8:30 a.m. taking an Introduction to Psychology course, especially since the professor never took attendance. I had never earned less than a B in a class, so when I got my first semester's transcript, my parents didn't have to lecture me about it at all because I beat myself up about it. Those grades remain the worst I had ever or would ever receive, and I spent the next 3 1/2 years trying to balance out their impact. Luckily for me, I eventually learned how to balance work and fun, responsibility and freedom, and eventually made Dean's List a few times. I felt like I was finally learning the same life lessons as everyone else, at relatively the same point in our lives.

UNIDENTIFIED: DISADVANTAGED

In thinking about my primary and secondary education, I realize that while I never specifically took an Advanced Placement or Honors course or was placed in a gifted program, all of my classes were, in essence, advanced because I was so much younger than everyone else. Beginning in junior high school, none of my teachers knew that I was younger (or at least never told me that they knew), and I never got preferential treatment. I was expected to do the same work as everyone else. More importantly, my parents also had the same expectations of me as my teachers did. I don't think my parents thought of me as a 12-year-old taking ninth-grade math, or a 14-year-old taking the SATs; I was a freshman taking freshman math and a high school junior preparing for college. I was in my own private gifted program for 7 years, from seventh grade through my PG year.

Given the community where I attended junior high and high school, being in a gifted program would have probably served to separate me even more from the people I most wanted to befriend—the other Black students. As it was, I was usually the only Black student in my classes, so being in a separate school community for the "nerds" would have probably made me stand out even more, and would have further underscored my differences. I wanted to blend in as much as possible during high school, and being placed in a gifted program would have done quite the opposite. It's clear to me now that, at that time, my priorities were a bit skewed, but it was high school.

I think that the biggest disadvantage about not being in a gifted program was a social one. Had I been placed in a gifted program, I'm sure my father would have applied the same dating rules, but I probably wouldn't have lied to all of my friends and classmates about my age because perhaps it would have been more acceptable. Had I been placed in a gifted program, I might not have been so prone to hide my accomplishments. Doing a PG year allowed me to gain some social ground before heading off to college.

I think that had I attended a more diverse high school, more like my elementary school, where there were students of every race in every class, I wouldn't have felt so insecure about my academic achievements. Everything changed for me once I got to college. No one cared how old I was; it was about grades, internships, and networking. I no longer needed to lie about my age, and following college graduation, I began to let my resume do the talking. After several years in the workforce, I decided to return to higher education. I again chose to attend nationally renowned predominantly White institutions for both my master's (private institution) and doctoral degrees (public institution).

Looking back, much of my insecurities stemmed from other Black people questioning who I was because I didn't fit into their traditional mold of what a Black person should be or what he or she should do. Most of my close White friends in high school knew how old I was, especially once they were old enough to start driving and I wasn't, but it was never really a problem with them. As I've gotten older and become much more open about who I am and what I've accomplished, I realize that I don't need to explain or justify my achievements because it may not conform to someone else's preconceived notion of Blackness. I'm happy to be a few months shy of receiving my doctoral degree, and believe that my past experiences, both positive and negative, helped me get to where I am now.

QUESTIONS FOR REFLECTION

1. How can parents and educators provide a positive social environment for accelerated gifted Black students who may feel like outsiders?
2. In desegregated schools (especially in those where Black students have diverse backgrounds), how can parents and educators promote healthy interaction between accelerated young gifted Black students and regular education students?
3. How can parents and educators combat the detrimental effects of social segregation among Black students?
4. How can parents and educators ensure that Black students who are not placed in gifted programs, yet excel academically, are adequately prepared for selective colleges and universities?

THE OUTCOME

Lily is presently enrolled in a doctoral program and looks forward to pursuing a career in research and teaching at the university level.

CHAPTER 11

TO BE GIFTED, BLACK, AND PREGNANT IN HIGH SCHOOL AND COLLEGE

by Candice Norris-Brown and Tarek C. Grantham

BACKGROUND

The school is located in a small southern city in Georgia. The school district has 21 schools: 14 elementary schools, 4 middle schools, and 3 high schools. The total number of students served in this county is 12,557 students. The demographic profile of the school district is the following: 2% Asian, 53% African American, 22% Hispanic, 19% White, and 4% multiracial. The total number of students served in the gifted program is 1,478. This county has one of the highest teenage pregnancy rates in a state that ranks among the top 10 in the nation. It is also one of the poorest counties for its size, with a poverty rate of 30%. The average monthly number of food stamp households for the 2011 fiscal year was 7,447. The school district is collaborating with several community agencies that have expertise in developing and implementing sex education policies, programming, and curriculum in schools to reduce teen pregnancy.

TIFFANY'S STORY

TIFFANY, TODAY AND YESTERDAY

Tiffany is a 24-year-old African American woman who is outgoing, autonomous, and confident. She was a high achiever throughout high school and is a recent graduate from college, with a degree in prenursing. She is currently preparing to take the MCAT and apply to medical school. She became pregnant at 18 years of age. She has one child, a 5-year-old daughter named Mecca. She currently resides with Timothy, her daughter's father and Tiffany's fiancée. Her goal is to "be able to provide" financially for her daughter.

Tiffany proudly shared her educational experiences, noting that she was an A and B student while in high school and that she met the requirements to be inducted into the Beta Club. She stated that she always aspired to be a doctor. When asked to describe her schoolwork habits, Tiffany politely responded,

> I did the minimum and that was enough to get into the Beta Club and honor classes. No one at home was pushing me to work harder so I didn't try. It [high academic achievement] was unnoticed . . . I think my mom was proud [of me] but I don't think she showed it as much as she should have because of my dad. I think he was jealous of his kids and that is ridiculous to be jealous of your own kids. I think he was mainly a big kid himself and wanted all of her attention.

It was evident that sharing this perspective about her parents was painful. She slumped her shoulders and unconsciously looked down while sharing this experience.

When asked to identify the person or persons who were most helpful to her in school, Tiffany recognized her science teacher and mentor for their unwavering support. She shared, "The only people that seemed to notice that I was doing the minimum were my science teacher Dr.

Bailey and her husband. They pushed me to take AP classes my senior year." However, even with their support and increased academic expectations, Tiffany indicated that she still only did the minimum in her classes and earned top grades. In fact during her high school years, she earned only two B's.

TIFFANY'S SEXUAL DECISION MAKING

Tiffany shared her prior sexual experiences, beginning with the time she started having sex up through the time she discovered she was pregnant. Unlike the stereotypes that are often reported about Black teenage mothers, Tiffany was not a promiscuous teen.

> I started having sex at age 18. My friends were having sex, so to fit in, I lied and told them I was having sex. Then one day, I finally decided to experiment and believed I did "too much" experimenting. I was just ready and everybody was talking about it, so I wanted to know what they were talking about.

When asked if sexual protection was ever a consideration, she interestingly shared that:

> The crazy thing is that I wanted to be an OB-GYN so you know I knew all about this. I think I just got caught up in the moment and thought it just won't happen to me. I've only been with one person. Most of the time, we used condoms.

TIFFANY'S FAMILY'S REACTIONS TO PREGNANCY

As Tiffany described her parents' reaction when learning that she was pregnant, she became very emotional and tears began to stream almost uncontrollably down her face. She recalled going to the emergency room for back pains. She explained,

I did not tell anyone until I was 5 months. I was small. I just had a belly button. It did not register to me that I was pregnant until I went to the hospital for back pain. I remember seeing my baby on an ultrasound and hearing the heartbeat. I was like "this is really real" and I probably need to tell my mom because not having prenatal care could really harm my baby. One day, I got tired of holding in the secret, so I wore a tight shirt so that my mom could see my belly. I peeped in her door to tell her that I was leaving, and she looked down at my stomach and asked if I was pregnant. I told her "yes," and she asked me how far along I was. I told her, and she almost fainted. My mom was surprised that I stayed in her house for that long, and she did not notice.

It was apparent that both Tiffany and her mother were in denial. Tiffany described her parents' reaction to her pregnancy.

She [my mom] cried at first and called everybody and told them. She was not proud. She called my dad and he said, "Well that's your problem! You deal with it." He told my mom that she had played a fool for me this long, so she should continue to play the fool by herself. Initially, the first few weeks my mom was excited, she bought diapers and clothes for the baby. She even went with me to my doctor appointments. Whenever she would hang out with my father's side of the family, she would return home upset and say many mean things about me and my boyfriend. My father's family is very jealous. They were probably happy that I was pregnant.

For Tiffany, becoming pregnant in high school and struggling financially were not in her plans. Adding to her stress, she could not depend on her family for emotional support or financial assistance.

Well, my mom was really negative. She felt that I was going to quit school. She doubted me many times. She did not think that I would graduate, and honestly she has done nothing to help me succeed at graduating. She constantly asked me how I was going to finish school with a baby but she never asked what she could do to help me finish school with a baby! When I would ask my mom to help, her reply was, "I'm a young grandma."

When I would ask my sister, my mom would say, "You better pay her." The Baileys have continued to support me and so did Timothy and his family. My mom was always negative, and she felt that I was going to quit school.

Mothers are a significant and powerful source of sexual health information. Oftentimes, the topic of sex is either not addressed at home or handled in ways that criticize the pregnant teen. It was obvious that Tiffany wished she could have had an open discussion regarding her sexual decisions with her mother. She was unable to communicate with her mother about sex with comfort and confidence. Tiffany believed that a conversation with her mother would serve as more of a source of potential reprimand than a source of information or support.

My mom never really opened that door. She told me whenever I was ready, I should come and speak to her. But my parents were so protective. It felt hard going to her because I knew she was going to take my car and put me on lockdown. They didn't want me to date at 18. No boys could call the house or take me out. I couldn't even go to my parents to tell them that I wanted to date someone. No one was ever good enough for me. When my parents did find out that I was dating, they called my boyfriend, who was 2 years older than me, at work and asked him if he was sexually active. "What do you want with my daughter?" It was really embarrassing. Clearly, they did not like my boyfriend, and they never took the chance to get to know him. I was growing up, and it scared my dad. He would have my mom follow me around town and call me constantly whenever

I was away from home. If I wanted to go out with my boyfriend, I had to lie and say I was going out with my best friend.

SCHOLAR MOM BEYOND THE STIGMA OF TEEN PREGNANCY

In college, Tiffany had an empty apartment and was unable to pay rent. She was a freshman at the local university and her baby was due in 4 months. College presented Tiffany with an array of academic and personal challenges. She had to balance schoolwork and motherhood. As a result, she was no longer able to do the minimum; she had to work hard. Oddly enough, the parenting, college academics, and financial hardships taught Tiffany how to effectively manage her emotions and remain focused on her goals. She stated,

I have to work really hard now. Organic chemistry, biochemistry, and genetics are not easy subjects, but I've done well in them. I actually made the Dean's List.

I only made two high C's the whole time I've been in school. I still have a good GPA, and my advisor tells me every time she sees me how proud she is with my GPA and being a mom.

QUESTIONS FOR REFLECTION

1. Being gifted does not inoculate Black teenage females from peer influences and making decisions to initiate sexual intercourse. How can teachers and counselors encourage Black mothers and fathers to be open to discussions about sexual decisions with their gifted daughters (and sons)?

2. Describe Tiffany's personal attributes that contributed to her academic success in high school and college.

3. Are gifted Black females more likely to have knowledge of sexually transmitted diseases and condom use than Black females in regular or workforce education courses? How can gifted Black female adolescents minimize their risk of contracting a sexually transmitted disease and pregnancy?

4. What factors predict high-risk sexual decision making among high-achieving Black females?

THE OUTCOME

In spite of obstacles, Tiffany was able to rise up and succeed.

I knew that I was going to graduate and so did my child's father. He was a little upset with himself for getting me pregnant, but he did not want for me to miss out on anything just by being pregnant. He worked two and sometimes three jobs to provide for our family. We were determined, despite all of the negativity. I had my daughter on Tuesday, I came home that Thursday, and then I went back to school on Monday. My daughter's father watched her while I was at school, and then when I came home he went right to work. His family was also a big help. They helped watch our daughter when she got a little bigger. His cousin became our number one baby sitter. We were barely making ends meet at that time. We never begged or asked anyone to support our child, but one thing we did ask for was a little help babysitting while I went to school for a couple of hours. I had to work really hard.

Being gifted and making high grades with ease in high school did not prevent Tiffany from making sexual decisions that impacted her college pursuit. She accepted the reality of her pregnancy and used it to rise above others and prove her self-worth to her family. Complimenting her intelligence, her high level of motivation and aspirations have been reflected in her determination to return to college soon after giving birth. She attributed an immediate return as a step closer to being in a position to provide a better future for her child by becoming eligible to pursue a college degree. Although Tiffany appeared to be happy with her decision to pursue a degree in nursing, she desperately wanted to become a doctor.

> After I had finished all of my prenursing courses, I sat in my advisor's office and cried when she told me that it was time to apply to nursing school. I knew that I wanted to be a doctor deep down inside. I told my advisor that I didn't want to be a nurse and that I wanted to be a doctor. She asked me one question, "Do you want to work for someone else or for yourself?" I clearly told her for myself, and she told me, "Okay, well this is what we have to do." I admire my advisor so much, because she believed in me even when I did not believe in myself. I will be studying for the MCAT and applying to medical schools this spring.

RESOURCES

Aspy, C., Vesley, S., Oman, R., Rodine, S., Marshall, L., & McLeroy, K. (2007). Parental communication and youth sexual behavior. *Journal of Adolescence, 30,* 449–466.

Bachanas, P. J., Morris, M. K., Lewis-Gess, J. K., Sarett-Cuasay, E. J., Sirl, K., Ries, J. K., & Sawyer, M. K. (2002). Predictors of risky sexual behavior in African American adolescent girls: Implications for prevention interventions. *Journal of Pediatric Psychology, 27,* 519–530.

Belgrave, F., Marin, B., & Chambers, D. (2000). Cultural, contextual, and interpersonal predictors of risky sexual attitudes among urban African American girls in early adolescence. *Cultural Diversity and Ethnic Minority Psychology, 6,* 309–322.

CHAPTER 12

"BLACK AND IVY"
BECOMING THE MODEL MINORITY

by Shani Harmon

BACKGROUND

Black students in predominantly White schools are inevitably viewed as an exception. The only question then becomes whether the Black student chooses to be a good exception—a model minority performing at above-average levels—or a bad exception—a minority perceived as having inferior intelligence and/or behavioral problems who possibly earned his or her place in school because of a perceived affirmative action quota.

When considering my relationship between my school and my peers, the choice to be an underachiever or overachiever has consequences. As an overachiever, I was less inclined to have an adversarial relationship with my teachers and the school at large, both of which had an interest in my achievement, particularly because I was a token model minority. But with many students vying for the few openings in the top schools in the U.S., I was more likely to be competitive with students who were somewhat racially charged, because they believe I had been "given" their spot because I was a minority.

THE STORY

To begin, I do not remember consciously choosing to be a model minority, and such a decision would only partially account for my success. As Malcolm Gladwell explains in his book *Outliers*, "It's not enough to ask what successful people are like. It is only by asking where they are from that we can unravel the logic behind who succeeds and who doesn't" (p. 19).

Gladwell is a model minority outlier. He was the son of a Jamaican woman, who was educated in an overwhelmingly White working class area of Canada. He excelled in school and ultimately became a prominent academic. He attributes his academic success in large part to the exposure to universities he received at a young age as a result of his father being a mathematician.

I grew up under similar circumstances. My mother is a university professor, and I spent many hours at the university at a young age. This gave me exposure to many academic fields, as well as high-achieving role models, some of whom were minorities. I also happened to have a high-achieving older brother who often set expectations for his younger siblings. There was never any question that I would go to college, preferably following in the footsteps of my brother, going to preparatory programs and ultimately the Ivy League.

My parents expected us to excel academically, and indirectly encouraged us to be model minorities with their instruction to give 110% because the teachers wouldn't believe that minorities are smart to begin with. They also explained that in environments where I was the only Black, I was representing the entire Black race; therefore, I should not play into negative stereotypes—in fact, I should do whatever I could to disprove them. My and my brother's natural intellectual inclination, combined with our parents who exposed us to high-achieving role models, ensured that we were challenged in school, and expected the highest level of academic success. It is in some ways not surprising that my brother and I were both academically successful and, consequently, model minorities.

ELEMENTARY SCHOOL

I attended elementary school in a suburb of Tacoma, a major urban Midwestern city. Around the time that I started elementary school, African Americans comprised about 4% of the state's population. The state's African American population at that time was concentrated in the city of Tacoma rather than its suburbs. Other than myself, there were three African American students out of approximately 80 students in my school.

In addition to African Americans, there were a handful of Asian and Latino students. The school was predominantly White, in the middle of an undeveloped prairie, in a predominantly White middle-class suburb.

Despite being one of the few African Americans, I never felt like I didn't belong there. I was placed in a gifted program and quickly made some of my closest friends there. The gifted kids were pulled out of class to do special activities—like logical problem solving and other challenging activities. The distinction of being a gifted and talented student, or a "GT kid," was the most meaningful societal distinction to me at that point. I liked being around kids who learned as fast as I did, were creative, and had a similar sense of humor. The other kids that were not in the GT program seemed to resent that we got to go off to do something special and they didn't. This seemed to strengthen the solidarity of the bond among us GT kids.

Having found my niche as a GT kid, I can remember telling my mom that race didn't matter any more—my friends and I didn't care what race we were. The first time that I remember thinking there was some significance to race was when my best friend, who was White, mentioned that her dad said I wasn't like those "other Black people." I asked her, "What Black people are you talking about?" and she said, "You know. Those rappers." On one hand, what she said was not disturbing to me because it was true—my family was not the epitome of rap culture—far from it. But the reference to "those other Black people" was a little puzzling and unsettling to me.

MIDDLE SCHOOL

For the first year of middle school, I remained in a school in the suburbs of Tacoma, despite my parents' wishes that I go to a school in Tacoma where the magnet programs were better and the students were more diverse. I didn't want to transfer to a school in Tacoma and leave my friends. But after one year—in which the school's gifted program consisted of exiling students to the hallway with harder work and my interest in hanging out at the mall began to surpass my interest in studies—my mom stepped in and made the decision that I would be transferring to a gifted program in Tacoma.

I was leery of transferring to a Tacoma school due to an interesting "misunderstanding" that occurred during the process of getting admitted into its gifted and talented program. The district was actively recruiting African American gifted students at the time. Initially, I was not accepted even though I qualified for the program. My mother was shocked and inquired into what happened. She was told that an error was made—they didn't think that I was African American due to my test scores. They apologized profusely and admitted me right away. The only hitch was that the program was full, so they arranged for me to complete coursework within both the general education class and the gifted program.

It was at this point that I began to notice a racial divide—the general program was predominantly African American, and I was the only African American in the gifted program. The students in the gifted program never made an issue of my race. But some of the students in the general program, particularly Black girls, were hostile toward me. I asked one of the girls why she didn't like me. She said it was because I had good hair. Another time, a classmate called me at home and didn't believe that it was actually me on the phone because she said I "sounded like a White person." Over the course of that year, I figured out that many of the Black students didn't think I was Black enough, and it was very upsetting. This was the first time I was able to interact with a group of Black students, but I didn't seem to fit in. My mom and her friends had very similar stories, so it didn't take it personally.

HIGH SCHOOL

For high school, I attended an International Baccalaureate (IB) program within a large high school in Tacoma. Every student in the IB program, including myself, was focused on one thing—getting into the best college possible. Every course and every extracurricular activity held far-reaching implications for the future. Everyone wanted to be the model student. I knew from my older brother, who completed the same program, that the model student was well-rounded—played sports, played an instrument, spoke another language, demonstrated leadership potential, and was at the top of the class. I played soccer, played violin, was active in Model United Nations, and studied hard so that I stayed at the top of my class. This same formula worked for my brother—he played in the band, played basketball, and interned with neurosurgeons and, as a result, he was a premed student at Yale. Given that students were vying for the same few slots in top colleges, it was no surprise that my relationships with my peers took on a more competitive edge. Interestingly enough, despite there being only a handful of minorities in my class of 100, the student I was most competitive with was not White—she was Southeast Asian.

In this fierce academic environment, racial divides did not seem relevant—until the school dances rolled around. People felt compelled to match up the two Blacks, the two Asians, and so forth, with one another regardless of whether we actually liked each other. But boycotting dances provided an easy solution to the awkwardness that ensued.

When I was accepted to an Ivy League school, most of my friends in the IB program were gracious, but some friends outside of the IB program were not—many of whom told my younger sister that I was accepted because I was Black and that they weren't accepted because I "took" their spot.

THE IVY ROAD

One of the reasons I was really excited to go off to Yale was that I thought I would meet students from similar backgrounds who were knowledgeable and culturally aware in general. However, I quickly learned that this was not the case. A fair amount of the students in Ivy League institutions came from insulated suburbs and boarding schools. Some of these students never had talked to an African American before. As for the students of color, many of them came from areas of the East Coast and the South that were predominantly Black, and it wasn't unusual for them to remark after finding out where I was from that they "didn't think there were any Black people there."

My freshman year provided me with many opportunities for personal growth. Being uncomfortable with having a racist roommate, I decided to become more active in the cultural houses and organizations. Although I had many positive experiences, I also had a contentious relationship with some of my Black peers—more specifically, those who felt the need to single out certain Blacks as needing to have their "Black cards" revoked. I tried to reason with some of these students, arguing that there wasn't just one standard for being Black and that there was a lot of diversity within the African American culture, but to no avail. One of my best friends, who was placed in the "not-Black-enough" category, simply told me that I was "being silly" and that I didn't "need to go to the African American Cultural Center to be Black" nor did I "need anyone's approval," that I was "simply Black." After some time, I realized that the students who were trying to define Blackness were the ones who were having issues with their own racial identity.

Another decision I made during freshman year was not to be a premedical major. Almost half of the incoming class was premed, and most of the other half were set on being lawyers or going into finance. Many students seem to opt for these careers because they promised the most security, prestige, and prosperity—which was a large part of my brother's desire to be a doctor. Because African Americans are underrepresented in these fields, there is sometimes even more pressure to go into them to increase the numbers of African Americans in these top-level positions. Interestingly, many high-achieving Blacks are an exception to this rule.

But I realized that there were other areas of study that I was more interested in and other careers that I wanted to pursue, besides becoming a doctor or lawyer, even if those were the most high-paying and secure options. I became interested in environmental studies and anthropology—environmental studies because it was a truly interdisciplinary field, and anthropology because it provided an opportunity to study and better understand the race and class dynamics that I was personally struggling with. Malcolm Gladwell began his research by looking at why he was successful academically and in his career and why other minorities were not. Similarly, I study race and class dynamics to better understand factors that explained why I was successful and other minorities were not. Both of the fields of study presented interesting experiences.

I was the only Black in the environmental studies major. To be fair, it was a small major—only 13 students in my class. The lack of diversity became very evident when certain racially charged issues came up—like racial determinist theories that argue Native Americans love the environment and Blacks hate it; that poor people either don't know how to take care of their natural resources or don't care to; whether minority and poor communities are disproportionately impacted by locally undesirable land uses that are health hazards, such as landfills and factories; and that institutional processes are definitely at play. Being the only minority, I was forced to speak up and point out when ideas had racist or elitist overtones, especially because I knew that no one else was going to.

On the opposite end of the spectrum, students of anthropology tried to be attentive to different cultures and viewpoints. All of us students of color were used as the spokespeople of Blacks and Asians. We often speculated that there must be a better way to do this than turn to the Black and Asian students in class and ask us to provide our perspective. I wasn't sure if the question annoyed me more or if my annoyance was more with one of my White friends, who one day remarked that she was jealous because I was always off doing cultural things—and that she wished that she had a culture, too.

In retrospect, I am glad I faced so many challenges during college—it prepared me for the harsh realities of the real world. I also was able to overcome the confines of being a model minority and model student in general and am more secure in my racial identity and career path.

QUESTIONS FOR REFLECTION

1. How important are early positive experiences in education in student achievement?
2. How important are parents' expectations and positive role models, like siblings, in shaping a student's academic goals?
3. Is the isolation high-achieving minorities experience in elite schools good preparation for the isolation they may experience in careers? Discuss.

THE OUTCOME

I graduated from Yale and continue to work in the environmental law and policy field.

REFERENCES

Gladwell, M. (2011). *Outliers: The story of success.* New York, NY: Back Bay.

RESOURCES

Grossman, L. (2008). Outliers: Malcolm Gladwell's success story. *TIME*. Retrieved from http://www.time.com/time/magazine/article/0,9171,1858880,00.html#ixzz1koCaLz6K

Grasgreen, A. (2011). *Opting out.* Retrieved from http://www.insidehighered.com/news/2011/12/02/new-book-says-elite-black-students-dont-try-high-paying-job

CHAPTER 13

GIFTEDNESS AND BLACK GIRLHOOD

by Delila Owens, SaDohl K. Goldsmith,
Rhonda M. Bryant, and Patrice S. Bounds

BACKGROUND

The community in which Tianna and her family live has deep roots. Initially an enclave for emancipated African Americans, the community has continued to remain primarily African American despite integration of other neighborhoods in this Midwestern city. Tianna enjoys the comfort of an extended kin network that includes her maternal and paternal grandparents and "play" aunts and uncles who are longtime family friends not related by blood, but who nevertheless provide guidance to her parents on educational and spiritual matters.

Similarly, the city leadership is also primarily African American. This is especially significant to Tianna and her family in that they have experienced the positive influences that African American leadership has provided in their communities. Where the leadership has been less than positive, the community generally regarded these shortcomings as related to leaders' poor choices or moral decision making rather than related to race.

The city has faced numerous challenges in educational funding. The city relies on neighborhood zoning to place students in schools; that is, students attend the schools in their neighborhoods. However, there are no magnet programs in Tianna's neighborhood and the closest program requires her to board a bus early in the morning. Some of Tianna's community members consider lack of magnet programs in poorer parts of the city as an inequity. Consequently, they have lobbied the school board to move magnet programs closer to the inner parts of the city; the board has refused, citing budget and physical plant limitations. Tianna has had to travel a long distance to get to the magnet program that she attends.

TIANNA'S STORY

Tianna, a 15-year-old Black female, is a freshman at a moderately sized high school. Her mother, stepfather, and siblings live in a modest income neighborhood. Her biological father passed away when she was 10 years old.

Seeking the input of her high school counselor, Tianna tells the counselor that she feels sad most of the time and that lately, she finds completing school and family responsibilities exhausting. After school, she picks up her two younger sisters (ages 6 and 8) and is responsible for their care until her parents come home from work around 6 p.m. Tianna finds it difficult to stay awake in class because she feels "bored" and this makes completing "a ton" of homework even more difficult. In particular, Tianna does not understand how her schoolwork relates to her life and responsibilities. She has told her teachers that she knows most of the material they cover, and she had a 4.0 average in middle school. Tianna's current grade point average is 3.7 overall, and she is enrolled in honors classes.

Socially, Tianna reports having few friends and not sharing much in common with her classmates. Tianna observes, "My classmates already have their cliques," and that most of these students have been friends since grade school. Tianna indicates that her middle school placed her in gifted education when she was in seventh grade. Her parents expressed their pride in her achievements and when she tells them about her feelings of social isolation, they stress the "importance of education" and tell her that she has "plenty of time for all that social stuff." Tianna knows that her parents are "right" but she feels that she is missing high school "fun" and that she is not fully equipped to negotiate friendships at school.

Tianna indicates that she was one of two African American females in gifted education and that while her gifted classmates seemed "nice," she felt more comfortable with her other classmates because she knew a few of them from her neighborhood. Tianna states that her teachers are "good" and that they encourage her. The teachers are concerned that recently she seems bored and that she daydreams during class. When we probed more about her classmates, Tianna sadly notes that she does not have much in common with them and feels uncomfortable because they are "extremely competitive" when discussing grades and plans for the future. She prefers cooperative learning assignments, but her teachers primarily have students work independently. Tianna wonders if her gifted education peers will accept her because she does not talk about her grades even though they are high and the students have been friends since elementary grades. Tianna has tried to make friends outside of gifted education, but her schedule does not facilitate this and she does not live in the school's neighborhood. Housed in a school located several miles from her home, Tianna has a long bus ride to and from school. This is the only place where the gifted program is available.

Given Tianna's feelings of disconnection from her gifted peers and a school culture that she believes values achievement over cooperative and student-led learning, we do not find it surprising that her transition to high school has been especially tough. Still, Tianna wants us to know that she "loves school" and hopes to become a successful business owner. If she could, she would go to a women's college like Bennett College or Spelman College so she can be around "positive young ladies." When asked to describe herself in a few words, Tianna uses words like "responsible," "friendly," and "shy." When asked how her classmates would describe her, Tianna responded that they would use words like "quiet" and "a loner." Tianna feels that her peers misconstrue her introversion as disinterest in them and social interactions. Nevertheless, she really wants to find a few friends to "hang out at the mall with" and "to go to sleepovers."

Continuing, Tianna indicates that her family and school responsibilities are so important that she has not had time to participate in extracurricular activities. When asked if she feels her responsibilities are too great, Tianna shared that her parents have made many sacrifices for her and her sisters. She feels good that she can help but wants to get involved in clubs (i.e., math club, pep club) now that she is in high school. Tianna does report that her life is very different from those of her peers because they do not seem to have to help with managing siblings and family chores because of their parents' work responsibilities.

As we came to know Tianna better, she shared fond memories of her father. His death was unexpected and the result of a stroke he had at work. Tianna "loves" her stepfather and he tries hard to make the family happy, but she really misses her father. She is afraid to bring this up because her mother was so sad after he died, and Tianna does not want to open an old wound. When we asked Tianna to describe her neighborhood, she painted a vibrant picture of many ethnicities living and working together. She notes that there are "more Latinos than before" and "people from the islands" in her neighborhood and that older women from these groups teach her how to play their games and how to cook food in according to their traditions. Although some of the boys try to "holler" at her, she knows her parents will not allow her to date until she is 16. Tianna has to get up early to get to school, and she cannot stay for afterschool activities because the activities bus will get her home too late to pick up her sisters. Still, Tianna seems to have rich experiences at home and in her neighborhood, which are in stark contrast to her school experiences.

Tianna, who is only one of two African American students in the gifted program, may feel pressure to perform because of her race. Interestingly, Tianna told us that her parents express special pride that she is African American and in the gifted program. Their expressions make sense to her because it seems like "some people don't expect Black kids to do well." This is a sentiment she has experienced from adults at church and in her neighborhood several times.

QUESTIONS FOR REFLECTION

1. What approach would you take to assist Tianna's integration into the school culture?
2. Who would your approach involve and how would you get them to buy-in to your approach?
3. Tianna reported sadness and difficulty concentrating. What would you do to address this?
4. What effect do you think that Tianna's emerging racial identity development has on her self-concept?
5. In your opinion, how have changes in the school, such as the busing of students from different neighborhoods, and changes in mandated instructional practices built community within the school and encouraged autonomy and cultural expression in gifted African American girls?

THE OUTCOME

Tianna, now a junior in high school, is doing well both socially and academically. She has become a member of the school's varsity basketball team. The differences in her abilities and personality have become more apparent to teachers and coaches. She is a natural born leader. She volunteers weekly for Big Brothers/Big Sisters, and today aspires to become an attorney. She is still enrolled in the gifted and talented program and has a 3.5 out of 4.0 cumulative grade point average.

SECTION IV

NEGOTIATING MULTIPLE IDENTITIES: ABILITY, RACE, CLASS, AND PLACE

CHAPTER 14

ON GROWING UP BLACK, RURAL, AND (UN)GIFTED

by Sheneka M. Williams

BACKGROUND

I grew up in a rural town that was comprised of approximately 12,000 people during my youth. Today, given the loss of manufacturing jobs and the declining need for the paper industry, the town's population has decreased to approximately 6,000. Due to the lack of job opportunities, many individuals who leave my hometown and go away to college are unable to return. Given that reality, I knew that when I graduated from high school I wouldn't be able to come back to my hometown.

My family is very close-knit. My parents have been married for 48 years, and I am the youngest of three girls. My father is a retired school superintendent, and my mother is a homemaker. My sisters and I are all college-educated, although I am the only one who received a doctorate. My paternal grandfather was the principal of a one-room schoolhouse, and his students called him "Professor." I often hear from relatives that I cherish education in the same way that he did, and I am sad to say that I never got to know him. Nevertheless, I realize that I am who I am because of who he was.

MY STORY

REALIZING I WAS ACADEMICALLY DIFFERENT

When I was 6 or 7 years old, I remember spending what seemed like countless hours sitting in a room with a man—a man who was a stranger to me. He asked me to put pieces of a puzzle together, and he tracked how long it took me to complete the task. He asked me what different words meant—words that I had not pronounced before. I spent time with this man—a psychometrician—more than once. Little did I know that I was being tested for giftedness. Regardless of the hours I spent with this stranger, I did not pass the test.

I progressed through my elementary school years not knowing that I had been tested for being gifted. I just knew that I had spent more hours than I preferred taking an assessment for "smart kids" that seemed a waste of time to me. I wanted to go to recess with other students, not take a test all day. I remember my parents mentioning the possibility of me skipping a grade, but I did not know that was one of the reasons I was taking a test. When I was in middle school, I realized that I failed the gifted test. I realized this when I witnessed some of my classmates getting pulled out of class for gifted coursework. I could not understand why they were going to spend time with the smart teacher, when it was evident that I made much better grades than all of them. I can see them in my mind now—they are all White, and I am Black. They were placed in the gifted program, and I was not. I felt less than—like I was not as smart or not as worthy as them.

REIFYING THE NOTION OF BEING DIFFERENT: GRADES 7–12

My middle school also had a practice that I came to understand later in life. The middle school I attended practiced ability grouping, or tracking. The tracks were literally labeled A, B, C, or D. I remember being in the A group. Most of the students in my group were White, but there was a core group of us who were Black—Reggie, Dennis, Pierre, Diane, Donna, Marie, Katlyn, and me. We called ourselves the Goonies. Oddly enough, we chose this name because of the movie, but I am not sure if any of us ever saw the movie; we simply heard about it. So I can't say our name had any particular meaning, but we made an informal pact to support each other, academically and personally. We went through most of high school taking the same advanced or AP courses. It is important to note that Reggie and Pierre dropped out of the Goonies as we entered high school. They no longer wanted to be labeled with us. In fact, it was not cool for them to be smart Black boys. Dennis, on the other hand, hung in there with us ladies. He persevered all the way through to his medical degree. In fact, three out of six of the Goonies received terminal degrees. That's not too bad for six Black students growing up in the rural South.

As we matriculated through high school and remained in segregated classrooms in desegregated schools, we experienced much success in the classroom as we competed against our White peers for grades, awards, and other recognition. However, our Black peers saw us as sellouts. Although they appreciated our academic talents, they saw our academic progress as "acting White." I remember vividly that one of my Black male friends, who is now deceased, called me "Oreo." That hurt my feelings, but I didn't let it stop me from pursuing my academic goals. While my Black friends were calling me "Oreo" or "sell-out," one of my White friends would often say to me, "You don't act like the rest of them." I didn't appreciate her comment at the time, but I didn't know how to respond to it. If she said that to me now, then my response would be different, and our friendship might be strained.

DIMINISHING MY DIFFERENTNESS: COLLEGE ADMISSIONS

Upon graduation from high school, there was only one college that I wanted to attend. I wanted to go there because it was the flagship university in my state. Moreover, I wanted to attend the school because of its great football history. I wasn't old enough to really understand the school's tainted, racist history. However, it seemed like a big deal for a Black person from my small town to attend there. My dad would say, "Baby, I remember the time when we [Black folk] couldn't go there." His comments made me feel like I was accomplishing something big by being admitted to the university.

While at the university, I felt like I was attending a school-within-a school, which was a good thing. During the time I was an undergraduate there, there were approximately 20,000 students. However, the students of color enrollment rates hovered around 10%, with a majority of us being Black. I was not called an Oreo in college, but that's probably because I was around more like-minded peers. Meaning, most of the friends I made in college had been at the top of their classes as well and had friends who were White. Now that I was in college, being smart was part of the norm. This meant that I didn't seem different because I was interacting with a larger group of students who were similar. It's significant to note that a large number of Black students, especially males, played sports and the other half were in fraternities or sororities. I was neither an athlete nor a sorority girl, but I still felt at home at a White public university. As I reflect on it, college was the first place where I experienced the interaction of race and social class in both my academic and social lives.

Despite the school-within-a-school model that Black students preferred at the university, we felt the university treated us fairly, and we believed that we received a quality education. Black student enrollment alone at the university was large enough to comprise a small college. We gave little thought or effort to cross-racial interactions because we felt we had protection in numbers. We also felt, from an educational standpoint, that attending a predominantly White university afforded us the same quality education that the White students received. This, we believed, was the ultimate purpose of us attending college there. As a result, most of my friends, especially Black women, who graduated from there moved on to very productive and lucrative careers.

Upon graduating from the university, I taught high school for 6 years. The high school's demographic was approximately 60% White and 40% Black. Less than 1% of the student body was of other races. Actually, the high school where I taught had a similar racial composition to the school I attended. Although I did not recognize it at the time, that probably made my adjustment there somewhat easier. It is also important to note that I student taught at the same school where I earned my first teaching job. This means that the students knew I was a recent college graduate. I was 22 years old teaching 18-year-olds, and that encouraged me to mature quickly. Although I did not teach advanced or AP classes, I coached a debate team. My debate team was mostly Black, and that made me really proud, particularly because we were in a majority White school. Also, research indicates that few Black students participate in school organizations like debate and student government. They were extremely intelligent students who understood the world in a way that I did not. Coaching them attributed to my growth in understanding policy and politics. Little did I know that while I was coaching them, I was inherently coaching myself. I often reflect on how the conversations I had with high school debate students 10 years ago inform some of my class discussions in the graduate-level courses that I teach today.

CAREER TRAJECTORY AND K–12 GIFTED PLACEMENT

I decided to leave public school teaching after 6 years. It was then that I entered the top-ranked college of education in the country. This private institution was a different kind of place for me. I had never been in any private school before; therefore, I had to adjust to the customs and traditions of the school. Although I had taught in a majority White setting and had many White friends, this school came with a sense of privilege that I had never experienced. For example, we referred to faculty members by first name, and we often had social time at bars and at their homes after class. This was culture shock for me, especially given my Southern Baptist roots. There was only one other Black student in my program who attended full-time, and he, like the majority of others, had attended elite private schools all of his life. In fact, I had never heard of some of their schools before. I realized that I was an outlier in this setting, especially because I was the only Black woman in the group. However, one of my mentors made me realize that being an outlier was a good thing. I will never forget the day that he looked at me and said, "They need your perspective. Don't ever forget that." From that moment onward I did not feel inferior as a Black woman. Being a woman was never a barrier because we were the majority in the program, although I must admit that it appears that more opportunities to publish and do other academic tasks went to the men. As I reflect upon it, my graduate experience provided me with a great formal and informal education that prepared me for an academic career. It prepared me for the politics of the "game" that pervades the academy. Additionally, this was another lesson in race and social class for me.

QUESTIONS FOR REFLECTION

1. How does the lack of social and cultural capital among many rural African American students impact their assessments for gifted programs?

2. In what ways might student relationships/friendships influence behavior and achievement, as is evident in the case presented here?

3. One's upbringing does not necessarily dictate one's trajectory. African American students from rural areas rarely see individuals with professional and/or terminal degrees. How might you increase opportunities for talented African American rural students to gain greater exposure to professional careers?

THE OUTCOME

I am currently an assistant professor in the College of Education at the University of Georgia, where I enjoy conducting research in the general area of education policy. My career goals are to attain full professor status and to either become a college dean or lead an education policy think tank in the future.

CHAPTER 15

FINDING MY IDENTITY IN A GIFTED MAGNET MIDDLE SCHOOL

by Dawn L. Curry

BACKGROUND

"Dawn. How are you?" Duane said as we embraced. I hadn't seen him in almost 20 years. Duane continued, "You were the girl that received all of the awards in elementary school. You were so smart—the smartest person in school." I laughed and shook my head listening to him describe me in that way. A long time had passed between our elementary school days and our chance meeting at a funeral. However, it made me think back on my elementary school years when I was a successful gifted student. I was at the top of my class at the time. Little did I know that after leaving elementary school, I would have to wrestle with myself to discover and embrace my gifted identity.

Growing up as a gifted Black girl—what does that really mean? I have come to accept that it means different things at different academic stages. My journey as a gifted student, which began in the second grade, can be compared to the experience of riding a roller coaster at an amusement park. The elation, fear, sense of the unknown, soaring highs, and deep lows are the images and emotions that come to mind when I recall my transition from elementary school to attending a talented and gifted magnet middle school. This transition forced me to embrace the multilayered identity that comes with being young, gifted, and Black.

MY STORY

ELEMENTARY SCHOOL

As an elementary school student, I loved school. I couldn't get enough of it. I enjoyed everything about school: my teachers, field trips, learning, homework, my friends, and being involved in numerous clubs and activities. I dreaded summers because that meant 2 1/2 months without school. I even remember crying hysterically when I was too sick to go to school. I cried so much that my mother threatened to give me a spanking, and I was willing to take it because I loved school that much.

I was blessed to be raised by two wonderful parents whom I still adore and admire to this day. I was comfortable in school, and this was very important because I was an extremely shy child. School was the place where I consistently experienced success, recognition, and admiration, and it was the place where I knew who I was. I remember being the student the teacher called on to answer questions, to run errands, or to take the speaking parts for assemblies. My identity as a smart girl was clear, and I embraced it fully.

I admired each one of my elementary school teachers, and I felt that they brought out the best in me. Each of them added to the confidence created from my school experience. I remember Ms. Newell allowing a few of us to stay after school and help her in the classroom. It was heaven on Earth to actually ride in her car as she drove us home. I can recall Mr. Green taking the top students to a local pizza place after school to reward us for being the "best students." These pockets of memories helped me accelerate up the hill of being gifted in elementary school.

Gifted wasn't a term that I remember being used in elementary school. I do remember TAG (talented and gifted) being used to refer to the few of us who were pulled out of our classroom on a weekly basis to attend a special class. The classes were fun and challenging and I enjoyed them.

Although I don't recall being called a gifted child in elementary school, I do remember understanding that intellectual abilities had benefits. One of the most vivid memories I have is winning the fourth-grade spelling bee. Afterward, I was thirsty, and although the class was lining up to return to the classroom, I asked my teacher if I could get a drink from the water fountain. She replied, "You can have whatever you want!"

Oh really? I thought. *Being the best speller could get me anything I wanted? Wow!* I was certainly determined to continue to be the best.

Life during elementary school was good. I was the top student, I loved my teachers, and they loved me. Race was not a factor during that time because in my world, it didn't need to be. My school had slowly changed from being a majority White school to being a pre-dominantly Black school as a result of the last phase of desegregation busing in my county. The bus ride to school was about 25 minutes. We passed several elementary schools that were close to our neighborhood. White children attended my school, but injustice was not a concern. I witnessed firsthand that being bright was rewarded.

MIDDLE SCHOOL

During my sixth-grade year, I was teetering at the top of the first roller coaster hill, and I left elementary school with an armload of awards, plaques, and recognition. I thought I was capable of anything and that my knowledge and hard work would pay off. But like a first time roller coaster rider, I was not prepared for the steep drop that would come. In this case, the steep drop was in the form of a magnet middle school for talented and gifted students.

In an attempt to provide more diversity in schools, the school district in which I was enrolled offered competitive magnet middle schools. My seventh-grade year was the second year of the program. All identified gifted students were able to select a magnet middle school to attend. My parents told me of the great opportunity it would be to attend a school where everyone was high performing and loved school just as much as me. I was 12 years old and was thrilled to be able to tell people that I was going to a TAG magnet center. I had been "chosen" to do something different, but it did not dawn on me that I would not be attending school with my neighborhood friends. I also didn't realize that I would meet different types of gifted students. Instead, I ignored the downward jerk on the roller coaster.

The school, which was about 20 minutes from my home, was in a neighborhood different from my own. Trees lined the street of my neighborhood that was solely comprised of single-family homes that mostly reflected two working parents, some with extended family members. Each home had a driveway and ample yard space, and it was common to see manicured lawns with lawn ornaments and small gardens comfortably nestled behind fences. The school I chose to attend was located in a low-income area and the students who were slated to attend were predominantly African American. Low-income apartments, duplex homes, and modest single-family homes surrounded the school. A once-sprawling mall that was the center of activity was on the decline. High-end anchor stores were quickly disappearing and were either empty or being replaced by discount clothing or housewares stores. In addition to the financial decline, crime was becoming a regular occurrence and the drug outbreak was running rampant in the area.

The magnet program was a court-monitored plan that provided more racial diversity in schools and an alternative to busing. The district wanted to balance the schools racially. In other words, the Black schools wanted to attract White students and the White schools wanted to attract Black students. The goal of the TAG magnet program was to provide academic rigor in all subjects. The programs also had a multicultural education emphasis. They offered foreign language options, assigned cultural projects designed to broaden our view of the world, and coordinated special multicultural events. At 12 years old, I was excited to have been selected to attend the magnet program and was unaware of the reasons behind its implementation.

The summer leading up to seventh grade seemed long. I was eager to start the new school year at a new school. A few days before the school year began, seventh-grade students were given the opportunity to attend an orientation. This was a half-day event that allowed students to meet their teachers, walk through their daily schedules, and become familiar with the school. Unfortunately, I boarded the wrong bus. One of the most embarrassing things that could happen to a middle school student is getting on the wrong bus and arriving at the wrong school and that is exactly how my orientation day began. I had been accepted into a magnet school for gifted students, but I managed to take the wrong bus! Little did I know that this was the first incident that would make me question my giftedness.

During the first few weeks of school, I took a math exam, and after the scores of the magnet students were disaggregated, I was placed in the low math class. What a reality check! I was no longer the top math student. Instead, I was one of the lower students with regard to math. That was the first sign that my roller coaster was heading downhill.

I remember questioning my ability, intelligence, and all that I had known in my safe world of elementary school. Was low performance in math an indication of how well I would do in my other courses? My mother would often say, "You just do the best you can. If a C is your best, then that is fine" in her attempts to comfort and encourage me, especially after I had begun to earn, C's, B's, and very few A's in math. Up until this point, I had *never* received anything less than an A. I was quickly losing my academic identity and hardly recognized myself.

I was confronted with accepting my little-fish-in-a-big-pond life and had to navigate between being a "magnet" or a "local." The line of declaration was clear between the two, because the local students were not in the magnet program but were attending the school because it was their neighborhood school. The line was only erased during lunch and elective courses such as gym and chorus. It was during these times of coexistence that I was faced with having to choose with whom I would socially "hang." Magnet students were already taunted for being smart. On top of that, the African American magnet kids were taunted for being smart *and* "acting White." I found that I began to question my racial identity, too. Did I belong with a group of students that could so quickly turn on me because of the classes I took or with whom I chose to hang?

In elementary school, I enjoyed friendships with people from different races. I was never made to feel like I was "acting White" or trying to be White because of the friendships I maintained. In middle school, I became increasingly aware that differences existed, and it was extremely important to let others know where you stood. I soon realized that my lower academic math class was filled with more African American students while the higher performing class was filled with White, Indian, and Asian students.

MAKING NEW FRIENDS, RECOGNIZING DIFFERENCES

Because I was no longer attending school with my neighborhood friends, it was extremely important for me to make new friends. I began to be exposed to the social ills of society, which were far from the beginning of the roller coaster ride I started in the safe haven of elementary school. I remember hearing racial jokes told by the African American students. I now wonder how Aaron, an Asian student, felt when an African American girl teased him because of the shape of his eyes. For the first time, I saw racial differences, a difference in abilities, and a difference in opportunities provided based on the differences in race and abilities. Was this what the world was about? I wasn't too sure that I liked this new world or what it was saying about my identity. Did my gifted identity supersede my African American identity?

This dark emotional period was like the surprise tunnel that often appears in the middle of a roller coaster. I began to wear a jacket during school. My classmates may not have seen the shirts I wore because they were always covered with the dark blue jean jacket that had become my source of comfort in school. My mom questioned my actions, but still issued daily words of affirmation: "I know you are doing your best." "You are in a very challenging school." "Your dad and I love you and are so proud of you." Although I needed to hear those words, they did not remove me from the tunnel I was in. Self-doubt screamed in my head and drowned out the positive affirmations that came from my mom.

In just a few months, I went from a happy-go-lucky high-achieving student to a student who was no longer considered high achieving enough to be afforded certain opportunities. High-achieving students were able to take the PSAT early and invited to participate in academic competitions. I slowly sunk into a pit, and I felt as if I had no way out as I questioned the world's attempt to highlight differences.

One of my most vivid memories of just how different my life had become occurred when my math teacher began the class period with a speech about how some students did not do well on a math test administered a few days prior. She continued on for about 10 minutes explaining that she was very concerned about the students who failed the test. Of course, everyone was nervous and wondered about his or her performance on the test. I remember having what felt like an empty hole in my stomach. I just knew that my teacher was directing her speech toward me, and it seemed like her footsteps were slow and thunderous as she passed out the tests. She made her way to me, and sure enough, I had failed. All I could think about was how I would be able to face my parents or anyone who had known me before middle school, for that matter.

I struggled in math that year. I was frustrated daily but I never sought out extra help. Looking back, it seems that seeking help would have been the obvious thing to do, but asking for help was such a foreign concept to me. I was accustomed to having academics come easy to me. I received top grades in all of the subjects in elementary school without studying. I had been the student used to tutor and assist other students or provide the answers to the examples so that the other students could see how it was done—asking for help was foreign and unfamiliar to me. It was my assumption that students who were accepted into a talented and gifted magnet school did not need to ask for help—even if they were gifted students in the "lower class." I saw the failing grades and lack of understanding as a new label that I *had* to wear, without question. I accepted this label and wore it the rest of the year in silent acceptance and agreement.

As an already shy girl, the academic difficulties caused me to close out the world even more. I volunteered less and less. Socially, I could count on one hand those I considered friends. I felt alienated from the neighborhood kids who were attending the neighborhood school, and I no longer played with them. For the first time, I was excited to see summer vacation arrive at the end of the school year. It was clear to me that I needed this year to end.

As the year ended I had begun to accept the distorted identity that had emerged. In my mind, I was girl who was "somewhat smart" who hated math and would never be good at it. I no longer saw myself as the award winner or a top student and although the next year was better, it would take a long time for me to see that my identity was greater than seventh grade, greater than the magnet program, and greater than any label that anyone could ever place on me. Unlike a roller coaster ride, I cannot go on the journey again, but I can share my experience with others who are waiting in line.

QUESTIONS FOR REFLECTION

1. How can schools support the social and emotional needs of gifted African American students when entering a gifted magnet program?
2. What are schools doing to address academic challenges gifted Black students face when being invited to take college entrance exams in middle school?
3. In what ways can schools support African American families of gifted students who experience failure and a deflated academic identity?

THE OUTCOME

Despite the challenges faced in middle school, I did experience academic and social success in high school. In addition to maintaining a high GPA, I was elected twice as a class officer and participated in many extracurricular activities. The turning point came in attending a high school that not only acknowledged but embraced differences. The administrators and teachers fostered a sense of community among students and parents. It is interesting to note that both schools were magnet schools for gifted students. The difference I came to understand through my experience was that the middle school focused on achievement scores and the high school focused on children.

RESOURCES

Davis, J. (2010). *Bright, talented, and Black: A guide for families of African American gifted learners.* Scottsdale, AZ: Great Potential Press.

Hébert, T. (2011). *Understanding the social and emotional lives of gifted students.* Waco, TX: Prufrock Press.

Jolly, J. L., Treffinger, D. J., Inman, T. F., & Smutny, J. F. (2011). *Parenting gifted children: The authoritative guide from the National Association for Gifted Children.* Waco, TX: Prufrock Press.

CHAPTER 16

FINDING AND REDEFINING GHANAIAN IDENTITY AS A GIFTED AFRICAN IN AMERICA

by Beryl Ann Otumfuor

BACKGROUND

Growing up in Ghana, West Africa, which has a largely homogenous race, I never had to educationally redefine my identity until I moved to the United States. There was never a moment where I had to question who I was and what I could do, let alone constantly question my educational aptitude. My experiences may be similar to an African American student in a predominantly White college; however, the path varies significantly due to our cultural differences. Although my parents had no formal college education, their zeal to ensure that I received the best education definitely provided me with valuable opportunities that have shaped my entire philosophy on the value of quality education and its advantages. It's amazing to find myself in a position to share the experiences that have compounded who I am and what I have become due to my solid educational background.

MY STORY

MY PAST, MY FOUNDATION

For the most part, my primary and secondary school education was in a private Catholic school. Due to the strict governing structure, attending a Catholic school made a momentous difference in my behavior and attitude and instilled in me a sense of accountability for all of my actions—more specifically for my learning. Combined with the rigorous West African academic curriculum, the Catholic school's provision of effective discipline prepared me to enter postsecondary schools and beyond with a sense of responsibility and integrity. I did not participate in any gifted, honors, or advanced programs, because they were not available in my culture. Hence, no matter how exceptional someone was, he still ended up in the general classroom, which was not as challenging as an honors class. Thus, the mandate to learn and accelerate my already developing gifts and abilities was not fortified.

At 4 years old, I could not only absorb difficult text with ease, but also possessed the ability to quickly recall dates and numbers associated with historical events. It was later in life that my mother discovered that I was a visual learner with an extreme photographic memory. Even when I excelled on my third-grade mathematics entry exam and was to be skipped on to the fourth grade, my father disapproved because he believed my social skills would be impacted, especially because I was already a year younger than my classmates. I sometimes wonder how different my life course would have been if that opposing decision had not been made. What would have happened, what other interests might I have developed, or would I truly have been so overwhelmed that I would I have fallen through the cracks due to the pressures to succeed? Or, would I have actually excelled beyond the point at which I stand? I believe more structured programs equipped for challenging young minds such as myself would have been essential in building on my extraordinary abilities, especially when I compare my experiences to that of the well-established gifted or exceptional programs in the United States.

I always thought I was a gifted individual, until I started high school. It was at this stage in my life that I realized I needed to put in some extra effort to achieve my dreams and goals. My school was among the top-tier programs in the nation and hence, all students accepted to enroll in my high school were all coming from top-quality middle school programs. Although I excelled in history, geography, and science during elementary and middle school, I enrolled in the science track because I initially wanted to pursue a medical degree (the Ghanaian high school systems were divided into different academic tracks: science, general arts, visual arts, agriculture, business, and home economics). Although my science high school curriculum was arduous, the experience better prepared me for college.

I realized that I was no longer interested in pursuing a career in medicine after high school and because psychology was not formally included in the university curriculum in my country, I chose to pursue my studies outside Ghana. I believed the United States was the best setting to help me accomplish my goals. During my first semester in college, I enrolled in a psychology course and became intrigued by the content presented. This newfound information encouraged me to pursue the field of psychology for my college career.

Once I arrived in the United States, I started to research the high school curriculum of a local school district, and I began to realize that the Ghanaian school system was acutely flawed. This is because a specific focus limited to one area of study forced individuals to only explore career opportunities for that particular sector of study. Even with a demanding curriculum, a lack of exposure to a well-rounded education can skew the worldview of young students.

REDEFINING WHO I AM

The academic competition encountered during primary through secondary school may have seemed overwhelming to some. However, when one enters college and graduate school, the competition intensifies and can lead to frustration or raise many doubts. When I started college at a predominantly White institution in rural Pennsylvania, the excitement of my freedom was shattered by the journey I had to take in the academic world. During my first year, I was assigned to a research mentor, Dr. Brown, who was extremely passionate about counseling. I felt that this was my calling to a lasting legacy.

Dr. Brown and I engaged in different research projects; however, it seemed as if every suggestion I made was received with some sort of reservation. This behavior continued for a couple of years, and I began to believe that I did not have what it took to be at this level of education. As time progressed, I came to the realization that the mentoring relationship was unhealthy and self-doubt had developed; thus, I decided to end the mentoring relationship.

Shortly thereafter, I found another advisor to whom I attribute a great deal of my graduate school success—Dr. Ruiz, a woman of Latina descent, with family from Cuba. She also lived in Florida for several years; hence, she could relate to my transposition experiences. Dr. Ruiz and I created a strong bond. Her belief in my abilities and her constant support of my uniqueness helped me to realize the potential that I had and could obtain. Also, her research interests ignited my interest in cognition and development, which ultimately led to my decision to attend graduate school with a focus in educational psychology.

After viewing the way research impacts our lives, I vowed to utilize my career to help the lives of others. From this point, I decided graduate education was the only way to make this possible. But I felt I had only scratched the surface of many research issues during my undergraduate career; hence, I believed in order to improve the contributions I could make in graduate school, it was essential to continue with a postbaccalaureate training. My training under the guidance of my advisor and research mentor strongly enlightened my desire for graduate education and helped me acquire practical skills necessary for a research career and also gain a huge appreciation for collaborative research work.

My graduate school experience led to a reconfiguration of my identity and a startling realization of what it entailed to do research, irrespective of my exceptional abilities. It was during my tenure in graduate school that I had to redefine who I was, in all aspects of my life. I found that I questioned myself more and more and wondered about my existence in a graduate program. It was then that I realized that even though the crème de la crème entered graduate programs, it took more than gifts and talents to succeed.

During my tenure as a graduate student, incidences that occurred greatly affected my outlook on education, specifically the biases in the classroom due to race and gender. As a Black student originally from Africa, I constantly try not to attribute all of my experiences to the issue of race and gender, but I had to face the truth—there were some individuals who could not believe that a Black person would be so equipped and disciplined to handle a rigorous graduate curriculum. Through research and being informed, I later came to understand where this misrepresented concept derived from. This was somewhat challenging during my first 2 years of graduate school and because the journey was relatively new, I expected my master's advisor to nurture me during the process. This, however, was not the case, and at the end it felt like I was being left at the altar. Although discouraging, this experience did not stop me from pursuing my dream.

I decided to further my studies and begin a doctoral program. The coursework, internships, and field placement lessons shaped my philosophy of gifted education. For a long time, I believed being gifted meant you excelled in all your academic subjects, by being in the top 10th percentile of your class. The courses and interactive discussions in my doctoral program precisely helped to broaden my understanding on the scope of intelligence. I realized that giftedness did not just encompass excellent academic ability but also artistic and creative abilities. People look at the great minds of the world like Einstein and Hawking and tend to equate their intelligence to scientific abilities, sometimes failing to realize it was their creativity that made them stand out from their peers.

QUESTIONS FOR REFLECTION

1. How can we remove the barriers experienced by gifted Black students with international backgrounds in higher education and build secure bridges toward success?
2. In what ways might we empower gifted Black international students in their development of a professional identity?
3. How can we address deficit thinking of professors regarding gifted Black students from other countries?

THE OUTCOME

A person does not really know his limit until it is tested. My hope is that everyone experiences at least one defining moment that makes their path in life clear. For me, this moment came as a result of the experiences I encountered during my master's program. Although the experience could have deterred me from focusing on the task ahead, I found that it served as a catalyst for me to investigate some of the critical issues in our educational system. I am happy to share that pressing toward my ultimate goal—receiving my doctorate—has qualified me to successfully defend my dissertation proposal. I am currently in the process of data collection and finishing up my dissertation writing. I am scheduled to graduate this December with my doctorate. It is important to note that I feel blessed because the culmination of my experiences made such strong impacts in my life and further strengthened the importance of education even for gifted students. Whereas when growing up, I associated giftedness to mainly academic tests, I have now come to appreciate the importance of creativity and other factors that make individuals unique.

CHAPTER 17

BECOMING COMFORTABLE WITH MYSELF, BY MYSELF

by Kiesa Ayana Harmon

BACKGROUND

I grew up in a middle-class community with my parents, two older brothers, and an older sister. All of my siblings were identified as gifted and participated in the gifted and talented program. I was identified as gifted and talented too, but I was also diagnosed with an auditory processing disability—which made me twice-exceptional. When I got into elementary school, I was the only African American student in the school, and that added another exceptionality to the mix. It was not until middle school that I finally experienced diversity among my peers and teachers, but, to my peers, I didn't act Black enough—yet another exceptionality. By the time I reached high school, my family relocated, but we moved to a state that did not support gifted students, plus I had to deal with the deficit thinking of culturally incompetent teachers. It wasn't until I reached college that I finally found my identity.

ELEMENTARY SCHOOL

My first elementary school was predominantly White and located in an upper class community. I always looked forward to kindergarten, but was not sure what to expect. I was the only Black girl in my class, but that didn't bother me because we were one of the only Black families in the neighborhood, so I was used to White people. At first, I thought nothing of how differently my classmates and teacher treated me. I was never chosen to be the line leader, no one would play with me during recess, and it seemed as if I was only allowed to play in the sandbox—by myself. I loved to swing on the swings, but I always had to patiently wait until everyone else finished, which left me with just a little, if any, time to swing. I had no clue about what happened or why it happened but, after a while, I realized it wasn't right.

My classroom had bulletin boards on every wall covered with students' work, but my teacher never put my artwork on the wall. The one time I felt very proud of a picture I drew, I shared it with my teacher and hoped that she would put it on the bulletin board. Instead, she examined my picture, looked down at me, and told me it was too ugly to go on the wall. I remember how disappointed and angry I felt—about myself.

During naptime, whenever I chose a spot next to a classmate, she would move their cot away from me. After this happened a few times, I asked my teacher if I could place my cot next to her desk so that I could sleep next to her as she worked. I saw other students do this in the past so I thought that it would work for me. But, she told me no and instructed me to lay in one of the far corners of the room where the "bad kids" slept. I wondered if being "bad" was the reason she didn't like me.

My favorite play center was the housekeeping center. Whenever I wanted to play with dolls in this center, my classmates only allowed me to play with the dolls that were Black and the dolls that were "messed up." Although I didn't mind playing with the Black dolls, I did mind being taunted and teased by my classmates who sang a song, "Baby, baby, dipped in gravy," because I sucked my thumb. The first time this happened, I followed my parents' advice and told the teacher. She listened to my complaint, smiled, and told me to stop sucking my thumb so they would stop teasing me, but she said nothing at all to them. I felt helpless.

The unfair treatment also continued in the afternoon when I attended a daycare that was across the street from the school. I was always fearful because if I didn't get to hold the teacher's hand to cross the street, I had to walk all by myself. All students were supposed to hold hands to safely cross the street, but no one would hold mine.

During science class, I would hear my classmates say that I was "dumb." But, this confused me because there were many things I knew about science that they did not. I did not know that I learned differently from my classmates, but a few days a week, the special education teacher would come and pull me out of class and take me to her classroom. She would talk and play games with me, and I would work on assignments that she picked out just for me. I felt safe with her, and I knew she really liked me. She told me I was very smart and that I learned in a different way.

I did not know why I was pulled out of the class to work. I remember wondering why, if I was so smart, did I have to leave class and work with her? But it didn't matter, because to me, that teacher seemed like an angel coming to my rescue. One of my fondest memories of her was when I drew a picture, and she told me it was beautiful—quite contrary to what happened when I shared my picture with my kindergarten teacher. Aside from the special education teacher, the only other friend I felt I had in my kindergarten class was the class pet, a huge rabbit with large floppy ears that hopped around the classroom. I knew how to lure the rabbit over to my table and oftentimes, when he got to me, he would snuggle up to me and nap. That rabbit somehow helped me relax and feel better about what was going on around me.

One day, I finally reached my breaking point as I gathered blocks to build walls for a house. I selected a big blue block, picked it up, and raised it above my head. As I was turning to add it to my house, I accidentally hit one of my classmates with the block. I apologized to him, but the teacher screamed at me! She asked me how I could be so mean and believed I hit him on purpose. She also stated she did not understand why I was such a bad girl and made me sit in the corner for the rest of the day. I never got the chance to explain anything. I remember putting all of the pieces together while I sat in the corner. I knew that somehow I had to get out of that classroom—away from those classmates and that teacher. I knew I had to tell my parents, but

I was terrified that I would get into trouble at home, because I got in trouble at school.

Up until then, my parents did not know how my classmates or teacher treated me. My mom would ask about my school day and would visit my classroom and the daycare at times. I wondered if she knew what was going on. I figured the way my classmates and teacher treated me was wrong or at the very least, not fair, but I didn't want to get them in trouble. I felt if I got them in trouble, they would treat me even worse. Nevertheless, I had reached my limit.

That day, when my mother picked me up, I told her that some older students harassed me during recess and the teacher and principal did not protect me. I hoped that story would cause her to take me out of that school. But my mom questioned me and finally got the complete truth about what happened. I was happy when she told me that evening that I did not have to go back to that school or that daycare. I knew the terror had finally ended! It was hard for my parents to explain to a 5-year-old child that she was being picked on because the shade of her skin was different from her classmates and teacher. But they reassured me I was loved and did nothing wrong.

After that, I was transferred to the same elementary school my older brother and sister attended, a predominantly White middle-class school where my siblings and I were the only African Americans in our classes again. Even though I knew I was in a safer place, I didn't trust anyone, including my classmates and teachers. I was scared to interact with my classmates because I didn't know how they were going to treat me. I didn't want to have people move away from me or tell me where I could go and when I could play. I didn't want to eat in the cafeteria at lunchtime or play outside for recess. My new teacher was understanding and allowed me to eat in the classroom with her and play with the musical instruments until I felt comfortable enough interact with my classmates during recess. She never asked me why I didn't want to go outside with my classroom. She praised my artwork and was impressed with my work. I remember wondering if she knew what had happened at my old school, but she never mentioned it at all. She actually cared about me.

The first time I went outside to play at recess, I could tell my teacher was happy for me. My sister's class had recess at the same time, and she and her friends would play with me and push me while I sat on the swing. It was at that point that I knew things were going to be okay. That same year, I met my best friends, Kayley and Samantha, and even though my skin was darker than theirs and I struggled with memorizing the same information they seemed to learn so quickly, it didn't matter to them. We all played together and accepted each other.

MIDDLE SCHOOL

I attended a different middle school from Kayley and Samantha, but I was excited because it was a school with diverse students and teachers. The school was in a middle-class neighborhood and had a magnet program for gifted students. Many of the students in the school looked like me, so to be among this type of diversity was great! But after awhile, I noticed I was still considered different.

Some of the Black girls in my class had issues with the way I looked because my hair was a different texture from theirs and my skin was lighter when compared to them. I also spoke differently and lived in a different neighborhood. This was a problem for some of my Black classmates, and they told me that I thought I was better than them and rolled their eyes at me. I was quiet, showed respect to the teachers, enjoyed learning, often completed my work early, and did extra work. In addition, I could leave the room to go the resource room if I needed any help.

I remember being accused of misbehaving by a substitute teacher. However, when my teacher returned, she rectified the situation and that angered some of my classmates. After school, two Black female classmates—who whispered horrible things in my ear that suggested that I thought I was better than they were and that I acted White—pushed me up against my locker. I was terrified and confused. I wondered why these girls were so mad at me and what it had to do with acting White. If there was one thing I knew, it was how White people acted, and that wasn't me! I managed to get away from them. I informed my father of what happened, and he assured me that I had done nothing wrong and that the girls were angry and tried to hurt my feelings. The next day, my parents met with the principal, who in turn, made the girls apologize and promise to leave me alone.

I still didn't understand what I had done to make those girls so angry and wondered what was going on. I didn't understand why girls who looked like me were so unwilling to accept me. I still tried to understand why girls who were White were also unwilling to accept me: I was too dark for the White folks and too light for the Black folks, and, it seemed I was too smart for both of them! My parents tried their best to reassure me that there was nothing wrong with me. They also reminded me to not let these types of things affect me. But I was very confused and tried to figure out who I was and where I fit in.

HIGH SCHOOL

Ninth grade was a good year for me. Our family relocated to a new state and the high school I attended seemed to be very diverse to me— even though it was predominantly White. It was located in a middle-class, college community. I was a member of the varsity gymnastics team and the school choir. I was one of the only Black students who participated in these extracurricular activities and, for the first time in my academic life, I was able to be myself and be a part of something that made me acceptable and popular.

I figured out early on that math and science were difficult for me, but when the teacher explained things to me in a different way, I did well. However, English was one of the subjects in which I excelled, so I was extremely proud when I placed into the advanced English class despite my disability.

Although I was only one of three African American students in my advanced English class, I enjoyed it. When we began reading *To Kill a Mockingbird*, my teacher informed us that the book contained some disturbing language. When we reached one of those chapters, the word "nigger" was discussed. The teacher asked for a show of hands of those who had been called this slur. I was not ashamed to admit that I had been. She then asked me to describe what happened and how it felt. Afterward, the teacher stated that she felt people didn't use that type of language anymore, but I became upset because it seemed she did not care or believed what happened.

Our final assignment for that class was a critique of our teacher's teaching style. The assignment provided a good opportunity for me to express how I felt about how she reacted to my experience of being called a "nigger" and was surprised to find out that she didn't know she was being insensitive and she apologized.

During my 10th-grade year, I wasn't as lucky. I felt from the very first day of class that my AP English teacher, Ms. Evans, didn't like me. She wouldn't call on me when I raised my hand, and she made me sit in the front row when all of the other students were able to choose their seats. The final straw was when I noticed items were marked wrong on some of my assignments when I knew they were correct. I wanted to double check and make sure I was absolutely certain before I told my parents what happened, so I compared my assignments to those of a few of my White classmates, and it became apparent that my teacher graded me differently.

My parents discussed the situation with her during Back to School night the next day. Every teacher had positive reports, but when we reached Ms. Evans, there was obvious tension. Ms. Evans went on to tell them that I was very disruptive in class and that I did not complete my assignments and as a result, I was earning a D in the class. My parents interjected and let her know they had some concerns as well and shared that I felt as if she didn't like me. They also shared the concerns they had about my grades and asked why she had not informed them of my academic status earlier. Ms. Evans then announced that she was leaving after one of her colleagues informed her that she didn't have to answer any questions. She told my parents that she would only meet with them with the principal present. My parents agreed and invited her to join them in the principal's office so that they could continue the discussion.

In the principal's office, my parents asked for an explanation for the disparity of grades in the teacher's grade book and my graded assignments (which they had on hand). Ms. Evans had no explanation. My mother told her that I felt that she would not call on me, even when my hand was raised. Ms. Evans responded that, at times, she did not think I understood her questions. My mother then asked if she was aware that I had an IEP and received special education support. Ms. Evans admitted she did not know and asked why I was in an AP class if I was in special education. My mother told her I was twice-exceptional and had every right to be in an AP class. At the end of the discussion, my parents asked that I be removed from Ms. Evans class, which was the only AP class available. The principal suggested that I remain in the class and assured that he would observe Ms. Evans weekly. Ms. Evans then announced that she was not prejudiced and that she had African American students in her class without any problems. My parents then insisted I be placed in a different class. Their request was granted, but I changed English classes two more times that year—because both teachers felt that I was too advanced and felt their classes were a disservice to me. It seemed, once again, I was different and did not fit in.

COLLEGE

I attended a state university and earned a bachelor's degree. While I was there, I decided I wanted to be part of a sorority. When I researched my choices, I became very discouraged and then angry because I felt that I should not have to choose to be in either a Black sorority or a White sorority. I could not belong to the White sorority because they did not want me as a member. But I also didn't want to join any of the Black sororities because I feared I would have experiences similar to those in middle school. So I decided to charter the first multicultural sorority on my college campus. My personal experiences were the passion that helped me decide to bring the sorority to campus. I wanted a place where people would be accepted for everything that made up who they were, and as a part of this sorority, I was accepted for who

I was—my race, where I resided, my level of intelligence, or anything else did not matter.

I will never understand people's hatred for those who are different. Although I now understand why my kindergarten teacher disliked me, I cannot understand how a kindergarten teacher could treat an innocent child the way she did. I still wrestle with the anger I feel toward those who are narrow-minded, but I do not know what to do about it. I am grateful that I have love in my heart and have forgiven those who have hurt me and, I can now say, I'm in a society that places me in many different categories, I have reached a place where I am okay with myself.

It'd be nice to think that maybe one day, when I have children, everyone could be accepting and get along with people who are different from them, but unfortunately I'd be doing a disservice to my children if I did not prepare them for what I'm sure they'll face. I will follow the footsteps of my parents and let them know that they are loved, that they are smart, that they should have pride and courage, and no matter what happens or what others say, I will always be proud of them.

QUESTIONS FOR REFLECTION

1. How do you think Kiesa coped with the multiple layers of being African American, gifted, and having a disability?

2. What qualities in Kiesa enabled her to deal with her twice-exceptionality and her encounters with racism and colorism?

3. Why was it so difficult for teachers to understand the needs and challenges of being African American and twice-exceptional? What was the most difficult aspect to deal with—race, giftedness, or special needs?

4. How should teachers be prepared to teach twice-exceptional students? How should teachers be prepared to teach African American twice-exceptional students?

THE OUTCOME

I received my bachelor's degree and, after a few years, have returned to school seeking certification and a degree in radiography. I continue to be active in the multicultural sorority I founded.

SECTION V

GIFTED BLACK STUDENTS
IN COLLEGE

CHAPTER 18

"BEING AN ONLY"

THE EXPERIENCES OF A GIFTED AFRICAN AMERICAN STUDENT IN AN ELITE SCHOLARSHIP PROGRAM

by Jocelyn D. Taliaferro and Jessica T. DeCuir-Gunby

BACKGROUND

The Smith Studies[1] program is a merit scholarship at a large, predominantly White, state university in the Southeast. The program selects outstanding students based on exceptional accomplishments and potential in scholarship, leadership, service, and character. The program develops and supports students in preparing for lifelong contributions to the campus and the larger community. Supports for these students include full tuition payment for 4 years, including fees, room and board, books and supplies, travel, and personal expenses. Students receive a computer stipend and opportunities for funded professional and personal development including, but not limited to, national and international research projects, service activities, and conferences.

Components of the program include mentoring, seminars, retreats, experiential learning opportunities, diversity activities, leadership development, and community engagement initiatives. Students participate in these varied activities throughout their eight semesters at the university. In addition to working individually on academic and professional activities of personal interest, the Smith Studies program

---

1   All names have been replaced by pseudonyms.

participants engage in several team and class endeavors during their time at the university. The participants are creative, smart, motivated, and service-oriented. They participate in a wide array of university and community extracurricular activities, including student government, varsity and intramural athletics, fraternities and sororities, and academic and cause-related clubs. Approximately 50 scholarships are awarded each year to outstanding high school seniors for undergraduate study in any discipline at the university. In any 4-year period, there are 200 Smith Studies students on campus. Fewer than 20 of those students are African American. Kordell Stuart is one of the few African American Smith Studies participants. Although this story focuses on one student's experiences, it is important to emphasize that his experience is not in isolation. Kordell's experiences reflect those of numerous African American college students throughout the country.

KORDELL'S STORY

Kordell Stuart is an undergraduate student at a large state university in the Southeast. He is a 20-year-old Black male who previously majored in engineering and is currently majoring in business with a minor in sociology. He considers himself to be a high-achieving student despite only having a 3.12 grade point average (GPA). His underachievement largely stems from his disconnection from the engineering curriculum. Unlike many of his peers, Kordell did not come to the university with college credits earned in high school. However, he was in his high school's gifted program and graduated at the top of his high school class. Kordell attended high school in a small town located in a relatively poor county within the same state as his university. He is the younger of his parents' two children, maintains close relationships with his family, and places significant value on his Christian traditions and beliefs.

Kordell sought out one of the authors to request that she serve as his mentor, a significant component of the Smith Studies program. Kordell was having difficulty in engineering, his chosen major, but really enjoyed sociology, his minor. This situation contributed to his relatively low GPA. Therefore, he often visited the author to discuss social issues, as well as his academic and personal development. As an easy mentor/mentee relationship emerged, Kordell readily agreed to be interviewed by the author. What follows is a transcription of the conversation:

Taliaferro: So Kordell, tell me what it has been like here at [the university].

Kordell: You know it was really hard when I first got here. There was nobody like me. I didn't know whether I belonged.

Taliaferro: What do you mean?

Kordell: Well, I'm from Harper County. Nobody gets out of Harper (laughter). You know it's just different. I didn't have all the things the other kids did. I even look back at myself at orientation when we did the video. I go up there in a beater [shirt] and shorts and Tims [Timberland boots]. I looked ridiculous. I was looking at the floor mumbling. I am so embarrassed at how I projected myself back then. I looked crazy (laughter).

Taliaferro: What do you think the other kids were thinking?

Kordell: Like who is this knucklehead? Where did they get him from? I couldn't even make out what I was saying on the video. I was looking down, not enunciating, and I sounded sooo country! Whew! It makes me laugh now!

Taliaferro: So what do you project now?

Kordell: I enunciate is the first thing! I'm working on it. I really try to speak clearly. At my last internship, a supervisor told me that "You've really have *got* to get that together." I really did. I tried as hard as I could to think about the way to talk and to think about what I'm trying to get across and to think about the way it sounds to other people. And I know that doesn't make it all right. And I know that I have a lot a long way to go, but I'm doing better. Much better.

Taliaferro: So let's go back to you not feeling like you belong.

Kordell: Yeah, I mean, everybody seemed to be *so* smart. And I know that I do really good in school. But I wasn't sure if I was as smart as everybody else. I made it from Harper County, and schools in Harper aren't really all that good, and I didn't take a whole bunch of AP classes. I was smart and in the gifted and talented classes. But we didn't have all that many classes that you could even take. I mean all of my peers came in with all kinda credits, and I wasn't like that. You see the other thing was that when I came into the Smith program I had already gone to an orientation. I came in to [the university] as an engineer and so the Black engineers had orientation and so I met all of those people. I started really hanging out with them. Those [students] became my people. That was my world. And then I had to leave that group and go to the Smith orientation over the summer. So I had to leave my friends [and] come with the Smith program to the freshman retreat. I didn't feel like I belonged. I didn't know those students at all. I didn't belong in their circles. I really didn't feel like this is what I wanted to do. It's a shame; I'm ashamed to say it that with all the stuff we do I really don't know the names of my classmates. Come on, we're only talking about 40 people, 45 people, and I don't even know their names. It's kind of embarrassing, but . . . that wasn't my group. And since I've been here I've been hanging out with the Black engineers. Not really the Smiths. I don't feel like I have a lot in common with them. When I first came it felt like I wasn't smart enough and that's why I didn't hang out with them. Now I know I am, but back then, I didn't think I was.

Taliaferro: You felt like you weren't smart enough?

Kordell: Well, kind of. I know that I'm smart, don't get me wrong. But I didn't feel like I was as smart as all the rest of them. And then I got into engineering, well, I came in engineering. I'm not in engineering anymore. It wasn't for me.

Taliaferro: What made you choose engineering?

Kordell: When I came here, I wasn't sure what I wanted to do, you know, which direction. I wonder though . . . when you come to [this university], you know, you choose engineering. And my parents made one thing clear, that I was going to have a good career—to be able to do something with my life. They didn't tell me to choose engineering. But I know they, they didn't want me to choose something like sociology. That's my minor—that's what I like. But I know they wanted me to do something a little . . . well, a little bigger . . . a little better. You see my dad is a minister. He cares about people; he dedicated his life to helping people. But he's not well-to-do; he doesn't make a lot of money. And I know they wanted me to do something that would make a lot of money.

Taliaferro: So that's why you chose engineering?

Kordell: Yeah, I chose engineering. That's what we knew. That's what people said I should do if I was going to come to [this university].

Taliaferro: So what's your new major?

Kordell: Business.

Taliaferro: What made you choose business?

Kordell: I'm not sure. I took a class and I really liked it. It was an accounting class. I liked it. Then I looked at my grades. Well, Monica and Lyn [Smith Studies staff members] made me look at my grades, and we had a long conversation. We talked about what I really like to do—about the stuff that really got me excited. We talked about the stuff that I really wanted to do for the rest of my life. Then I figured I could go into business, and do some things to help people to bring businesses back to Harper County. You know, I don't want to live there immediately after I graduate, but I definitely want to go back to that community, because they have so many needs. You know? Kids in that community, they don't have anybody to look up to. Nobody, anybody to say, "Hey, you can do better, you can get out of this community." I do know that I have something to offer. And I want to give it to that community. I would really like to start a business in that community and then take on some interns. So students can get the same opportunities that I got and have somebody in their community who can mentor them and show them how to get along and how to do better. When I was young I couldn't wait to get out of the county and do better but I want to teach people how to make a living *in* the county because I don't think that we should all leave.

Taliaferro: Is that what prompted a sociology minor?

Kordell: Yes. I really have a heart for people, for young people, especially. I want to make a difference. I wanna know the reasons why people are in situations like that. And I want to understand what's going on with people before I start going in trying to fix it. I want to figure it out. All of that aligned with the sociology and the business. I want to have understanding of what people need in communities. So that everybody doesn't end up in a bad place. So the whole community isn't down-trodden like that.

Taliaferro: Do you have any other thoughts about being a Smith Scholar as an African American student?

Kordell: It's just, it's just hard.

Taliaferro: What do you mean?

Kordell: It's hard to be here sometimes. It's hard to have to worry about what other people think and if you mess up . . . you know . . . you've messed up for Black people everywhere. It's hard having to make all these new friends and not really know if they'll get you or understand where you came from. I know we're more the same now, but when I first got here, well I had no idea. I thought we were all so different.

Taliaferro: Do you regret any of it?

Kordell: Naw, I mean no. I don't regret it. I think it's hard, but I wouldn't change it for the world.

QUESTIONS FOR REFLECTION

1. How can high schools better prepare gifted African American students to transition to college?
2. What role does racial identity play in gifted African American students' feeling of belonging at predominantly White institutions?
3. What resources or activities would be helpful for African American families as they prepare to send their children to predominantly White institutions?
4. The Smith Studies program requires that all students find a faculty mentor. What strategies could be promoted to foster a healthy and engaged mentor relationship with African American students entering predominantly White institutions? Should all students be required to have a mentor?
5. Explore the impacts of the sense of responsibility to the African American community expressed by Kordell.

THE OUTCOME

Kordell has successfully graduated from college. He has accepted a position in the private sector where he can use his degree. He continues to mentor youth from his alma mater and home community.

RESOURCES

Brotherton, P. (2001). It takes a campus to graduate a student. *Black Issues in Higher Education, 18*(18), 34–43.

Davis, M., Dias-Bowie, Y., Greenberg, K., Klukken, G., Pollio, H. R., Thomas, S. P., & Thompson, C. L. (2004). A fly in the buttermilk: Descriptions of university life by successful Black undergraduate students at a predominantly White southeastern university. *The Journal of Higher Education, 75,* 420–445.

Fries-Britt, S. (2000). Identity development of high ability Black collegians. *New Directions for Teaching and Learning, 82,* 55–65.

Olenchak, R., & Hébert, T. P. (2002). Endangered academic talent: Lessons learned from gifted first-generation college males. *Journal of College Student Development, 43,* 195–212.

Schwitzer, A. M., Griffen, O. T., Ancis, J. R., & Thomas, C. R. (1999). Social adjustment experiences of African-American college students. *Journal of Counseling & Development, 70,* 189–197.

Mentors Inc.—http://www.mentorsinc.org

Open Society Foundation, Black Male Achievement Initiative—http://www.soros.org/initiatives/usprograms/focus/cbma/about

Urban Leadership Institute—http://www.urbanyouth.org

CHAPTER 19

JUMPING HURDLES, BEATING THE ODDS

by Karen Harris Brown

Learn all you can, so you can contribute all you can.—Ron Goch

BACKGROUND

I always knew that I would go to college. With my Caribbean father, there were no other options. Although he did well with a high school diploma, he was determined that his children would be more successful, and education that resulted with a college degree was the only way to do this. For him, academic achievement was synonymous with success. His expectations were high, and we were expected to always excel.

I was born on the Caribbean island of St. Thomas, the capital of the U.S. Virgin Islands and a territory of the United States. Most residents of the U.S. Virgin Islands are descendants of Africans who were brought to the Caribbean by Europeans as slaves during the slave trade. Born on the island of Saint Kitts in the West Indies, my parents are now naturalized citizens of the United States. They both come from a modest upbringing. Both are considered blue-collar workers. Neither is college educated, which makes me a first-generation college educated student.

MY STORY

ELEMENTARY SCHOOL

Although most of my schooling experiences occurred in the territory, it began on the U.S. mainland. I moved with my parents to Brooklyn, NY, at 1 year, 6 months of age and returned to the Caribbean at 10 to complete my last 2 years of elementary school, as well as junior high and senior high school. Throughout my elementary schooling experience, I made the honor roll consistently. Fascinated with science, I entered many science fairs and remember on one occasion that my entry placed, resulting in a prize. In the fifth grade, I placed second in a spelling bee at the school building level. I would have won had I simply asked for the word to be used in a sentence; it was a homophone. A few weeks after entering the fifth grade in the U.S. Virgin Islands, my parents received a letter from the principal to let them know that I was performing at an exceptional level and would be moved to an advanced class. I thought that I was a good student when completing school in my first elementary school in Brooklyn. This validated that belief for me. It probably fueled my desire to perform well. I continued to do extremely well, confirming that the decision to advance me was the right one.

JUNIOR HIGH SCHOOL

My junior high school experience was similar to my elementary experience. I had supportive teachers with high expectations of my abilities who were dedicated to my overall success. It was during this time that I excelled in courses outside of the traditional academic subjects as well. I learned to sew and proudly wore a skirt that I created and added to the school's uniform requirements (beige shirt and rust skirt). Additionally, I learned how to play the clarinet and joined the band. This was such a great experience that I continued to play the clarinet after graduating from high school. My band teacher sponsored many concerts for the band, both on and off campus. I was picked by the director to perform with the band at every concert. My proudest moment as a member was when I played during my graduation ceremony from junior high school. Although my father reminded me that my academic work should be my priority over extracurricular activities, my parents supported every concert. All of my teachers had nothing but great things to share with my parents during parent teacher conferences.

HIGH SCHOOL

The "Community High School" teachers were nurturing as well. They encouraged me to excel and always pushed me to do better. As a result, I believed they cared about me and my future. After completing my freshman year at Community High School, I was inducted into the National Honor Society. The advisor for this organization provided me with an invitation letter to join the organization. The letter stated that I was receiving this invitation as a result of my academic excellence, based on my grade point average and honor roll status. During my sophomore year, school administrators made the decision to place me in an advanced biology class simply due to the overcrowding of regular biology classes. I demonstrated the ability to keep up with my peers in this fast-paced, advanced environment and earned an overall average grade of a B. Prior to being placed into this class by the school principal and class teacher, I was told that the class would be challenging and was questioned by the teacher and principal if I would be up to that challenge. At that time I was very confident that I would be successful, so my answer to the question was "Yes!" I'm not sure if I was picked solely because of overcrowding or because of a combination of space issues and my prior academic record. That was the last and only time that I was questioned about my ability. While in the class, my male biology teacher treated me the same as my peers. He held high expectations, and I proved to him and the school administrators that this was a correct placement for me; perhaps it should have been my original placement. My educational experiences to this point had been positive.

A lover of the Latino culture and language, particularly the Afro Caribbean influences, I chose Spanish as my foreign language to study in school. Learning this language came naturally to me. I did well, earning the grade of A in these classes. My Spanish teachers always complimented me, stating that I spoke the language with native proficiency. By the end of my sophomore academic year I was scheduled to be inducted into the National Spanish Honor Society, effective during my junior year. Unfortunately (I would later learn just how unfortunate), my family moved to another location, and I was forced to transfer to "Popular High School"; although my academic records transferred, my National Spanish Honor Society induction did not.

Popular High School had a larger student body, an elitist mindset, and less nurturing teachers. They often made comments about being the better of the two public high schools. In fact, to this day they are simply referred to as "High School." There is no need to differentiate to *which* high school a person is referring.

I was placed on a college preparatory track and vaguely remember choosing college preparation over cosmetology. Although my records transferred to my new high school, my status/history with the National Honor Society and National Spanish Honor Society did not. Back then I was very much an introvert, and I did not know to fight for myself. At that time, I didn't think that it was my place to question those in charge of my education regarding my placement. In my mind, they must have received my records from Community High School, but administratively decided that I needed to qualify for this honor at their school. I assume that my parents did not have the wherewithal either because they never said anything.

Remarkably, I did not fare as well at this high school. I did not get the same support from the teachers. It is not what they did; it is what they did not do. They never attempted to get to know me as the transfer student. No one asked me about my previous high school experience or bothered to determine why I was performing lower at this particular school. I can only assume that these teachers did not look at my previous school records to determine my baseline academic skillset. These teachers did not provide additional instruction, offer tutoring assistance, contact the school's guidance counselor, reach out to my parents, or pair me with an academically stronger peer when they noticed that I was struggling. This was my junior year, and I felt as if I was on my own. Many of the students, who had been at Popular High School since their freshman year, had formed solid relationships with the teachers, as well as one another. I now feel that things would have been different had the teachers known *me* since *my* freshman year.

Also, for some of the students, their friendships had been cultivated from elementary and junior high school because they attended feeder schools and were automatically enrolled in a particular junior high school and subsequently enrolled in Popular High School. This allowed them to easily form study groups and elite cliques because of their history. No one was looking for a new friend. This even manifested itself during our senior introductory night show, which highlighted various dance acts, plays/skits, and other productions, when the student body was divided by these student-established cliques. The few friends that I did have at Popular High School were the result of being a former band member of a steel drum band/steel orchestra and participant of the Upward Bound Program prior to transferring high schools. Additionally, some members of my church attended this school, and while a few of us were classmates, we did not have the same instructors.

Not feeling supported in this new environment, I struggled with studying on my own and did not feel comfortable asking my instructors for assistance outside of the classroom. I became an average student, and my grades dropped. I failed my first class ever, trigonometry, and had to retake it the following year. I even made lower scores than what I was accustomed in English, a subject that I loved. My academic performance brought down my self-esteem and my GPA. I internalized this as a personal failure of my abilities and questioned the decisions made previously to place me in gifted classes. How was I successful at all of my previous schools, but not at Popular High School? Based on general negative comments made by students at Popular High School about Community High School, I began to believe that my previous schooling experiences must have been substandard and inferior. However, this reasoning did not account for the fact that I performed very well academically at two elementary schools, thousands of miles apart from each other, and one junior high school.

During my senior year, I became more acclimated and sure of myself. I took advantage of the tutorial services offered by an external resource, the youth steel orchestra. However, during the latter half of my high school experience, I took the two college entrance examinations, the ACT and SAT. I never received information from any school administrators regarding preparatory courses for these exams, retaking the exams to achieve a higher score, or applying for a waiver for the fees for taking the exam. I scored so low on the ACT (in comparison to my peers across the United States and its territories) that the comments found next to the results recommended that I seek another career option besides going to college. According to the ACT, my scores suggested that I might not be successful in college. I did score better on the SAT, but my scores were still not great. My self-esteem was at its lowest during this time of my young life. My dreams of going to college were shattered, and I no longer believed that I was good enough. After spending most of my life thinking that college would be my next logical step I was at a loss with what I would do with my life if I did *not* go to college.

I also took another exam, the Armed Services Vocational Aptitude Battery (ASVAB). Administered by the U.S. Military, it is used to determine qualification for enlistment in the United States armed forces. Prior to taking this exam, I had no desire to join the armed forces. I took it because it was offered. But I scored very well and was contacted by the U.S. Coast Guard and given a personal invitation to join after graduation. My self-esteem was on the mend. Excited about the career possibilities and armed with the news that my college tuition would be paid for, I presented this information to my father on more than one occasion. However, he would not hear of it. For him, there were no other options but a college education. He feared that the Coast Guard would keep me so busy that I would not complete my education. The discussion was over.

To add insult to injury, the African Caribbean American guidance counselor at my high school withheld information from me to ensure that other students she favored had the opportunity to apply for and receive scholarship funding. By listening to my classmates, I began to see the evidence of scholarships she never bothered to mention to me. Naturally, I was upset and began to question her motives to myself. Had she looked at my prior records and academic history? Did she consider my potential, based on my previous demonstrated skills? Why didn't she meet with me when I first transferred to PHS? Why didn't she schedule a meeting after seeing the significant decline during my junior year? I sought her for guidance and assistance more than once during the college application process, but she did not help me. Was her mind already made up? I mentioned this to the program director of the youth steel orchestra. She mentioned it to the program developer who, in turn, suggested that she schedule an appointment to speak to the counselor with me in attendance. The program director followed suit and when the counselor was questioned about this action on my behalf, she remained stoic and unapologetic and admitted nothing. I believe the program director placed a call to the principal, but I was not made privy to that conversation. Regardless, this meeting and phone call made me feel vindicated and supported. On my many visits back home, I secretly wish to run into the counselor to let her know about my accomplishments despite her efforts to prevent my success. But that has yet to happen.

Although my grades improved significantly during my senior year, one year was not enough to make a significant impact. I graduated without the honors received previously. Regardless, I kept my National Honor Society pin, patch, and induction ceremony document. It served as a reminder of my capabilities. I then applied to and was accepted for admission into three colleges, one in the territory and two on the U.S. mainland, one of which was a flagship institution. This did wonders for my self-esteem. After conducting my own *limited* research to fund my education, I applied for and received a scholarship, grants, and student loans. On my college applications, I indicated my participation in the Popular High School band as one of my extracurricular activities. I wanted to appear as a well-rounded individual. Although I was offered an additional scholarship to participate in the marching band at one college (I played the clarinet), I turned it down. My father thought it best to "concentrate on my studies" because the goal was to complete my undergraduate degree within 4 years.

COLLEGE

When I arrived on campus, I made an appointment with my academic advisor, who advised me on what course sequence to take. It was then I realized that I was required to take and pass a noncredit basic math course before enrolling in math courses for credit. I thought that this must have been an error because I took trigonometry in high school. However, my performance on the college entrance exams made a huge impact on course selection and the areas of which I could choose to major. I became irritated and extremely frustrated. Those in charge of *guiding* me to this point had failed miserably. I passed the noncredit math course successfully. However, it didn't count. Taking this initial math course was a setback for me, both time wise and financially. Still, I needed to meet the math requirement for credit *and* graduate within 4 years. Additionally, I had to pay the out-of-state tuition rate for a class in which I received *no* credit. I questioned my place in college and didn't think that I was good enough and began to regret the decision of not accepting the offer made by the Coast Guard. I began to question myself, "How did I go from being inducted into the National Honor Society and actively recruited by the U.S. Coast Guard in high school to taking a noncredit college math course?"

I went on to successfully complete college algebra and trigonometry (with the urging of my father), but, following my freshman year, my interest in the military resurfaced. By this time I became aware of the option to join the military as an officer once I completed my baccalaureate degree. I made an appointment with an on-campus Air Force ROTC representative, who just so happened to be a Caucasian male. I was a premed major and told him of my potential plans, seeking advisement for next steps. However, he advised me to change my major to nursing and become a nurse instead, but I did not let this man's or any other instructor's perceptions of my abilities deter me. Although I am not a medical doctor, I have earned a doctor of philosophy degree and, as a college professor, I teach courses with a strong foundation in the biological sciences.

In retrospect, I have never been a stellar standardized test taker. The purpose of college and graduate school entrance exams is to determine an individual's success at those levels. My performance on these exams indicated that I am not supposed to have an undergraduate degree, let alone a master's degree with a strong foundation in the biological sciences, and a terminal degree. Inconsistencies throughout my schooling experiences in helping me reach my potential are clearly evident. These personal experiences fuel my passion to prevent similar experiences from happening to others who look like me.

QUESTIONS FOR REFLECTION

1. Discuss the mindset of the guidance counselor. What could have been her motives for withholding information?

2. How can Black students be empowered to advocate for themselves?

3. How can parents of gifted Black students, with and without a formal education, be empowered to advocate for their children?

4. How can Black civic organizations advocate for gifted and high-achieving Black students and their families?

5. How can schools nurture high-achieving Black students *consistently* and *effectively* to realize their advanced abilities?

THE OUTCOME

I graduated with a bachelor's degree in speech communication. I was able to graduate within 4 years, despite having to take a noncredit remedial math class during my first semester as a freshman. I entered a graduate speech-language pathology program and earned a master's degree 3 years after earning my bachelor's degree.

I worked as a successful speech-language pathologist with stroke patients in hospitals and skilled nursing facilities and with students with special needs in school districts for 9 years before enrolling in a doctoral program. Upon entering the doctoral special education program, I was awarded the Cathy Lynne Richardson Endowed Doctoral Scholarship and Project LASER fellowship. Project Linking Academic Scholars to Educational Resources was a $5 million U.S. Department of Education grant focused on funding the education of doctoral students of color and those interested in conducting research related to cultural and linguistic diversity. I was the first LASER scholar to defend her dissertation and graduate from the program. My dissertation is still used as a model for other students.

CHAPTER 20

GIFTED BLACK MALE ATHLETES' INTERCOLLEGIATE EXPERIENCES NEGATE THE DUMB BLACK JOCK STEREOTYPE

by Billy Hawkins and Joseph N. Cooper

BACKGROUND

Athletic talent is seldom considered in the dialogue regarding gifted students. Often, in educational institutions, and in the broader society in general, athletic ability is viewed as an antithesis to intelligence and academic achievement. Despite the space sports occupy in this culture and the premium we place on athletic achievement, the label of the "dumb jock" has been pervasive. These personal narratives and experiences of Black male athletes who attended predominantly White institutions (PWI) provide critical insight into their lived experiences. Note that all of the names used are pseudonyms.

EDDIE MACK

My name is Eddie Mack. I am from a small town in South Carolina. I started playing sports when I was 5 years old. Coming from a family of athletes, I played baseball, basketball, and football. My family played a major role in supporting both my athletic participation and my academics. Even though education was important in my family, college was not a number one priority for me coming out of high school. In high school, I was a standout football player and earned a full athletic scholarship to a major Football Bowl Series (FBS), formerly Division IA, school in the Southeastern United States.

EDDIE'S COLLEGIATE EXPERIENCE

I would describe my transition to college as "different." One major challenge I faced was adapting to the strenuous schedule of being a student-athlete at a big-time FBS school. Due to the time constraints, I had to deal with staying up late many nights and waking up early the next morning to attend athletic workouts and practices. In high school, I was able to sleep around 8 hours a night, but in college, my nightly sleep time decreased to about 6 hours or less. After I adjusted to my schedule, I was able to manage my time and responsibilities effectively. Overall, I would say my college experience was positive.

The two factors that I would attribute to my success in college would be my support system and my personal determination. I had to learn from other people's mistakes. When dealing with a team of so many people with different cultural backgrounds, personalities, and attitudes, you find that most form into small groups or cliques and conform to that group's beliefs and behaviors. After observing some of my teammates getting arrested for numerous reasons, I made a conscious decision to not follow suit. Another factor for me was my personal determination. Throughout college, I had to deal with tough challenges as a student-athlete at a major FBS school, but I was determined to succeed.

For example, I knew I was a minority as a Black male at a PWI, but I used that as a source of motivation for me to excel academically. I felt like I did not want to be the stereotypical "dumb Black jock" in the class with the lowest test score. As one of the few Black males on campus, I felt a sense of obligation to be a positive representative for all Black males. I felt like it was my duty to do well, academically and athletically, and stay out of trouble. Although there were times when I wanted quit playing football, I did not because I had a strong support system, and I was personally determined to succeed.

MY FRATERNITY AND FAITH

My involvement in extracurricular campus organizations such as my fraternity, the use of my network from my athletic experiences, my never quit mentality, and my desire to be well-rounded contributed to my success as a student, as an athlete, and, more importantly, as a person. Most athletes hang around athletes *only*. Participating in extracurricular activities gave me a chance to feel like a "normal" student. My coaches were not so happy about me joining a fraternity because they thought it took away from the brotherhood of the team. They always said that football is your fraternity. My teachers just wanted to see me succeed, and my teammates were curious about the fraternity life after I crossed.

As I look back on my success and think about how I made it, I realize that I learned from my experiences that surrounding yourself with positive people who hold you accountable for your actions is the key to staying out of trouble. In addition to surrounding myself with positive people, the most important relationship in my life is my relationship with Jesus Christ. Both my relationship with Jesus Christ and with positive social groups on campus contributed to my academic and athletic success in college.

FRANK BRANTLEY

My name is Frank Brantley. I was born in a metropolitan city in the Midwest. My family moved to Florida when I was in middle school. After finishing high school in Florida, I moved back to the Midwest to live with my grandmother. I started playing sports when I was very little. I can remember playing basketball with my brother and my cousins when I was in elementary school. We would play football in the streets during the day when there were not many cars going by. We played baseball for a while and then somebody hit a baseball through a neighbor's window, so that ended our desire to play baseball after we all got home and got a whipping. Growing up in Detroit, basketball was the most popular sport. During that time, the Detroit Pistons were winning championships, and it was all about basketball. I played football, but it was just something to do until it was basketball season again. I did not start playing football seriously or running track until I moved down to Florida.

Unfortunately, growing up I did not have a major supporter. My father passed away when I was 7, and my mom did not come to many of my games. I felt really sad at some games when I would look up in the stands and see everyone else's parents and not see my own. She wasn't working at the time that my games started, and we only lived 5 minutes from the school. After the games, I would see loved ones waiting for the other players, and I did not have anyone waiting for me. My mother was never really interested in me or in anything that I participated in. I played sports because I wanted to and I loved it. Sports were a way to escape the reality of my harsh home life, and I was actually good at sports, so I loved doing well. I hated going home because my home life was rough. After practice, my friends would offer to drop me off, but I would rather walk because it took longer to get home. I grew up in an abusive home, and I just hated being there because my mom hated me so much. The story goes that my mom hates me because I remind her of my deceased father who she really hated.

I always did well enough to play ball, and I could have done so much better if I was pushed to do better. My teachers were happy that I was sitting in my seat and that I was not "acting a fool." My teachers did not push me to do better because they did not think I was smart. Every time I did well on a test or on a paper, they were surprised. I remember after turning in a paper that I worked really hard on, one of my teachers asked me if I wrote it. I guess I was just another "dumb jock" to the teacher, but I was content as long as I was eligible.

Academically, I regret not taking school more seriously in high school. I did well in regular classes, but I regret not taking honors and gifted classes. I wish my mother would have pushed me, but she did not care what kind of grades I brought home or if I was in honors or gifted. I loved all of the accolades that came along with winning.

FRANK'S COLLEGIATE EXPERIENCE

In college, education was a priority, but only because I wanted to continue playing ball. Education was second to how much I wanted to play ball and, if I could do it again, my priorities would be different. My transition to college was a difficult experience. I did not go to college right after high school for myriad reasons. After working for a year, a college coach remembered me from high school and recruited me to play football at a small private Catholic college (PWI) in the Midwest. It was not a big school, but I did not care because it would give me a chance to continue playing sports and I could get an education along the way. I moved more than 1,000 miles away from home, and I did not know anyone. I was one of the few Black students on campus, and it seemed like all of the Black students there played some kind of sport.

When I look back on it, I think my decision to go to that college was more positive than negative. I got a chance to live somewhere I had never been before, and the people were nice. The opportunity to go to college for me was something special. Before college, I was at home working at a local store, and my life was going nowhere fast. I think that if I did not go off to that small college and played football

I would not have continued through school. With regard to balancing academics and athletics, I did not have much difficulty doing that. I am a very regimented type of person, so athletics kept me in check. I knew I had to lift in the morning, go to school in the afternoon, go to practice later, and then do homework before I went to sleep. I had a strict schedule every day, and I had to follow it so that I would not fall behind. My strong time-management skills enabled me to manage my multiple responsibilities.

The factors that contributed to my success in college were the environment at the historically Black university (HBCU) I later attended and my strong work ethic. I did not do well academically until I transferred to the HBCU. When I was at the HBCU, it felt like they expected more from me because they looked at me differently. They saw something in me that I did not see. I remember turning in a paper and my professor giving it back to me and telling me that I could do better. I could tell that they believed in me and they raised my expectations for doing well in the expectations for doing well in the classroom.

When professors believed in me, it made me try even harder so that I would not let them down. They made me feel like I was doing this for a greater cause. I had to do this for my ancestors, my family, and future generations. I never felt that way at the other university (PWI) I attended. Whatever I did was good enough, as long as it kept me eligible. I loved that all my professors were Black and so smart. It made me want to do better in school.

As far as doing well athletically, I had a great work ethic and my pride would not let me give anything but my best. The year that I went to nationals in track I trained extra hard. I changed my diet and I stayed at school for Christmas break instead of going home and getting fat. I made some sacrifices, but they all paid off. My family even came to cheer me on at nationals, and they could not have been more proud of me.

TEACHER EXPECTATIONS AND GIFTED CLASSES IN DETROIT

Personally, I do feel my race affected my academic experiences. I feel like teachers did not push or expect much out of me in school because I was a Black male. The fact that they questioned whether I wrote a paper or that they were so surprised whenever I did well on a test bothered me and made me feel like maybe I am not that smart. I feel like if they were more confident in me that I would have tried harder and done better in school. The fact that I was quiet and stayed in my seat was good enough for them.

I remember being in school in Detroit and being in gifted classes and loving every minute of it. I was never accused of acting White because everyone in my class was Black. The phrase acting White means that you are acting smart and thus not fulfilling the negative stereotype that Blacks are unintelligent. I feel like the phenomenon of acting White mostly occurs in integrated schools. Being smart was just being smart at an all-Black school; it wasn't something that had to do with race because we all looked the same. I did not feel that way about school again until I transferred from my small Roman Catholic university (PWI) to a HBCU. With regard to my athletic experiences, I do not think race affected it too much because I was big and Black so it was the expectation for me to play sports. I did not receive any special treatment from teachers, but I did not receive any unfair treatment either.

SAMUEL HAIRSTON

I am from a metropolitan city on the West coast. I started playing organized sports in elementary school. Growing up, I primarily played basketball, but I also played flag football. My major supporters growing up were my older siblings. They played basketball. My parents supported me in my athletic endeavors, but education was the top priority to them. My parents were always intentional about placing an emphasis on education first and sports were secondary. As a result, going to college was always my number one priority.

SAMUEL'S COLLEGIATE EXPERIENCE

With regard to my transition to college, I would say my experiences were both positive and negative. It was negative because I had to deal with all of the talk about how schools could prepare me for the National Basketball Association (NBA). I was offered money under the table and that element wiped away the innocence of the college selection process for me. All of the coaches were like used car salesmen; although there was excitement about going to college, I just felt like I was signing my life away to dishonest people. Going from high school where academics were pushed to a big-time program where it was all business and I had to deliver athletically or else I would not have my scholarship renewed was an adjustment. Some of the positives, though, were that I was able to attend college and meet my teammates, whom I grew close to and still keep in touch with today.

The main challenge I faced in college was the fact that my coach couldn't care less about my life off the court. His athletes had a very low graduation rates, and he showed no interest in what we did as students. It was difficult to invest in that part of your life when so much of your energy was devoted to the basketball side. The 20 hours per week rule is a joke. No one can account for the mental and emotional attention student-athletes give to their sport. In addition, if practice is 2 hours long, you usually have to get there 2 hours before to make sure that you are seen as a devoted player.

BEYOND SPORT PARTICIPATION

The key factors that contributed to my success in college were my parents and other role models who helped me look beyond my sport participation. With regard to race, I do believe my race affected my academic and athletic experiences in college. I was identified as an athlete automatically because I was tall and Black. I would hear all of the time about basketball players and how they do not have to work hard academically or that we had academic inadequacies as students. For example, people would always say to me "You are so articulate, not like I thought you would be." I felt my race and all of the implications when I was in academic settings as well. It caused me to try to stay in the shadows because I often felt I did not belong.

MICHAEL ROBINSON

For as long as I can remember, I have always been a football player. It is all that I have ever wanted to be, and I will always be a football player, until the day that I die. It is who I am and what I am. Football is life. I was born in Trenton, NJ, and I can remember very few days that I did not play sports. Even though football is, and always has been, my favorite sport, I also played basketball and baseball growing up. In my apartment complex, I would play with my friends and even play by myself—playing catch against a wall.

As a youngster, my father taught me how to catch and throw a ball, but he did not do much more than that. I remember the catching sessions with him; they were special, but my coaches played much more influential roles in my athletic career. My coaches were mentors and father figures who are still influential roles in my life. My offensive line coach in high school taught me the value of hard work and accountability. My head coach in high school taught me the importance of setting goals and achieving those goals. We won a state championship my senior year, and every week we had to set and obtain goals. No one outside of the team gave us much of a chance, but we believed in one another and played for one another every week and the hard work paid off. We did not lose a single game, the only undefeated state champion in the history of Mercer County.

MICHAEL'S COLLEGIATE EXPERIENCE

When I was being recruited to play college football, I met my offensive line coach, who was the recruiter for my region of the country. The opportunity to work with him was the reason I chose to attend the college that I did. He was the only person who I trusted and respected during the recruitment process. I made a good decision because my college offensive line coach and my high school football coach are still active in my life, and I still consider both of them mentors.

The transition to college from high school had positive and negative effects. The difficult part of the transition existed because football was no longer a game; it became a business and that was difficult to accept. It was not as fun as it was when I was growing up. It had become work, a job.

Because I had been taught a strong work ethic in high school, I was successful very early in my athletic career. I was used to working very hard. I simply outworked my peers and was able to play pretty early in my career. Unfortunately, early in my college experience, I worked much harder on my social life and athletic career, and my grades suffered my first two or three semesters. When I learned that to be successful academically I would have to spend as much time studying as I did practicing, my grades began to improve. Eventually, the business side of athletics taught me that my athletic career would soon be ending and that I would need to develop skills to help me survive after my playing career was over.

RACE, TEAMMATES, AND CULTURAL NORMS

Race, in my opinion, played a major role in my academic and my athletic experiences in high school and college. As a young Black man, I believed that I would not have many chances to succeed. I felt that I had to take advantage of my opportunities when they presented themselves. There were dozens of teammates that I grew up with who were much more talented than I was academically or athletically but who did not make it. Some were killed, some were incarcerated, and some simply ended up bitter and angry at the way that their lives turned out. I was fortunate to learn at an early age that the world was much larger than Martin Luther King, Jr. Avenue (the street that I grew up). I wanted more from my life than to spend it on the street that I was born on.

After middle school, I was given the opportunity to leave my urban school system and matriculate into a private school. I used my opportunity to attend a predominantly White Catholic high school as an ethnographic opportunity to study and learn White culture. It was a culture shock. I had entered a paradox, an alternate universe where everything was the opposite of the world in which I had grown up. In my studies, I learned what Whites valued and how these values were different from the cultural norms that I grew up learning. As I learned, understood, and accepted these differences, I began to excel in high school and I later excelled in college as well.

Football made all of this possible. I was able to go to a highly competitive college because I played football and because I was Black. Being Black in America can be very challenging. It is a very dangerous occupation. However, today, many opportunities that are afforded to African Americans academically were not available to my parents. I understood these advantages and took them. My children will as well.

QUESTIONS FOR REFLECTION

1. What are some of the salient themes across each narrative?
2. What polices and practices regarding improving academic achievement and overall college experiences for Black student-athletes should be addressed?
3. How did the positive support systems of these athletes impact how they dealt with being Black, male, and an athlete at a PWI?
4. Discuss how each of the participants created alternative positive self-identities for themselves.

THE OUTCOMES

Eddie Mack's work ethic in athletics and academics has provided him with a master's degree, and he is currently an account executive working in the sports industry. Frank Brantley is finishing his doctoral degree with aspirations of being a university professor. Samuel Hairston is currently working as a college athletic administrator and completing his doctoral degree as well. He has aspirations of being a university professor or an intercollegiate athletic director. Finally, Michael Robinson is currently teaching at the high school level, while completing his doctoral degree.

SECTION VI

VILLAGE PERSPECTIVES ON GIFTED BLACK CHILDREN

CHAPTER 21

KNOWING, BUT NOT KNOWING

LIVING WITH A HIGH-ABILITY CHILD

by Toni Jones

BACKGROUND

How do you know your child is smart, has high ability, or is a genius, for that matter? Some parents know right away that their child is really smart. Likewise, they know right away when their child has a special need. My husband and I did not know right away that our African American male child was really smart, was of high ability, or that he was very active. We thought that all children were like him—always asking questions, always answering questions, engaging everyone in conversation (no matter what age, gender, or race), always moving, reading books and magazines that children his age wouldn't even look at, and remembering everything.

I recall our son at age 4 asking my husband to read him a book that we both felt was more appropriate for an older child. He looked at his dad and said, "I want you to read that book, Daddy." My husband looked at the book and scowled, "Hmm. I think we probably should wait on this book." But Hezekiah insisted. We bought the book without looking at the recommended age level, and he was curious about the book. My husband read the book to him and later asked his preschool teacher if it was okay to read a 4-year-old a book that was recommended for a 6- or 7-year-old child. The teacher said, "Yes. If he expresses an interest in the book, read it to him and question him about it." That evening my husband read the book to our son again and asked him questions about it to determine his understanding of it. To our surprise, our son fully understood and comprehended the theme of the book, was able to talk about the characters, and presented a new ending to the book. We scratched our heads and said, "Hmm, that's interesting."

A few weeks later, we were having breakfast in a restaurant, and I told my son that we were going to work on writing and spelling his name so he'd know how to do that when he got into kindergarten. We had been typing it on a text-to-speech computer because he struggled with shaping the letters since he was 2 1/2 years old. But we had not written it or spelled it without the help of the computer. I also knew that most teachers want students to know how to spell their name by the time they are in kindergarten, so now seemed like a good time to broach the subject. My son stood up on the restaurant chair and said, "I already know how to spell my name! H-E-Z-E-K-I-A-H-J-O-N-E-S! And I can write it too!" That's when we began to wonder about Hezekiah's ability. But our assumption still was that most children were like him.

OUR STORY

BEGINNING TO KNOW

As Hezekiah progressed through preschool, people would say that he was very smart and extremely busy. His preschool teacher also described him as impulsive. We were puzzled about the extremely busy and impulsive comments because we did not have another child with which to compare him, but as we observed him with other kids we saw that he was pretty active. We didn't think anything about it; instead, we attributed it to his being smart and curious about the world. When he got in kindergarten, the teacher told us that he was very smart; performed at a high level in oral language, memory skills, and problem solving; and had lots of energy.

I recall one day my husband and I went to the school for a kindergarten play (we had no idea what it was about). The kids were doing a reenactment of Rosa Parks and the bus she was on. The kids were lined up as if on a bus and Hezekiah was at the front of the line. Suddenly, one of the kids "got on the bus" and, to our surprise, we heard, "Go to the back of the bus!" It was Hezekiah! We had no idea he was in a play! While driving home we asked him why he hadn't told us about the play and his role in it. He said, "I don't know. I knew my line."

While in preschool and kindergarten, Hezekiah had behavior problems—talking too much and too loudly, running in the hall, getting up when he should be sitting down, and even kicking the teacher once. He got into even more trouble in first and second grade. Our friends suggested that maybe he was bored due to not being challenged. Or perhaps he had ADHD, or that nothing was wrong with him and that he would grow out of it. Then a school psychologist told us that if we "didn't get him help who knows what would happen to him!" We both were in tears when we heard this information. We began to get really worried and spoke to one of my colleagues who said that she would test him. After the testing, she spoke to us about Hezekiah being twice-exceptional. It made sense because I had learned that many twice-exceptional students also have issues such as Oppositional Defiance Disorder (ODD), Attention Deficit/Hyperactivity Disorder (ADHD), and Obsessive Compulsive Disorder (OCD).

Next, we took our son to a child psychiatrist who said that he was a smart boy but that she didn't think that he was ADHD. She also indicated that he might grow out of it. Our response was "Then why is he so busy and always getting into trouble in school?" We were so frustrated that we asked her to put him on Ritalin. She reluctantly did, and it made him lethargic. I recall looking at him at the kitchen table one morning after giving him the Ritalin. His body slumped in the chair and his head rested on his chest. "Are you okay, Hezekiah?" I asked. "Un-huh," he replied without even lifting his head. I was so hurt to see my child this way (usually, I was gone to work before he was given his medicine). We took him off of Ritalin after a few weeks.

In our conversations with one another, we questioned how a child could be so smart and yet so troublesome. My husband and I began to read books, articles, brochures, and websites about children with ADHD, gifted/talented children, defiant children, and twice-exceptional children. Our hope was that we'd get a better understanding of who our son was and why he did the things he did. We were beginning to know, but were afraid and didn't want to know at the same time.

AFRAID TO KNOW

In second grade, we enrolled Hezekiah in a different, tuition-based school that espouses to the Rudolph Steiner philosophy of teaching. Our thinking was that in this environment he would be accepted for who he was—smart, energetic, a leader—and would be nurtured academically. Such schools focus on educating the "whole child": "head, heart, and hands" and "spirit, soul, and body" (Nicholson, 2000). The teachers were predominantly (about 90%) female and White. They ranged in age from the late 20s to 50s. Teaching experience varied from being fairly new to having many years of experience. Likewise, the students were predominantly (about 95%) White and female, coming from middle- to upper class two-parent homes. Most of the students had siblings.

What we found was an environment that was mired with concerns and issues for us and our son. In addition to being one of the few African American males in the school building, he was a loud talking, high energy, smart boy. Reading is typically not introduced until first or second grade. Our son was an advanced reader while in a traditional school environment and as a result really excelled academically and artistically. This seemed to create concerns for some of the parents and their children. When he was selected to participate in a string competition through the school's music teacher, his classmates asked, "Why was he selected?" He on the other hand was very excited to have been selected and very nervous at the thought of performing by himself in front of an unfamiliar audience. As parents, we held similar emotions. Nonetheless, he did perform and did well. While he was at this particular school, he was excluded from some birthday parties or play dates and his classmates seemed to want him to know when there was an event to which he wasn't invited to. He actually didn't seem bothered by it or, at least, he didn't say anything about it. I was more upset about it than my husband and Hezekiah because I had expected more compassion from such an environment. I soon got over it, though. Hezekiah and another boy connected, and they had play dates and celebrated birthdays together. The boys were of similar intellect, energy, and disposition. I formed a relationship with the mother. As parents, we shared similar concerns about our children and were able to talk about them with each other. Eventually, both boys were invited to parties, and Hezekiah even had play dates with two other boys.

In the third and fourth grades, the boys and girls begin to realize they were the opposite sex. We got complaints that Hezekiah was bothering the girls (although some of the girls didn't seem to leave him alone). One of his teachers indicated that because he was a big kid (and therefore, more visible) that if he was in the vicinity of an altercation (and he often was) he was identified as being part of it. Sometimes he was part of it, and sometimes he wasn't. One parent even indicated that he was afraid that our son would "hurt" his daughter.

On another occasion, he asked his teacher if he could start a library and have cards that students could use to sign out/borrow books. She said yes, but that he would have to put the cards together. After school that day, he and I were in the school's knitting club and he was telling some of the students about his plan. "I'm going to start a library in our class, and I have to make some library cards tonight" he told them. One of the girls told him that she'd help him do the cards. They decided who would do which cards for which students and agreed that they would bring them back to school the next day. Our son went home and created the cards for the students who were on his list and returned to school the next day with his cards. He gave his cards to the teacher who looked them over and proceeded to bawl him out because there weren't cards for everyone. The girl who volunteered to help him sat there and said nothing, and the teacher did not allow him to explain. When I arrived at the school at the end of the day, the teacher proceeded to tell me how disappointed she was in him for not doing cards for everyone in the class. I was shocked, but maintained my composure and explained that an agreement had been reached between him and another student and that apparently the other student didn't do her cards. The teacher then asked the girl, who confirmed that she had forgotten about it. No apology was given to our son by either the teacher or the student, and the concept of the library and borrowing books was dismissed. In the car with him, he said,

> Mama, I tried to tell her that Veronica was supposed to do some of the cards but she wouldn't listen. She just kept telling me how inconsiderate I was to just pick and choose who would get library cards and then told me to sit down.

My husband and I tried to convince ourselves that none of this was racist, but at times it felt like it and, at other times, it just simply felt mean spirited and the result of jealousy because he was smart, loud, and full of energy. No matter how we looked at it, it was painful for us as his parents to watch him try to be accepted, and I believe painful on his part to go through it, even though he didn't talk about it. On the positive side, while being in this environment, our son learned to play the cello and did well at it, learned about his ability to act and did well at it, and was affirmed in his abilities as a chess player. The administration suggested that he be examined for sensory integration disorder, and we learned that he does have sensory integration disorder, although a mild form of it. We, as a family, also learned about sensory integration disorder, homeopathic medicines, and healthier ways to eat.

After being in this environment for 3 years, we pulled Hezekiah out of the school and put him in an African American all boys' Christian school. We were trying to better understand what we knew about Hezekiah and didn't want anyone else to know. We were trying to get him into an environment where he'd be accepted and academically challenged.

Hezekiah's next school experience at the African American all boys' school was the best learning and social experience he has had as a student. There were no suspensions at all, the students accepted him for who he was, and the teachers and administrators loved him, admonished him, and helped rebuild his self-esteem. I recall going on vacation, and he would talk about his teacher and what he'd be doing at that time of day; he missed the boys, the teachers, and the school. (He still talks about the teachers, staff, and his peers.) The only problem with the school was that it only went to the sixth grade.

When Hezekiah entered seventh grade, all hell broke loose! He had behavior problems galore and was asked to leave the tuition-based pre-K–12 school that he was attending during the middle of his seventh-grade school year. The school had a student population of about 40% African American and 60% Caucasian students, with 98% Caucasian teachers. All of Hezekiah's teachers were Caucasian and mostly female. At the end of the school day, I would arrive at the school early and wait for Hezekiah to come to his locker. In one week, I saw two students wrestling on the floor, another two students throwing one another's books down the hall, and several students shouting at each other. The day the two students were wrestling on the hallway floor (right in front of a teacher), Hezekiah came down the hall and shouted "Hey man!" and gave a student a high five. The teacher who didn't see the two students wrestling in front of him immediately told Hezekiah to stop shouting and stop running. I was stunned! A few weeks later, he was in trouble for something else, and the principal requested my husband and I come to the school. During the meeting Hezekiah told her, "Other students have done things like I've done and didn't get in trouble." Her reply was, "We are not perfect here." More problems and several in-school suspensions continued until he was told that he had to leave. As we were walking out of the school he said, "Mama, I didn't want this to happen! I tried to be good. What's wrong with me? Why am I so bad?" My heart sank to the floor, and I tried to encourage him and myself.

The next day we put Hezekiah in our neighborhood middle school, which was predominantly African American. Although he was enrolled in advanced/honors classes, he was not challenged academically except in mathematics (which has always been a problem area for him). He was like "hell on wheels" behaviorally while at school and home. Hezekiah often said, "I'm different. I want to be with the cool kids." In his mind, being smart and cool was a no-no. He often said that students told him that he "acted White." He wanted to be popular and have lots of friends. We think that his desire for popularity and friends has contributed to him "acting Black" (Ford, Grantham, & Whiting, 2008)—not wanting to be considered smart/intelligent, wanting to speak "ghetto," and behaving poorly by being rude and disrespectful. He even began to pull his pants below his waist, whereas when he was about 8 years old he questioned a friend about why boys pull their pants below their waist, saying that he didn't think it looked good. We could say without a doubt that we now knew about his academic abilities and his challenges and realized that others needed to know, too. Nonetheless, we still struggled with it.

GETTING COMFORTABLE WITH KNOWING AND TELLING OTHERS

Currently, Hezekiah is in a pre-K–12 charter school in an urban setting with a student population that consists largely of African American students (98%) from mixed social and economic backgrounds and teachers and administrators who represent diverse cultural and ethnic backgrounds. The school has an advanced/honors curriculum of which he is a part. We love the school, but that's not to say that his time has been without struggles. As has often been the case, he struggles to be and feel accepted by his classmates and in mathematics.

His behavior, as of late, is improving but he continues to have problems. One teacher recommended him for out-of-school suspension because he was not in line when walking down the hall. I actually thought that I had misheard this but I didn't—he was, indeed, suspended for not being in the line when passing through the hall. He was suspended for playing with a female student when the teacher thought that he was touching her behind. Upon further investigation, it was determined that he didn't touch her at all, but he was so indignant about being accused of touching the student that he was suspended again. Each of these offenses occurred with the same (Caucasian) teacher. Hezekiah told us, and the principal, on the day he was about to get the second out-of-school suspension, "I'm different and I don't want to be. I want to be popular. People don't like me." We reminded him that his peers are smart like he is and that most seem to like him (according to previous conversations we've had with him), but, no matter, what he must behave and respect everyone. We continue to encourage him to do well in school; his job is go to school, get good grades, and stay out of trouble. We buy him lots of books to read and/or listen to, limit his television and video game time to the weekend, monitor his computer use (e.g., Facebook, e-mail), and pray for continued strength to get through this. He gets good grades and poor citizenship marks. The frequent comment regarding his citizenship is "excessive talking." During the last parent-teacher conference, most of the teachers said that Hezekiah's citizenship is improving and that they often find themselves engaged in interesting, intellectual discussions with him.

QUESTIONS FOR REFLECTION

1. How can one determine whether a student is facing racism, bullying, dislike, or just plain old jealously? What should be done about it?

2. What aspects of Hezekiah's challenges resulted from his being smart or from his being an African American male?

3. Hezekiah's parents seem to be afraid to admit that he is smart. Why do you think this is the case?

4. Hezekiah's mother implied that he was being singled out at school. How can a parent help a child to not be singled out?

5. How could Hezekiah's parents help him resist the need to "act Black" and just be himself even if his peers describe him as "acting White"?

THE OUTCOME

We now know who our son is, and we are learning and growing from what we know while laughing and loving each other all the more. He is articulate, humorous, and mischievous. He is also a knowledge seeker and gregarious. We hope that this mixture will enable him to navigate his way through life's challenges including racism and feeling different as he goes forward in life.

REFERENCES

Ford, D. Y., Grantham, T. C., & Whiting, G. W. (2008). Another look at the achievement gap: Learning from the experiences of gifted Black students. *Urban Education, 43,* 216–238.

Nicholson, D. W. (2000). Layers of experience: Forms of representation in a Waldorf school classroom. *Journal of Curriculum Studies, 32,* 575–587.

RESOURCES

Martin, A. D. (2012). *The 2e dilemma: Understanding and educating the twice-exceptional child.* Retrieved from http://www.2enewsletter.com/article_2e_dilemma.html

Nicpon, M. F., Allmon, A., Sieck, B., & Stinson, R. D. (2011). Empirical investigation of twice-exceptionality: Where have we been and where are we going? *Gifted Child Quarterly, 55,* 3–17.

CHAPTER 22

THE POWER AND PENALTY OF ENSURING EDUCATIONAL ACCESS AND RESOURCES FOR ONE'S OWN CHILDREN
A MAD MOM'S MEMOIR

by Robin Vann Lynch

BACKGROUND

Authentic parent engagement and the building of family-school partnerships are never by accident. Instead, it is the conscious intent of school district administrators, teachers, and staff who acknowledge the power of alliance and the importance of conceptualizing student achievement in a way that honors the needs and desires of all stakeholders. I am a "mad mom" who, at times, feels angry and crazy because of my unwavering quest to support the academic and social success of my children who are educated in an affluent, suburban, public school district. My husband and I were thrilled to have our children enrolled in one of the best school districts in the country. We believed that our sacrifices (financial and otherwise) were worth it. However, much to our dismay, our thrill turned to madness as both of our daughters encountered obstacle after obstacle throughout their academic journeys.

Throughout this chapter, I will share my perspective as both a parent and a teacher. I will also describe my ensuing madness as I attempted to make sense of exactly what my daughter Tracey was experiencing by consistently being overlooked for advanced math placement (my other daughter was denied gifted support services, despite testing in the mentally superior range, thus both encountered obstacles toward their success). What I will try to describe is the madness of the educational system that often promotes and perpetuates a deficit model for even high-achieving African American students. In sharing the story, I hope it adds to the many testaments of resilient parents who try desperately not to "go mad" as they work to ensure access to academic opportunities for their children in K–12 schooling and beyond.

MY STORY

LESSONS FROM MY MOTHER: AN EARLY MODEL OF AUTHENTIC PARENT ENGAGEMENT

I am a proud product of urban public schooling. As early as elementary school, I can recall my divorced, single mother being keenly aware of her power as a parent. Although her professional obligations did not always allow her to be visible within the school setting, she made her dreams for us (my sister and me) known at the beginning of many conversations with teachers and counselors by simply stating, "She is going to college." As a child, I observed my "mad mom" engage the school system on numerous occasions, as a means to ensure my educational success.

My fifth-grade math teacher always used a stern voice. One day, during math class, he stated, "Miss Vann, go to the board." He bellowed out the problem, and somehow I managed to record it. With some trepidation, I began to solve the problem. But I made a modest error and in the midst of trying to make a speedy correction, I heard my teacher shout out at what seemed like the top of his lungs, "Are you stupid?" In an instant, I felt both my confidence and spirit physically leave my body. I quickly corrected my mistake (which I was already in the process of doing before he berated me in front of the class) and returned to my seat. Completely deflated for the remainder of the school day *and* on the bus ride home, I wondered if I should tell my mother what happened since she was often so busy and stressed and I tried desperately to make her evenings with my sister and me less so.

As we sat down to eat dinner, we began to share our day with Mom, and I told her what happened in math class. She sprung from her seat, looked up a couple of telephone numbers, made some arrangements (of which I was not fully aware), and told me that she would take me to school tomorrow. I was even more terrified now as I was unsure what would come next. On our way to school the next morning, I pleaded with my mother not to embarrass me. She remained silent and pensive and did not respond.

Once we arrived, I was seated in the lobby as my mother met with the principal. I was then invited into the meeting because it seemed as if my mom wanted me to be aware of how she thought the previous day's events should be best resolved. My mother explained to the principal in a professional manner, but with a sound of disbelief and anger, that I informed her that my teacher called me "stupid" when I was trying to work out a math problem. The principal did not seem surprised. My mother went on to explain that she doesn't call her children "stupid," nor should anyone else, especially their teachers.

The principal said that she would talk to Mr. Barns that day. My mother sternly replied, "That is not sufficient! Mr. Barns owes Robin an apology." Again I felt my spirit leave my body. I wondered what in the world my mother was talking about. There was no way that Mr. Barns would ever apologize. At some point during the conversation the principal agreed, and the three of us walked to Mr. Barns' class, with the principal leading the way and my mother and I side by side.

The principal motioned for Mr. Barns to come out into the hallway and took him aside. He then brought my mother over to join the conversation. Never once did my mother yell or lose her composure. She was the picture of professionalism, but I am certain that her concerns were taken very seriously because she demanded an apology on my behalf. Mr. Barns walked over to me, looking somewhat apologetic; a look I had never witnessed on him before. He bent down and said to me, "Miss Vann, I am sorry that I called you stupid. I do not think you are stupid. In fact, you are one of my best students." He put out his hand to shake mine. I shook his hand and said, "Thank you." Still, I did not look him directly in his eye. I still lacked the confidence that left my body the day before. My mother thanked Mr. Barns and the principal and then she asked to speak to me alone. She took me to the end of the hall, smiled, and said, "You are not stupid and no one has the right to call you that. You are the smartest girl in this school, and don't you forget it." She kissed me on my forehead and with both of us holding back tears, she shooed me back to class. We never discussed the incident again except when Mom would conduct check-ins to discuss my progress in school. Like the home in which I was raised, we, too, have a house rule that we don't say or call anyone "stupid." The power and mean spiritedness embedded in this word can be extremely hurtful, even if only stated in jest.

Now that I am a parent myself, I look back on that day and often wonder what Mom was thinking when she returned to work on the day of that meeting. I shared this personal narrative because it helped me contextualize the role that parents have in the scholastic success of their children. It also showed the critical role of parent advocacy—where to go for what, who to contact, with what purpose, and how to advocate for one's child both effectively and efficiently. What my mother did for me and modeled for my elementary school teacher and principal represents an example of authentic parent engagement, a process by which parents and schools develop a reciprocal relationship and partner in multiple ways to ensure the academic and social success of their children (Hale, 2001; Henderson, Mapp, & Johnson, 2007; Lawrence-Lightfoot, 2003).

ADVOCATING FOR MY OWN: TRYING NOT TO REALLY GO MAD

Although the personal narrative shared happened more than 30 years ago, I have used it as my template for how to engage my children's teachers, school staff, and district administration to ensure their academic success and to acknowledge the power of an engaged parent. For nearly 7 years, our family has been situated in an affluent suburb of Philadelphia with our children attending a high-achieving school district with approximately 12% African American students. Our move from a more financially affordable suburb was both by design and with some calculated risks. We specifically made the decision to move because of the educational resources that our children would gain. Our girls, Tracey and Rhonda, were in first grade and preschool, respectively, at the time. There were numerous sacrifices, financial and otherwise, that led us to this point and while we made few assumptions regarding a hands-off approach for our girls, we certainly had no idea that advocating for our children could be a daunting, time-consuming, and sometimes "trying to find a needle in the haystack" endeavor. In retrospect, I was not prepared for what I encountered, some of which required mental gymnastics to fully conceptualize what student success might "look like" for Tracey and Rhonda. All we wanted was for the educational system that we selected to see the brilliance in our children and share our hopes and dreams for them (Lawrence-Lightfoot, 2003).

Nonetheless, we recognized at the beginning of our girls' educational journeys that advocating for them would need to occur early and often within this new school district. As an educator and researcher, I have found that there is a distinct level of acknowledgment and respect for the children whose parents who are even somewhat visible. With my mother's example in mind, I made it a point to meet teachers, the principal, and other key school staff. My challenge, even as someone who studies schools and the processes that occur within them, is that parent advocacy and engagement needs to be studied more in depth. We must begin to uncover some of the quiet and deliberate strategies that parents and school advocates utilize to provide students, particularly African American students, with the educational access and resources that they need to be academically successful as well as college and career ready.

TRACEY'S STORY: ACADEMIC POTENTIAL, PROMISE, AND PURPOSE

Tracey is our first-born. She currently is in sixth grade and is doing well both academically and socially. She began school at Pinewood Elementary in first grade having attended a private preschool and kindergarten prior to our move into the district. Like most African American parents at Pinewood, we were thrilled to be in a place that at least on paper offers every child the chance at success. The district prides itself upon its graduates, many of whom are National Merit Scholars and go on to some of the best universities in the country. However, what became an important data point as Tracey began her early educational experience at Pinewood was the looming achievement gap that existed for a relatively high percentage of African American students in the district. Although my spouse and I self-selected both the district and the elementary school based on both achievement data and the percentage of African American students enrolled, we were still concerned with the way in which this high-achieving district had both students who went on to Ivy League institutions and students who were barely graduating, most of whom were African American. With these and other imminent concerns, Tracey's journey began.

Tracey is what I term a quiet learner. She is a bright girl who often needs to have her brilliance acknowledged and pulled out of her from time to time. Her reading levels have always been far above grade level, so this was an area in which I felt we had little to worry. Our major challenge with Tracey came when we realized how soon our district began tracking for math, which is in fourth grade. To my benefit, I had many informal conversations with other parents within the district and was able to gain understanding about the process and which students were afforded access to the advanced math curriculum in fifth grade.

Once I sorted out the stories of other parents, I was better equipped to ask Tracey's teachers relevant questions as they related to her progress, particularly in math.

In first grade, Tracey's teacher boasted about her being on or above grade level on several mathematical concepts, so I had no reason to question her developing math ability. However, during Tracey's second-grade year, I began to notice that there was not a lot of emphasis on basic math skills. Furthermore, some of the math concepts that were actually addressed seemed to only scratch the surface level and when Tracey would attempt to do her homework, it was clear that either there was limited direct instruction or she missed some key concepts in class that day.

One day, Tracey came home and told me in a cheerful voice, "I saw that math specialist today." I probed further and she said she and some other students needed some extra help on a lesson, and they were pulled out to see the math specialist. I was concerned that I was not made aware that she would be pulled out of class, especially because I was in the building that day for a volunteer activity and spoke briefly with her teacher. I was also concerned about the stigma attached to students needing extra help and wanted to get a sense of the student demographics regarding who was getting pulled out to see the math specialist. So, I e-mailed Tracey's teacher, who assured me that she was doing fine and just needed a little extra support that the math specialist was better able to provide. I then reminded her to notify me whenever Tracey would be pulled out of the classroom in any capacity.

Once I realized the added value of having Tracey meet with the math specialist, I began to request that she be provided this level of support periodically. My requests were usually accommodated; however, my primary concern was that as early as second grade, Tracey was not developing a conceptual understanding or the related math skill set that I felt would enable her to access a more challenging curriculum in later grades, particularly at the end of fourth grade, which was already on my radar although it was 2 years away. Additionally, as we became more integrated into the school system, and I became more involved in both school and districtwide activities, I began to hear many parents casually speak about obtaining outside tutoring for their children. I thought to myself, "Certainly they are speaking of middle and high school students. Why would elementary school students need outside tutoring?" However, my assumption was wrong. As I began to ask more direct questions to parents who had students in the school, I found that, like myself, many parents quietly complained that the math instruction did not allow their students to have the ability to test into advanced math in fifth grade, so they decided to provide their children with weekly supplemental math instruction outside of school.

This was the first of many epiphanies for me as we continued to find our way through the district. I now knew firsthand that many of my more affluent, mostly White, neighbors had both the financial resources and insider knowledge to access the system in ways that many African American parents could not, particularly those new to the district. Armed with this information, I was adamant that Tracey would continue to see the math specialist and that I would pay close attention to her performance on both classroom and state-level assessments, in case we too needed to provide her with outside tutoring. Although I disagreed with the way in which students were being tutored outside of school and gaining access to an accelerated academic curriculum as a result, I also realized that this is the system that we were in, and in order to set my children up for academic success, it would be necessary to play both within and against the system. That is, we had to be vigilant, as well as provide our children with any resources that we could afford to enable them to fully integrate into a system that builds and perpetuates such systemic inequality.

Tracey continued to perform well in the classroom with extra support, which usually consisted of 30 minutes per week within a small-group setting of students, most of which had a documented need for this support, although my daughter did not. This continued on throughout her third-grade year. At the end of that school year, I was still concerned about her grade-level appropriate skill set in math. This was even more important because at the end of her fourth-grade year, she would be assessed for advanced math placement.

Tracey clearly demonstrated her ability to be successful in mathematics. She scored in the advanced range on statewide assessments as well as consistently earned A's each marking period while she was in the third and fourth grades. So, it was much to my surprise when I received a nebulously worded letter the fall of her fifth-grade year explaining that, based on her performance on various math assessments, Tracey would be placed in a fifth-grade math class rather than the sixth-grade math class I expected. And so it began: My quest to clearly understand how these particular decisions were made, find out who the key players were, and what this meant for Tracey's access to advanced-level courses in math and science as she matriculated through the school district.

The summer prior to receiving the letter, I began to inquire about the advanced math placement assessments as well as the criteria used to place students. I also asked for additional meetings to express my concern about the three math tracks (grade-level; one grade level above; two grade levels above). More specifically, I wanted to know at what level (building, district, or otherwise) placement decisions were made. I met with the school math specialist the summer before Tracey entered fifth grade to clarify questions I had regarding the placement process. Also, prior to the end of her fourth-grade school year, I attended a districtwide meeting that addressed the achievement gap. At that time, I began to get a better sense of what I now refer to as the "manufactured achievement gap." This gap existed simply because of a lack of access, information, and opportunity, particularly for parents new to the district and especially for parents of color who were not always welcomed as partners in their children's academic success. As I sat in that meeting, I thought about the number of parents who hired outside tutors and how that correlated with the number of students in advanced math. I also thought about the need to demystify the entire process for parents so that they would not be blindsided, as I was that summer.

I felt it important to examine the assessments for advanced math placement and repeatedly made this request. I wanted to know what math knowledge and skill set fourth-grade students were being expected to demonstrate on these assessments. I was given extensive push back and experienced difficulty with scheduling meetings and limited discussion once I was afforded face time with the math specialist and the elementary math curriculum supervisor. However, I did not waver in my now honed, investigative reporting skills during the process, which took place over an approximately 15-month period. I felt a strong sense of advocacy and began to think that if the outcome was like this for a parent like me, who had an educational background and understanding of how schools operate, then I could only imagine what a parent who did not have my background had to face.

After many meetings and pulling in key district-level administrators to view Tracey's file, she was eventually allowed to sit for the advanced-level math district-level assessment. This was at the end of fifth grade. Tracey had certainly grown academically. She also began to understand that many of her peers in advanced math were not smarter than she, and she felt that she could do the work in an advanced math course. Her father and I shared with her in an age-appropriate context our next steps regarding her placement.

My overall concern was that as early as second grade, I recognized growing gaps in Tracey's developing math skill set, and I raised questions that were often discounted, I believe in part, because Tracey was a compliant student, never complained, and was somewhat reserved in her demeanor. In most cases, she performed above grade level. However, the game changed dramatically when math tracking or accelerated math placement was being considered. I was even told, during more than one conversation with the building math specialist, that math ability is part of some students' makeup and those are the students that they want identified for advanced math. When I heard that statement, I decided that my husband and I would continue to advocate for advanced math placement for Tracey. That statement, which was made by a White female, was one of many racial microaggressions that I confronted during this quest.

As I reviewed the notes I had recorded during my meetings and thought about next steps, I remember thinking, *Is she really telling me that performing at an advanced level in mathematics is not part of Tracey's makeup?* I became astounded, irate, and found myself slowly "going mad." This conversation represented another epiphany for me, as it was at that moment that it was less about Tracey's math ability, and more about the math specialist's perception of her ability and perhaps about the abilities of many African American students who do not meet the district's rigid, almost exclusionary, criteria for accelerated math placement.

By the summer of Tracey's fifth-grade year, I was both confident and savvy in my dealings with the district. I knew who would hear my concerns regarding Tracey's math placement and how I could have someone review Tracey's file with a fresh set of eyes. By this time, I had met a number of key-level administrators, I attended various meetings as the token parent representative, and I had reached out to an African American administrator to share my concerns and bring him up to speed on what I had endured for the past 18 months. He asked a number of questions for clarification and agreed that my concerns were indeed valid, admitting that my experience was common practice in the district. I asked if he would be willing to sit in with my husband and I in an upcoming meeting with the math curriculum director to discuss the written request we made to place Tracey in the accelerated math curriculum. He agreed.

As we prepared our talking points for the meeting, my husband and I reviewed her file, which was, by now, about 5 inches deep. Armed with the supporting data that included advanced-level scores on the statewide assessment, above-average scores on the districtwide assessments, and report cards since fourth grade with all A's, we were ready. I also had a separate file with an evaluation from Tracey's math tutor stating that she would be successful in an accelerated math course. With my mountain of supporting data, my husband by my side, and my administrator colleague present, it was decided within 10 minutes that Tracey's roster would be changed to place her in either seventh grade or advanced math. The math director warned me, however, that this was a major exception and that Tracey would have a difficult time getting up to speed and would potentially struggle in the course.

I requested all of the sixth-grade math materials so that Tracey would be able to work on them with her tutor during the summer. Tracey's dad and I exchanged a high five in the parking lot and went back to the jobs for which we get paid. That night at dinner, we shared the news with Tracey. She beamed with pride and joy. I told her we would continue to work on sixth-grade math that summer and that she would do fine. Later, I thanked the district staff and sent a thank you card to the administrator for bringing a distinct dynamic to the table as an African American administrator.

QUESTIONS FOR REFLECTION

1. Sara Lawrence-Lightfoot (2003) in *The Essential Conversation: What Parents and Teachers Can Learn From Each Other* encourages us to consider ways in which school districts build partnerships that support school and family engagement in an authentic way. How can school districts build and sustain capacity among teachers, school, and district staff to understand and be responsive to both the academic and cultural needs of African American children?

2. How can parents and guardians gain access to necessary resources and develop strategies that will allow them to effectively advocate and ensure academic opportunities for their children and avoid "going mad" in the process?

3. Perhaps many of the issues regarding the underidentification of African American students could be mitigated by a reevaluation of the ways in which teachers and instructional leaders are trained. What role do teacher training and educational leadership programs play in this regard?

THE OUTCOME

These days I am less mad and more empowered. I know where to go and who to call for help, and I share this information freely with any parent who asks. I advocate early and often for all of our children and try to keep my finger on the pulse of both the district and my children's learning needs. Tracey maintained an A average in her advanced prealgebra course. She also made the honor roll each marking period. She has never questioned her ability to be in an advanced math class. She also shared that there were eight other students who were not previously in advanced math and were moved into the advanced prealgebra class for sixth grade. What made me feel most confident about Tracey's success was a statement that Tracey's math teacher made during an open house that took place in the beginning of the school year. She stated, "Somewhere along the way your child has shown that she is good in math. Now, my job is to make her better." I was so excited about her positive tone and high expectations, both of which seemed to be part of her repertoire. I knew already that Tracey would connect and perform well for a teacher like this. Recently, my husband and I received an e-mail from her math teacher stating, "I just wanted to let you know that Tracey scored a perfect score on the math test and I am pleased with her progress." So far, so good!

Tracey has a younger sister and a younger brother; I am prayerful that someday, all teachers and school staff will not have to be reminded to see our children's brilliance. That way, there will be far fewer "mad moms."

REFERENCES

Hale, J. E. (2001). *Learning while Black: Creating educational excellence for African American children.* Baltimore, MD: Johns Hopkins University Press.

Henderson, A., Mapp, K., & Johnson, V. (2007). *Beyond the bake sale: The essential guide to family-school partnerships.* New York, NY: The New Press.

Lawrence-Lightfoot, S. (2003). *The essential conversation: What parents and teachers can learn from each other.* New York, NY: Ballantine Books.

CHAPTER 23

MY CHILD LEFT BEHIND

by Samantha Elliott Briggs and Ursula Thomas

BACKGROUND

More often than not, the classroom experience can be oppressive to an impressionable young mind still in its formative years, especially when met with a biased teacher and hidden curriculum that reinforces societal norms without giving thought to the individual or his or her cultural experience. It is safe to assume that the teacher lacks the cultural awareness and sensitivity necessary to be a culturally responsive employee whose goal is to see each child receive an equal educational opportunity to succeed. In such a case where the teacher is ill-equipped or lacks desire, the parents must be conscious enough to ensure their child receives the proper social and academic nurturance within the school setting by acting as the child's advocate. With such attention, a child's success is unlimited; without, the success can potentially be unfounded. Our society has both consciously and subconsciously set African American males up to fail. Although a history of systemic racism can predisposition a Black male to fall short, individualized experiences and interventions can determine the ultimate outcome, whether it is positive or negative. Whereas racism may not always be the root cause for the "teacher as oppressor" dynamic, the resulting implications are far greater and much more devastating for an African American male than any other child of a different race or gender.

MY CHILD LEFT BEHIND

"Mommy! No! *Please* Mommy, don't make me do it!" All too often, this cry has been heard bellowed out from the battlefield of life—especially the highly intense, ever changing, dramatic life experienced from a wee one's point of view. More often this plea comes from a point of extreme desperation, a cry for help, or perhaps as a last ditch effort to be pardoned from a presumably unfair responsibility. Oddly enough, my personal experience with such petitioning comes each night that math homework has been assigned.

My third-grade son, Brent, has nearly exhausted himself in a variety of attempts to get out of math homework this year. He has tried not writing the assignment down in his homework planner, but that only lasts until the next day when I'm alerted that he didn't complete the work and it's sent home a second time. He's tried leaving his homework planner at home so that he wouldn't have to write anything down in it; however, the teacher has him write the homework assignment down on a piece of loose leaf paper instead. On three separate occasions, Brent has gone so far as to leave his math folder at school, believing that would get him out of the chore. In turn, I headed right back to the building promptly upon finding out. The third (and last) time he pulled this stunt, I did not find out until 5 p.m., and I had to ask the custodian to let me in to gather the materials necessary to complete his homework. When all else failed, Brent has taken to hiding, crying, and begging me not to make him do his math homework.

If I share this series of events with a friend, a colleague, or a family member who all know Brent well, they would pass on the mainstream assumption of a behavior issue and rightly relate these outbursts to anxiety, which is exactly what we are dealing with. However, if I shared this anecdote with any random stranger off the street, they would probably label it a discipline problem on Brent's part and a parenting problem on mine. In cities above the Mason-Dixon Line, along with those out West, Brent's behavior would seem normal for the free-spirited, independent, gifted child that he is. In the Black community (despite the region), Brent's behavior would be deemed irreprehensible; such a "temper tantrum" is more commonly considered a reflection of a White family aesthetic, and it would be met with a swift hand in many Black homes. Likewise in Southern culture—despite race and oftentimes despite economic standing—children are expected to know their place as subordinates and must comply immediately upon first command with an appropriate, "Yes, ma'am" or "Yes, sir" attached as if a punctuation mark at the end of every sentence.

Conversely, I am of the belief system that for every action there is a reaction and a behavior is oftentimes environmentally produced. My job as a mother is to identify what within the environment has caused such a reaction in my otherwise well-balanced, well-mannered child. Several things I know for sure about Brent and his relationship to academics: (a) Brent has a remarkable aptitude for mathematics; (b) he is the product of two parents with doctoral degrees—one of whom happens to teach math at the collegiate level; and (c) like most children, Brent has a natural curiosity that wakes him up each morning, ahead of the alarm clock, eager to soak up the world and all of its offerings.

So what environmental factor pushed my gifted 9-year-old son to the edge of doubt, rebellion, and academic failure? Surprisingly that was an easy answer—it was Ms. Deville. Ms. Deville is Brent's 20-something-year-old, White, female teacher, who upon first impression gives off the stereotypical personality of not only a SEC-university-sorority-row-legacy, but she also fits the mold of a proud multigenerational elementary school teacher who dutifully followed in the footsteps of her foremothers. Now mind you, my children have been raised in Southern suburban public schools, so all but three of their collective teachers have fit this profile. This isn't our first turn up to bat, and, by all means, we know the rules of the game.

Although each school year seems to bring its own challenge of Black, educated, middle-class family versus White, average, "teacher class" (but thinks she's upper class) teacher, we have typically won the upper hand by laying down the law upon the earliest confrontation within the first grading period—therefore, our children have come out relatively unscathed. You know the confrontation—the one where you have to let them know that your child is not that kid they were referring to on page 262 of the "How to Teach the 'Other' Child" manual. In other words, my child is not a statistic.

It is clear that as a first-year teacher, Ms. Deville bought into the predictable wisdom handed down from classroom veterans: "Don't smile until Christmas." This schoolhouse lore is meant to curtail student mischief and bolster teacher authority. To this end, during the first 90 days of school, a stern Ms. Deville managed to call Brent a failure, a liar, and a cheater who failed to live up to his potential. She did so to his face and to us over the telephone, via e-mail, and through typewritten notes sent home. Our first encounter stands out as memorable as the last. It was a day last fall when my telephone began vibrating while I was at the university teaching my first class at 10:30 a.m. I looked down and saw my son's picture smiling up at me, indicating the call was from his school. My heart dropped as I excused myself from the classroom and dashed into the hallway, expecting the worse.

"Hello, Dr. Briggs?"

"Yes, this is Dr. Briggs, who may I ask is calling?" I replied.

"Dr. Briggs, this is Ms. Deville, Brent's teacher. Do you have a moment?"

Anxious for her to get to the point, I answered, "Yes, of course! Is Brent okay? What's wrong?"

Perhaps aware that her call caught me off guard, Ms. Deville said, "Oh, yes, I'm sorry; I didn't mean to alarm you. Brent is fine, however, I was calling to let you know that he's failing."

In 13 years of parenting, I'd never heard that word attached to either of my children. So I asked, "Failing? What do you mean, failing? What exactly is Brent failing at?"

"He's failing math," Ms. Deville answered.

"Ms. Deville, as you are well aware, Brent's father has three degrees in mathematics and is a math professor at Midtown State. He takes great pride in helping Brent with his homework each night and would never send him back to school without making sure that it is 100% correct. So how exactly is it that he's failing in math?" I snapped in turn.

"He's failing because he is not showing his thinking when he works out the problems. Knowing your high expectations, I thought I should warn you in advance of his failing grade before he brings it home this evening for you to sign."

"Ms. Deville, I know for a fact that my husband makes Brent show his work for every problem, so forgive my ignorance, but what exactly does it mean to 'show his thinking?'"

Quite dismissively, Ms. Deville responded, "Yes, Dr. Briggs, he did show his work. To 'show your thinking' means something entirely different. Brent is in class when I teach the lessons—he knows what it means, perhaps you should ask him when he comes home this evening."

I could have been mistaken, but it sounded as if Ms. Deville felt quite satisfied after giving her report.

The moment I ended the call with Ms. Deville, I began a call to my husband. I gave him a quick summary of Ms. Deville's report and told him to meet me at the school in 30 minutes so that we could have lunch with our son. I dismissed my class early and was at Brent's school by 11:15 a.m. My husband met me in the parking lot, and we were able to sign in and walk to the cafeteria together. The looks on both Brent's and Ms. Deville's faces were priceless! Brent was elated by our presence; Ms. Deville was deflated.

Brent quickly grabbed his lunch tray and moved eagerly to the parents' table where children can enjoy lunch under the spotlight and away from their assigned seat with the class. He gave us both hugs and kisses and asked why we were there. We told him about Ms. Deville's phone call and asked him what was going on. Brent explained that he did not understand this "new math," where he was required to show his thinking and that Ms. Deville never fully explained it. According to Brent, whenever he raised his hand to ask Ms. Deville a question for clarification, she would quickly shoot him down, thereby discouraging him (and others) from asking any questions at all. We asked Brent if she said anything to him about his most recent math grade. He said, yes, that in fact, Ms. Deville called him to her desk earlier that morning to tell him that he failed the test. Wanting to know the specifics, I asked, "What exactly did she say? Was anyone else near the desk? Did she speak softly to keep the conversation private, or could others hear her?"

Brent said that Ms. Deville spoke to him in front of several other students in line at her desk and that she was loud enough to capture everyone's attention. Brent recalled her asking, "How does it make you feel to know that you're failing?" When Brent told her that it made him feel sad, Ms. Deville replied, "As well it should."

Crushed, I asked my son with genuine concern how her questioning made him feel, and he answered, "Mommy, I was so embarrassed and sad. I just listened to her and kept telling myself not to let her see me cry. I didn't want her to see me cry." I held back my own tears because I know that Brent was relying on the wisdom I give him when he and his older sister fuss and I tell him that his reaction gives her power. In that moment, my brave 9-year-old son was trying not to give Ms. Deville any undue power.

Ms. Deville's tone and choice of words to describe my son and his efforts were inaccurate and inappropriate, to say the least. Although my husband and I could handle harsh words and adult confrontation, my 9-year-old son should not have been subjected to such unfounded criticism from someone he is not only taught to respect and trust, but someone who he looks up to for guidance, modeling, and affirmation.

In the midst of all this, I called a colleague to talk about what had been happening in order to get an alternate perspective. Dr. Montgomery was teaching a math methods course for education majors at a regional university. As I laid out what happened with Brent, Dr. Montgomery asked questions like, "How many models did his teacher provide?" and "How did she unpack the standards?" She also asked, "Did Ms. Deville offer time for the children to choose a problem-solving strategy and explain their rationale for choosing that strategy to solve that problem?" Dr. Montgomery talked about how the national math standards valued differentiation and multiple ways of thinking of mathematics and problem solving were encouraged. Ms. Deville graduated from a large, well-known university and she should be more familiar with this philosophy—more than the veteran teachers should. Why did Ms. Deville not think enough of my son to step outside the box she was in to better support him?

In dual mommy/teacher mode, I contacted Ms. Deville immediately following her first outburst in an effort to both reprimand and scaffold. I simply told her that her poor choice of words could have irreparable damage, if they fell on the wrong set of ears. I explained that children should never find themselves associated with the concept of failing or being a failure. I also explained that if a child was truly performing less than expected, there were more approachable means of getting their attention.

Unfortunately, Ms. Deville refused to learn from my wisdom, and she failed to leave well enough alone. Feeling quite self-righteous, Ms. Deville chose to prove to us who the real teacher was and who was really running the show. To make sure that she had proper evidence to support her smear campaign, Brent suddenly began bringing home failing grades across all subjects—not consistently, but just enough to catch our attention. Ms. Deville became unforgiving on assignments, taking off points for misspelled words (even though in third grade phonetic spelling was still encouraged), or giving partial credit on answers where he may not have erased an error thoroughly enough. My son never received a grade higher than an 85% on his reading response for one vague reason or another.

There were two final straws that broke the camel's back (my math-teaching husband being the proverbial camel in this scenario). The first was Brent receiving (not earning, receiving) multiple grades of 60%–68% on his math exams. On average Brent would have the majority of the answers correct, however Ms. Deville did not approve of his problem-solving methods, citing "He could have shown his work differently" or "He didn't show his thinking." Most recently Ms. Deville wrote of Brent:

I wanted to send a note home to discuss with you some concerns that I have with Brent's teaching test from Friday morning. When grading, I noticed that he did not show his thinking on 8 out of 10 of the problems. Of course I want Brent to be successful; therefore I talked with him and asked him to review the noted problems and to please show me his work. When given the opportunity to show his work on these problems, Brent instead tried to correct the problem that was already marked wrong.

I discussed with Brent the importance of honesty and how this act was dishonest. Rather than allow him the chance to correct his problems, I feel now that it is more appropriate to take points off of his paper. I am concerned that I tried to provide leniency with his work, and rather than rise to the occasion, he tried to change his answers. I am disappointed by his choice, and I have talked with him about being untruthful.

I am sorry this has come up again, however, I knew that you would want to be informed.

Ms. Deville

This letter contradicted itself within its content; a follow-up meeting with Ms. Deville did not make it any clearer. The way we interpreted Ms. Deville's "help" was that she allowed Brent an opportunity to correct his mistakes. However, when he followed up to correct the mistakes by going back to show his thinking, Ms. Deville declared it cheating.

The second straw was finding out from Brent that when Ms. Deville did not approve his homework, she made him sit out from recess or from another fun elective to erase every answer on his homework page only to rework the problems under her watchful eye. Twice Ms. Deville said simply, "You did it wrong"; the other two times she said Brent didn't show his work properly and, most recently, she said he wrote the problems horizontally instead of vertically. As if it hadn't already been made clear, we now knew that this was personal.

Ms. Deville knew she had pushed us to the limits, and she was ready for battle. Before we had a chance to voice our concerns in a meeting with her and the school administration, Ms. Deville had already begun decorating for her self-initiated pity party. "Have you asked previous teachers about this family?" Ms. Deville wondered aloud to the principal before going on to say that we had a "reputation." Apparently, we believed Brent could do no wrong, and we liked to intimidate teachers and put them down in the face of our own personal and professional achievements. The very presence of my 6' 3", African American, bow-tie-and-suit-wearing husband was a threat to Ms. Deville, who had already been rumored to say that she felt as though we were at the school too frequently having lunch with Brent, volunteering, and trying to check up on her.

In our first meeting with the school administration, Ms. Deville had a sole interest of self-preservation, while my husband and I had a sole interest of Brent-preservation. I began the meeting by describing my son's plans to one day become a veterinarian. I let them know that Brent and his sister wanted to go into business together and that they already knew what college they wanted to attend. They knew that in order to get into the college of their choice, they had to maintain good grades, good citizenship, and community service. I reminded Ms. Deville and the others present that in order to become a veterinarian, Brent would need a solid foundation in math and science—both intellectually and emotionally. In case she was unaware, I also informed Ms. Deville that the third grade was quite pivotal in a young person's educational career and that her methods could either make or break Brent.

Unlike the one year Ms. Deville had underway, my husband and I had nearly two decades of experience in the field of education. We were well aware that key predictors of gains in academic outcomes were high-quality instruction and close teacher-child relationships.

During the 6 months following the initial meeting, Ms. Deville became more negative toward Brent. She allowed negative impressions and perhaps hidden biases to foreshadow a quality, equal educational opportunity for my son. After countless attempts to repair our broken relationship with Ms. Deville on our own and with administrative intervention, we finally sent the following letter to the administration:

Thank you for taking the time to listen to the concerns that we continue to have about the difficulties we are facing with Brent's academics as well as our parent/student/teacher relationship this year. While I know that you take great pride in the selection of every teacher and you are careful and thoughtful in the placement of every student . . . sometimes when the two come together it's a hit, sometimes it's a miss. I believe in some circumstances the "miss" can be tolerated and everyone involved can grow through the process—we did so already in both first and second grade—however, there are other situations that are a bit more trying and we have to look out for the best interest of the child. We have nurtured our son through a variety of circumstances at Hopewell Elementary that we wish we never encountered; however at this point we have reached our limit, as our son is not the same person he was when we placed him in Ms. Deville's care in August and we are not the same parents. If we had a Plan B, we would withdraw Brent from school today in order to preserve any sense of self-worth/ esteem/efficacy that may be remaining . . . we are that distraught over this year.

After five conferences and countless e-mail exchanges we do not believe this current situation can be repaired and we do not believe that Brent can be successful in his environment. As a result, we are making a formal request that Brent be moved to a new classroom first thing Monday morning. We trust that you will keep our circumstances at the forefront as you select a new teacher for Brent, and we expect that you will keep him safe from any teacher that has been too close to the negative attention their colleague has placed on him this year.

With only 3 months remaining in this academic year, we feel as though it isn't too late for Brent to have a fresh start and a clean slate. It is our hope that Brent can go into the spring testing season with the confidence he once had, and that he be well prepared for and excited about the fourth grade.

Thank you for your time and close attention.

The Briggs Family

We were grateful when the principal responded to our request before the close of business that day and Brent was moved the following Monday. Brent's new teacher had nearly a decade of classroom experience and was Nationally Board Certified. Although she closely fit the exact same description given of Ms. Deville earlier in this story, Ms. Miller had a certain confidence that translated into flexibility within her professional definition of completion and success. During the first few weeks in his new class, Brent was not a different learner any more than he was a different boy. As such, his way of solving math problems and completing class work was no different for Ms. Miller than it was for Ms. Deville. Strangely enough, Brent's grades spiked immediately, with his confidence soaring alongside.

I recall a day that Brent and I were sitting in the car waiting on his older sister to get out of school. As always, during our daily 30-minute wait for Althea to be dismissed, I suggested that we get started on his homework. Brent happily complied, pulling out his math homework first. I was caught a little off guard that he actually *wanted* to work on his math—it had been so long since he showed such enthusiasm for his once favorite subject. I asked Brent if we should work on spelling and hold off on math until we were home and he had a snack and the chance to relax. He said, "Nope! I'd rather get it done now so that I have more time to play when we get home." Brent proceeded to solve the problems with ease and was finished in no time. As I looked it over with pride and joy, I asked, "How on Earth did you go from not knowing how to subtract larger numbers from smaller numbers without regrouping just a week ago, to now knowing how to solve it not one, but *two* different ways?" Brent shrugged his shoulders and matter-of-factly replied, "Because Ms. Miller actually teaches us how to do it." Without any further prodding, he added, "Ms. Deville never really taught us how to solve a problem. She would write it on the board, solve it herself, and then tell us to 'wonder' about how she got the answer." Properly restraining myself from sharing the expletive that was on the tip of my tongue, I appropriately replied with a simple, "I'm so glad that Ms. Miller is such an awesome teacher," and "wondered" to myself, "Out of the mouths of babes . . ."

QUESTIONS FOR REFLECTION

1. What do you think are the long-terms effects on the third grader's educational experience considering his parents' "reputation"?
2. What do you think the role of school administration should be in this situation?
3. Should this child have been removed from this classroom? Why or why not?

THE OUTCOME

Brent successfully completed the third grade in Ms. Miller's class. He went from "failing" math under Ms. Deville's watch to earning a solid A with Ms. Miller. The school principal retired and the assistant principal, a young African American woman, filled the position. The new principal worked tirelessly to find the perfect fourth-grade match for Brent, a teacher that we were sure would produce the only type of F's we could tolerate, Fair and Firm. Although Brent was a bit apprehensive that his fourth-grade year would be any different from the past, we collectively worked toward changing his mindset. His grades are exceptional, and he has joined several school clubs in addition to earning a spot in the school choir. Brent's sense of self (both academically and personally) is on the mend . . . and so is my heart.

CHAPTER 24

KNOWLEDGE DENIED
AN INFORMATION DIVIDE

by Kristina Henry Collins

BACKGROUND

It's about 6 weeks into the school year, and I have been called to attend my first stakeholders' conference. As tradition has it, a stakeholders' conference is a collaborative conference held when the parents request to meet with all of their child's teachers as a result of concerns in multiple classes or when a teacher has concerns about discipline issues and attempts to show a pattern within all classes, specifically the core academic areas. They are typically scheduled right before the school day starts—usually around clock-in time for working parents—and convene in the counselors' conference room.

Those summoned to the meeting (or trial) are the parent(s), the arbitrating counselor, and the student's academic teachers outfitted with a defensive "snapshot" of the student's inadequacies (e.g., last progress report with grades and behavioral indicators, some work samples, attendance report). Ideally, these meetings are deemed necessary only after initial interventions such as individual teacher-parent phone conferences, notes home, and/or some other action such as afterschool tutoring or detention have failed to correct behavior.

Nonetheless, stakeholders' conferences can provide a great opportunity for the school and the home to connect so that parents are fully equipped to make informed decisions about their child's educational process once professional recommendations are considered. Unfortunately, however, this is not always the case. And on this particular day, this stakeholders' conference represents what is all too often the norm for parents of gifted Black students in Title I schools. In this Title I school with a student population of about 2,000, 64% of students receive free or reduced lunch, and the racial distribution of the student population is 74% African American and 17% White. Approximately 14% of the student body is identified with disabilities, 8% in remediation programs, 4% enrolled in alternative school, 46% on vocational lab focus/track, and only 7% identified as gifted.

ISAIAH'S STORY

THE SPECIAL EDUCATION DILEMMA

"That ADHD medicine makes me feel like a walking zombie and gifted classes in high school are too hard so I'd rather be in regular classes with my friends. In there I won't need medicine anyway—all the kids have ADHD," defended Isaiah to his mom as they discussed what prompted his latest suspension. This was the conversation and "last straw," as his mom put it, that led to the conference that we are having this morning.

Isaiah had been diagnosed with ADHD about 5 years before he was identified as gifted. So he definitely has more years under his belt as a "special education kid" with a behavioral disorder, coached and trained how to properly act in a classroom, than he does on how to maximize his gifted abilities in the classroom. For years, Isaiah learned that he did not have to study or do much to pass a class as long as he behaved. Furthermore, Isaiah learned a long time ago that he—in his words—
" . . . is definitely not one of those geeky White students that leave the

classroom once per week to learn things that other children are not able to learn." Isaiah learned the hard way from a former teacher that, "Bad children who do not know how to act in class are not rewarded with enrichment time." This response was to Isaiah's request to get out of boring classes by any means necessary.

So here we were, sitting in a parent conference with Isaiah's single mother, Mrs. Langford, and without the student, as it is traditionally done. Mrs. Langford's stress was evident with every gesture and movement. Desperation was written all over her face. Her hands, excessively wrinkled and scarred for such a young mother, tell a story all in themselves—a story of struggle and constant fight.

"I want to do what is best for my son, but I don't know what to do at this point. I guess I have to just trust your judgment, but please know that my son is not a thug, and he is smart," explained Mrs. Langford. Because these were her introductory comments, she obviously perceived us as a "panel of judges" to oversee her situation. I immediately thought, "Wow, Isaiah is already doomed with these opening statements."

Recognizing that her efforts were ill-informed at best, she continued,

I have tried my best to help him, but it doesn't seem to help anymore. He liked the gifted program when his fifth-grade teacher, Mrs. Brown, had him put in there; she was his favorite teacher. Then he went to middle school and went to a different room for science and English. He said he liked it because he didn't have to stay in the same room all day. We even tried once to stop the medicine, but he still did not do well in regular classes. So, the counselors thought we should start back again.

With tears in her eyes, it appeared as if Mrs. Langford knew that she found herself at the mercy of the knowledge and recommendations of those who sit with her. She trusted that we would decide what is best for Isaiah, her youngest child and only son, who she has struggled with ever since she could remember. I, as only one of two gifted math teachers for ninth grade, have Isaiah in my class; he comes to me around the middle of the day. And because I live in the same community as most of my students, I also remember Isaiah from a couple of encounters with his mom within the community setting several years ago when he was no more than 5 or 6 years of age. This was around the time when he was diagnosed ADHD. This is my third year teaching as a designated gifted teacher, but I have been teaching math for a long time. I am also one of two African American teachers that Isaiah has this school year; the other is his science teacher. As a matter of fact, and until the latest efforts of the district to certify most of our teachers through a local program, it would not be uncommon for gifted students to be enrolled in classes/services with only White female teachers up to this point in their educational careers.

Also at the table is Mrs. Johnson, his gifted science teacher, who is in her second year of teaching in the gifted program; Mr. Ramsey, the gifted ninth-grade government teacher, who has the most experience of all of us with teaching in the gifted program; Ms. Newman, the gifted ninth-grade literature teacher, who is teaching freshmen for the first time; and Isaiah's guidance counselor, Ms. Blanch.

"Well, Mrs. Langford, I have Isaiah during the first hour, and he is constantly acting up. There is a power struggle, and it is hard for him to understand that I control the class," explained Mr. Ramsey, the discipline referral teacher. Ms. Newman, Isaiah's last period teacher, chimes in: "Mrs. Collins can attest to his behavioral issues because I usually use her room when I put him in timeout at least once per week because he talks and jokes around inappropriately." With agitation still in her voice, Mrs. Newman continued, supporting her claims with the presentation of Isaiah's progress report, "He sits at the front of the class, but as you can see he cannot or will not do the work"

It is at this point, during the usual process and progression of this type of meeting, that the parent responds to the initial teacher's report. Mrs. Langford began by apologizing on Isaiah's behalf, reassuring us that she expects him to be respectful of all of his teachers and do his work. She stressed,

I don't know what has gotten into him this year. All of a sudden he does not seem as interested in school as much as he does socializing with his friends. He has one friend, Lance, in his classes this year. But Lance does so much better because both of his parents are home and they don't play when it comes to school. They have him in all types of other afterschool activities, but I can't afford that since I work part time and have my older daughter, Sheila, in college. That's another thing I don't understand—Sheila never got invited to participate in the gifted program, but she is smart and never got into any trouble in school.

"Mrs. Langford," Mrs. Johnson interrupted in her natural soft voice that matches her laidback demeanor. "I have no major problem with Isaiah in biology. His grade could be higher if he made a commitment to finish his projects but he is within the 80% that is required to remain in the gifted program." She continued with a bit of laughter,

There are times when the class gets talkative, and Isaiah will get off task, but a quick "mama look" with the eyes seem to work. Isaiah has even commented at times how I give him that look just like you do sometime. But more seriously, I am, however, concerned with his multiple absences that could affect his grade later on as a result of getting behind in class. We have talked about it and discussed a plan to make sure he still obtains the work when he is absent.

"Yeah, he really likes science so I expect him to have a better grade in your class," Mrs. Langford responded with a smile. "He is excited about his science projects and starts strong but has a problem finishing them. It's partly my fault because when he tells me he needs materials I can't always get them."

This leads into a conversation about how hard it has been financially trying to raise him without his father and the current living situation that is not good for him. By this time, Mrs. Langford was crying apologetically as she describes how Isaiah hardly sleeps—citing 3 to 4 hours nightly—and how it's so hard to wake him up in the morning that he often misses the bus and she can't always get him to school. "He always says 'Mom, I can't sleep because I can't stop thinking,' so I started giving him extra doses of his medicine so he can go to sleep and then one in the morning. We don't give him one after lunch anymore." She said that this might be the issue in first period with the lethargic behavior and then polled the group to see if she should ask the physician about increasing his dosage so that he can start back taking it after lunch, which might be a solution to the seventh-period woes in Mr. Ramsey's class as well.

Mr. Ramsey and Ms. Newman immediately agreed that a dose of the ADHD medicine should be added during the day. Mr. Ramsey added, "Gifted classes might be too much stress for Isaiah right now," and suggests that we seriously consider Isaiah's request to be removed from the gifted program.

Looking right at Mrs. Langford and in his most authoritarian voice, he said, "After all, Isaiah knows best if he can handle it or not." I reactively interrupted and asked Ms. Langford, "Are you familiar with twice-exceptionality and what is called overexcitabilities in gifted students?" She said that she was not. Mrs. Blanch added, "I'm not either and there is no mention of twice-exceptionality in Isaiah's permanent file." I briefly explained more about twice-exceptionality and Dabrowski's overexcitabilities.

As an attempt to provide what I think is a fair report of the situation as a whole and before any other comments could be offered, I began to provide my official "snapshot" of information. Considering that the focus thus far has been on Isaiah's behavior and performance, I decided to add to that information within the context of my classroom environment. "Isaiah actually sits in the back of my class when in alphabetical seating order. During our study buddy or quadrant group arrangement he usually chooses the back of the class area as well."

I went on to explain,

As students enter my room, they know to copy the instructional plans for the day that includes activating, teaching, and a closing strategy along with time frame and predetermined seating arrangement. Because my content is rarely delivered in simple lecture or single format, discussion, collaboration, and self-regulation are a big part of the class. As a result, talking is not an issue and movement is constant. Isaiah consistently adds to the discussions of the class and often volunteers to answer questions. He has an A in my class, even though his absences are a concern for credit purposes. As a matter of fact, he has come back to school on a couple of occasions and aced a test after several days of absences and missed lectures. I do admit, though, that I don't give a lot of rote practice problems to be turned in weekly but instead more independent work and provide several resources including a virtual classroom that offers other ways and choices for the student to learn the material based on their individual assessment.

Mrs. Langford responded with a slight smile that carries with it a hint of hope.

I know all about your class because Isaiah brings home the interactive notebook that I have to grade using that rubric that reminds me that I'm not good in math. He talks about the class all of the time—he thinks you are funny and makes learning math fun. But you are the strictest teacher he has ever had. He complains about your ZAP [zeros aren't permitted] policy, making them redo assignments over and over until they learn the information.

Once we discussed the situational causes surrounding Isaiah's underachievement and behavioral issues, Ms. Blanch ended the meeting by asking for recommendations and follow-up instructions.

PROFESSIONAL RECOMMENDATIONS

Mr. Ramsey quickly chimed in, "Mrs. Langford, we have talked on a couple occasions. Although Isaiah is failing my class and has behavior issues in my room, I want to assure you that we will work it all out."

I now thought, *All teachers present have taken the required special education course and have been certified as gifted teachers, so it should be obvious that we have observed a classic and almost textbook example about common issues within gifted education.* Like any good plot with a happy ending, I had already attempted to predict the next comments in anticipation to what would logically follow as a plan for Isaiah similar to that in special education known as an Individualized Education Program (IEP). Even though our district does not offer any type of formal parent indoctrination (orientation or education) about our gifted program, nor does it provide any common literature or framework by which all schools are required to follow in its own indoctrination program, I felt certain that we were going to make sure that this parent left confident and equipped with the information she needed to make informed decisions in the best interest of her son.

To my disappointment, there were no new recommendations offered. So as it stood, the information provided in this conference and the solutions offered during the earlier discussion were all that Mrs. Langford had as her resource for decision making. Those suggestions were to consider increasing Isaiah's ADHD medicine to include lunchtime dosage and to approve Isaiah's request to be removed from the gifted program, if that indeed made him most comfortable and happiest.

Encouraging Ms. Langford to review some possible resources about gifted education before making any final decisions, I stated,

> I will send home the list of gifted resources that we discussed in class at the beginning of the year that might be helpful in further explaining what is expected and suggested to be included as part of the gifted child's programming and curriculum.

I also added, "Maybe we, as his teachers and counselor, could also review those items as well before we make any further recommendations that could affect the student in such a significant manner." Once we were all in agreement, I made one other suggestion that Isaiah join the SECME (Science, Engineering, Communications, and Mathematics Enrichment program, formerly known as Southeastern Consortium for Minority Engineers; visit http://www.secme.org) club and meet Mr. Harris, who would make a great mentor for Isaiah. Mr. Ramsey asked Ms. Langford if he could speak to her in private as we adjourned the meeting; no other recommendations were offered.

QUESTIONS FOR REFLECTION

1. What are the causes of underachievement and behavioral issues for Isaiah? Do the professional recommendations address these causes?

2. What is the relationship between parents' knowledge about gifted education and the retention of Black gifted students in the program?

3. Does lack of knowledge about twice-exceptionality and social-emotional issues of gifted students significantly affect decision making that influences retention of Black students in gifted programs?

4. In what ways might formal parent education about gifted education and its resources enhance the partnership between home and the school to provide a more positive experience and subsequently increased retention of Black students in gifted programs?

5. Should support services that include parent and student orientation within the school system be required at each level of K–12 education to ensure parent empowerment and equity in gifted programming? Why or why not?

6. To what extent would provisions for effective support services for parents of gifted Black students affect the parents' perception of their ability to confidently address the social-emotional and academic needs of their gifted child?

THE OUTCOME

Isaiah is currently enjoying his sophomore year in high school and still enrolled in the gifted program. Taking a more personal role to manage his twice-exceptionalities, Isaiah started his new school year with no major infractions, nor has his mom been called in for the dreaded parent conference. Redirecting his unchallenged energy, he has joined the school's soccer team and does very well. Moved by the commitment to better inform her of options for her son, Isaiah's mom has since opened a small academic center that offers tutoring and support for younger students and their parents that find themselves in similar situations as she and Isaiah.

CHAPTER 25

PARENTING GIFTED SIBLINGS

by Sonja L. Fox

BACKGROUND: OUR STORY

MALLORY SPEAKS

In our house on Burberry Lane, Tory was babysitting us while our mom and dad were gone. Tory (my older brother), Ashleigh, and I (Mallory) were in our room when Tory said, "I bet I can flip from this bed to the other one."

"You can't do it," Ashleigh said.

I kept saying, "Do it! Do it, Tory!" I wanted to see if it was actually possible; however, Ashleigh thought that I shouldn't be able to see the spectacle and decided to put me in the closet. I guess she thought that if I saw him do it, I might tell and get us all in trouble. Well, through the crack between the doors, I could see the space between the beds. So he jumps, flips through the air, and lands with a thud. Because of my limited view, I couldn't see the landing. I burst out of the closet to congratulate Tory. I then saw the hole in the wall by my bed that his foot had left. Panic ensued at that moment as we began thinking of ways to hide the hole. We remembered that Dad had recently repaired a crack in the wall made by the doorknob at the garage door entrance. Tory went to the garage and got some of Dad's plaster stuff and was going to attempt to cover it with that, but because of how deep the hole was, the plaster sunk in, so we had to figure out how to fill in the hole. Voila! Paper towels to the rescue. After the hole was stuffed, we covered it with the plaster and hoped it would dry quickly. But another problem arose when we remembered Dad comes in every morning to say "bye" before he drives to work. That's when it was suggested that we put my pillow over the spot, so that he wouldn't see. Unfair if you ask me because the person least involved had to sacrifice her pillow, so everyone else wouldn't get into trouble. Surprisingly, the hole and the botched-up repair job went unnoticed for a while.

MOM SPEAKS

It was several weeks before Mark and I discovered the hole in the wall and the story behind it. As parents we felt obligated to "get in his stuff," as Tory was supposed to be the responsible older brother and knew better.

"You could have broken you neck!" came out of my mouth more than once. Privately, Mark and I had to laugh. "Can you believe they pulled this off?"

This is our story of raising our family of gifted learners.

TORY'S EXPERIENCES IN SCHOOL

Our son, Tory, is introverted, quiet, and always thinking. From second through fifth grade he attended the school where I taught. The school enrollment was 90% African American with a majority participating in the federal lunch program. He was a high achiever and came within a few points of the required scores needed for him to be labeled gifted. He was placed in a class of students with similar intellectual needs led by a teacher masterful in executing strategies that challenge students. The principal and teachers recognized that they had a group of Black students who would not be able to meet the required scores set on the gifted evaluations, yet who obviously exhibited intellectual qualities above the norm and needed instruction that would maximize their learning potential.

Tory was shorter than the average fifth grader and would question us about why he wasn't growing. We would try to redirect his focus to his other attributes such as his academic capabilities and leadership potential instead of his height. He had developed a specific set of skills for handling other children who thought they could bully him because of his size. Once, in his fifth-grade year, while his class was walking in line around the school grounds, one of his male classmates kept pushing him. Their teacher observed Tory step out of his place in line and move himself to the end of the line. She told me later that when she asked him why he had done so, Tory replied that the boy was bothering him and that he didn't want to get in trouble by responding. Tory was a successful elementary school student and well-liked by students and teachers.

When Tory looks back on those years, he says,

> One of the things I remember most was when I won the young author's contest with my story about two knights, and that's what I wanted to do, to be a writer, but you guys told me that writers don't make that much money, so I started thinking about doing something else like working with computers.

Tory had no difficulty transitioning from elementary to middle school in a new state, but we had to closely monitor his academic progress in math and emphasized to him that giving his best effort in school was paramount. During this time period, we were involved as a family in different activities as members of a revitalized United Methodist church. He became a role model for some of the African American youth in the neighborhood, as they all participated in a mentoring program. I used this program as an opportunity to help Tory develop some attributes he didn't realize he had.

In sixth grade, Tory had difficulty understanding math concepts as one particular teacher taught them: "Ms. Hodges would never explain anything, so I didn't understand. Then you guys had a conference with her to find out why I was getting low grades. I ended up with a B in the class." With our support and a team of caring teachers, our son stayed on track academically. About his middle school experiences, he adds:

> When I was on the Odyssey of the Mind team, the best part was the practice sessions where we thought of ways to solve our long-term problem and had fun working to get ready for competition. At the regional event, I liked the spontaneous challenge even more, because my teammates and I were used to how one of us would say something and another would try to top it with something even crazier. I was also on the Math Counts and a member of the Quiz Bowl team where we divided up into categories so that we could become experts. I studied random categories, because they realized I knew about a lot of different things.

We also supported Tory as he played flag football and then as he joined the same group of close friends on the eighth-grade football team.

The summer before we moved to Columbia, SC, where Tory began high school, he was diagnosed with juvenile onset diabetes. Our son was now insulin dependent, and he had a difficult time adjusting to the daily demands of proper diet and insulin injections. As a family, we adjusted our eating habits, so that we all had a healthier diet, and gave him a lot of emotional support and reassurance.

As Tory began high school, he struggled to maintain high grades. We found out that he had been incorrectly placed in a foreign language class. The high school was on the block system, so he completed the Spanish and algebra courses in December and started a new schedule in January with improved grades and confidence.

"My favorite class was world history. Dr. Felkel made the content humorous and relatable because he didn't just teach from the book like other teachers did " shared Tory. After his sophomore year, he was selected for Who's Who Among American High School Students.

When our family was confronted with a choice of moving, the greatest impact on this decision was the academic consequences of moving our son in the middle of high school. When we figured out that Tory was going to miss his junior year of math and would have to graduate the year after his class, we outlined a plan to remedy the mistake. We paid to have Tory attend summer school. This meant he could not continue on the wrestling team or pursue any other extracurricular activities. At his previous school, he'd taken several AP classes. After we moved, Tory continued with honors courses but missed out on the opportunity to obtain several college credits. Ironically, after his struggles with Spanish as a freshman, he was inducted into the National Spanish Honor Society.

Tory's resilience amazes us. He not only became an A-average student, he was selected for a regional program in computer technology at Georgia Southern University, through which upon completion of the program, he would earn a degree from Georgia Institute of Technology.

Tory did not adjust well to the college environment. Once he arrived on the college campus, he struggled with the transition from high school coursework to more rigorous curriculum expectations. He also did not monitor his blood sugar levels, so they fluctuated, making it difficult for him to get out of bed to attend class. Missed classes and assignments led to failing grades and a defensive attitude. We questioned him about his inability to function in the college environment. We refused to pay for another semester of poor choices and explained to Tory that if he wanted a college education, he was going to move home, enroll in the technical college, make up the courses he had failed, and get a job. We told him we would help him to pay for tuition and books as needed. He didn't want to continue to live under his parents' roof with the accompanying rules. Now he recognizes that it was not our refusal to pay for his college tuition that prevented him from obtaining a college degree, but the personal choices he made in how he wanted to live his life. He chose not to accept our expectations for his life and worked to live on his own terms no matter the struggle.

He did not feel that he was prepared for the level of work the instructors expected and he didn't feel like he had anyone he could ask for help there. He came home after the first semester and attended the technical college for three semesters and worked part time. After a few years of working various jobs, he decided he would like to study aviation mechanics. He is at the top of his class, has earned an FAA license, and will finish the program of study in June of 2013. Starting salary for aviation mechanics is $65,000 for those working on jets.

ASHLEIGH'S AND MALLORY'S EXPERIENCES

ASHLEIGH AND MALLORY: THE EARLY YEARS

Our two daughters, Ashleigh and Mallory, were born 14 months apart and exhibited high ability and motivation even before entering school. They have always been very close, so I often cannot talk about one without mentioning the other. During their preschool years, my husband noticed several instances when our oldest daughter, Ashleigh, exhibited a precocity that he thought unusual for a 3-year-old.

Once, when our children were visiting our neighbors, whose children were slightly older than Tory, their father kept beckoning our Mallory to come to him. Ashleigh asked him, "What do you want with my sister?" Rightly or not, she had analyzed his actions as suspicious and acted to protect her little sister. Mark's reaction when our neighbors shared what happened was, "I'm not surprised. She's just doing what she usually does, being protective of her sister."

Tory and his sisters would play outside in the afternoon with other children beside our apartment building. When their dad would pull into the parking lot after work, Ashleigh would always ask, "Daddy, do you want me to tell Mallory and Tory to come inside?" She understood that Daddy coming home meant dinner time and family time, and she again took responsibility for her siblings.

Ashleigh's problem-solving skills were also evident at an early age. Once, my husband was trying to open the twist top of an energy drink without much success. I handed him a dishtowel. When he still couldn't open the bottle, Ashleigh, age 4, went into the kitchen and brought back a rubber glove. "Try this, Daddy." "That was so smart of you, Ashleigh. I didn't even think of that!" I exclaimed. Of course, the lid came right off. Once, while going through the fast-food drive-through lane, Ashleigh told her dad, "Daddy I want to pay the lady." He did not want to have to unstrap her from the car seat, so he told her, "Ashleigh I have to pay, because the drive-through window is on the driver's side of the car." She replied, "Turn the car around and back it up to the window, so I can pay the money." On another occasion, as her dad drove down the nearest main street, past a convenience store, Ashleigh called out, "Our apartment is behind that store, Daddy, and that's the street where you turn."

I frequently took our children to the library to encourage reading. Both girls were reading before they were enrolled in school.

ASHLEIGH AND MALLORY: THE ELEMENTARY YEARS

All of our children were enrolled in the elementary schools in which I taught. When I asked them how they felt about it, Mallory said, "I felt different because you taught at the same school and most kids' moms worked somewhere else. I felt special." They were both blessed to have the same encouraging kindergarten teacher. She recognized their exceptional ability immediately and provided enriched instruction and additional reading opportunities for them.

Mallory shared,

I felt like I didn't learn much in kindergarten. I already knew everything, especially writing the alphabet and numbers and tying my shoes. The first time I learned anything was in first grade. I learned vowel sounds and cursive handwriting. I was an Accelerated Reader star. I liked reading science and animal books about cats, monkeys, and reptiles, but I didn't like bugs. I felt like I could have skipped a grade. I was not a big fan of toys and not into Polly Pockets or Beanie Babies like everyone else. I liked boys' toys like remote controlled cars and trucks. I like playing board games and my favorite was Payday. I remember following my big brother and sister around a lot because I had nothing better to do. I was never really a fan of Barbies. I just played because Ashleigh wanted to play. I loved the set of musical bells. There were only three music cards for the bells, and I always wanted more cards.

In first grade, the schoolwide composting project that provided nutrients for the school garden captured Ashleigh's interest. She was fascinated with the process of taking lunchroom leftovers and turning them into rich compost. She also enjoyed using math flashcards—"I guess I liked testing myself." As parents we encouraged excellence in all subjects and tasks.

During our first 2 years in North Carolina, I accepted a position as the TAG teacher for a small, rural, predominantly African American school where I facilitated gifted resource and enrichment classes for kindergarten through sixth grade. This year would be the first time that my daughters and I would not be at the same school, so I enrolled them in the YMCA afterschool program. Ashleigh was the ever-protective sister but bossy. Mallory says. "At home she was bossy. At school, she would look out for me. At the 'Y' there was a girl who always tried to talk junk, so I talked junk back to her and then I told Ashleigh." Ashleigh remembers telling Mallory not to be friends with the girl. When I asked Ashleigh why she advised Mallory against being her friend, she said, "I thought she was straight up mean. She didn't talk to people in a nice way."

Because students are not formally evaluated for gifted and talented programs in North Carolina until third grade, primary-age children with high potential must have their talents and interests nurtured by knowledgeable teachers and involved parents. I discovered Odyssey of the Mind and decided to coach a sixth-grade team at my school as well as help parents at my daughters' school organize a team that included my own daughters. The team meetings with other high-potential, motivated children allowed Ashleigh and Mallory to display their creativity and have fun with like-minded children. They successfully solved their long-term problem, and experienced what it was like to work as a team to create a performance that entertained a live audience.

GIFTED EVALUATION IN SECOND AND THIRD GRADES

We remained in Rocky Mount, NC, for 3 years and then moved to Columbia, SC. We now had a high school freshman, a third grader, and a second grader in our family. The two schools were right next to each other.

Our daughters were recommended for an evaluation for the gifted program. I was grateful to be able to understand the evaluation process, the assessment instruments, and how to interpret the scores. After they qualified for the program I remember thinking, "Now Ashleigh and Mallory can experience the challenge of units of study designed for students with their intellectual and creative abilities." They also participated in several clubs that the school had to offer including the P.E., chorus, and art clubs.

During our time in Columbia, Mark shared,

I didn't really understand just how smart or how gifted they really were. I just knew they were bright, and that something special was going on. I didn't realize until I heard our daughters' conversation in the car one day when I was picking them up after school.

Once I got them strapped into their booster seats and we were on our way home, I heard Mallory ask Ashleigh, "What is the difference between transparent and translucent?"

"Transparent is when you can see all the way through it, translucent is when you can almost see all the way through it."

I thought this was unusual for a second and third grader to have this kind of conversation.

At this time we began to see some differences in our daughters' attitudes toward schoolwork. Ashleigh was a perfectionist, and Mallory would complete the work, but did not have to try very hard to be successful. The latter concerned us, as we knew eventually that Mallory's laid-back attitude in her study habits would eventually catch up with her. I think we accurately, but perhaps at times, unfairly, compared Ashleigh's award-winning, focused achievement with Mallory's comparable academic achievement without the same level of sweat equity.

Our children learned that their parents were going to want a summary of each day's learning experiences, and no matter how painful, they were required to satisfy our interest. Mallory enjoyed attending the advanced class. Ashleigh, on the other hand, became fully immersed in a unit on architecture. Creating the models, displays, and projects were her favorite activities. She particularly enjoyed the design of structures through different stages and the thought process involved. This interest would lead to her accepting a full academic scholarship to Hampton University's master's in architecture program. After a year of study, Ashleigh decided that this field was not what she ultimately wanted to pursue. I am grateful that through her own academic effort, she at least had the opportunity to explore the possibility.

FAMILY VALUES

In order to help our children avoid the pitfalls of middle and high school, we endeavored to keep them busy. I encouraged them to enroll in band or orchestra, as I had enjoyed playing clarinet from sixth through ninth grade.

When our children were younger, we explained our expectations for behavior at home and away from home. Our children were more susceptible to shame with their father, as they did not want to disappoint him. The minute we began to talk to Mallory about what she'd done wrong, she would begin to cry. We could talk to her, and she would be remorseful. She now often offers a strong retort in defense of her actions. Ashleigh was a bit more sensitive to criticism or discipline, and we had to be more careful what we said to her to correct her behavior. She would and still does take things to heart.

We've had to maintain a heightened sense of awareness in gauging their moods, as all three of our children often lapse into deep thought about an event that is troubling to them. Thankfully, they usually felt comfortable enough with one of us to ask our opinion about a dilemma concerning friends or with a class at school. At times, we had to explain to them that although their school environment had a diverse student population, there were only a few African American teachers at their school who could relate to their experience as Black, highly intelligent students.

"Some teachers are not going think you have parents who expect you to perform at the highest levels and expect the best from yourself," we explained. We told them that although they were to be commended for having a variety of friends from several ethnic and religious backgrounds, ultimately they could only truly depend on family and that White friends in particular would not have their back when it came down to it. We explained that we knew these statements seemed harsh and maybe prejudiced, but we were speaking from our own life experiences and wanted them to at least be aware of the possibility of disappointment and betrayal from so-called friends as a part of life, and we knew we could not always be there protect them.

Fortunately, our daughters were selective in choosing friends; however, on occasion, they have had to put a White acquaintance "in check" to ensure they were respected. During her sophomore year in high school, Mallory told us about one incident in particular that occurred during a band rehearsal:

> When I meet people, I get an idea if I want them to be my friend, an acquaintance, or if I even want to associate with them at all. A lot of people I meet I keep as acquaintances, because usually there is a phoniness about them. One of these people was a girl on drumline, who would try to boss me around and talk to me any sort of way. I chalked this up to be because I'm Black because she only talked to me and one other guy like that, Holland, who also happened to be Black.
>
> During rehearsal for our next Friday show, we were going over a drill that we had already learned and what we were supposed to do. I knew my spot and at the time I was center of the bass line, so we were supposed to be doing one move where we had to guide right according the bottom (largest) basses. So we do the move, I'm guiding right like I'm supposed to, but it's supposed to be curved and Glenn and Hannah decided that they weren't going to do that, so the curve ended up looking a bit funky. So, the drum captain John, calls it out because it's not looking right.
>
> And Hannah decides she's going to blame it on me and that I should guide left to them. She said, "Mallory you're supposed to guide left, you're not supposed to follow them." She was very attitudinal about it! She wasn't trying to correct everybody, she was just yelling at me. Then I told her, "In fundamentals you are supposed to guide right, because the way the move is executed, you can't see over your left shoulder, so you have to guide right."

She barked back, "I don't care, you guide to me." Because I didn't want to hold up rehearsal, and we were supposed to listen to our section leader, I just did it the way Hannah wanted.

I waited until practice was over, and then said to her, "I don't know what your problem is, but I'm not going to let you yell at me for no reason. There is no need for you to get an attitude with me when I was doing what I thought I was supposed to do. Next time, fix your tone, because next time I'm not going to be so nice. You're just lucky I didn't embarrass you in front of everybody like you tried to embarrass me."

From then on she was much nicer to Holland and me. During the next full band rehearsal, our band director told us that it looked like we were having trouble seeing and wondered if it was because we were guiding to the left. He directed us to just remain stationary for this part of the show.

TWICE AS GOOD

As our children continued in gifted and AP courses in high school, we pushed them to continue their high level of achievement. We wanted them to understand that they had to demonstrate consistent ability if they wanted to be considered and nominated for awards and opportunities by their teachers. "You have to be twice as good and work twice as hard as the White children in your classes," we told them. These were hard lessons for our daughters to learn.

ASHLEIGH

Mark recalls Ashleigh's journey as an athlete, and the challenges she faced in playing for her middle and high school coaches, both of whom were White males:

Ashleigh did not get serious about playing basketball until the seventh grade. She came to me one day and said, "Dad! I think I want to play basketball." I asked her why now? She told me she beat a boy in a game of one-on-one during gym. By the time most serious female basketball players reach seventh grade, high school coaches are recruiting them and college coaches have them on their radar. I recognized Ashleigh's athleticism and how hard she worked at everything she attempted. We decided to expedite the training to improve her basketball skills. We immediately enrolled Ashleigh in Duke University's Women's Basketball Camp. She began camp the summer after her seventh-grade year. Ashleigh fell in love with basketball and Duke University. Little did we know that just improving her skills would not be enough.

Ashleigh made the eighth-grade team, but played very little. The highlight of her season occurred when they played against Maya Moore (currently an Olympian and WNBA star), and Maya's defense was so good our point guard could not advance the ball across half court. Ashleigh entered the game, broke Maya's press, and scored 3 times. The eighth-grade coach took Ashleigh out of the game, so that the other players on the team, all White players, would get more playing time. She did not play the rest of the game. The momentum of the game shifted in favor of the opposing team. They lost the game by 20 plus points. The favoritism and politics were evident early.

Entering Parkview High School, Ashleigh made the ninth-grade team. She continued to attend Duke's basketball camps and began making a name for herself as a very good defender. Over the next couple of years, she continued to improve her shooting and ball-handling skills. After attending camps, playing club ball, attending basketball showcase tournaments, and working with a shooting coach, she was ready for her junior year. She had worked on everything her high school coach asked her to focus on over the summer. The summer prior to the start of her junior year she played in the AAU Nationals in Orlando, FL, where she and her teammates made it to the Sweet 16.

She began her junior year at Parkview playing in the tournament that our program hosted. In this tournament, the girls made it to the championship game against Wesleyan, who had two very good guards. Wesleyan was up in the end of the second half with just a few minutes left in the game when Ashleigh hit a string of 3-point jumpers to get Parkview within striking distance. They lost the game, but this was the first time she recognized she could play against the best. She made the all-tournament team. She got off to a great start, but you could tell things were changing. Lots of bickering began in the locker room because certain players were threatened by Ashleigh's emerging talent.

In the next tournament, Ashleigh scored 18 points in the first game and was interviewed by a reporter from the *Gwinnett Daily Post*. The next game, she scored 13 points on her way to a second all-tournament team, possibly MVP. In the championship game, the coach decided to start a freshman (the sister of the best player of the team) instead of Ashleigh. At the time, Ashleigh was their top scorer and best defender. They went on to lose that game, and the coach lost Ashleigh. This was a huge hit to her confidence.

The next tournament was in Henry County. He started Ashleigh, but really limited her playing time. She played well, but I could tell she did not feel as much a part of the team as before. The talk was that the senior center and the freshman point guard were jealous of Ashleigh's accolades, therefore causing locker room issues. Coach approached me after one of the games in Henry County and asked me what was wrong with Ashleigh. I explained to him that I would not allow him to place blame on Ashleigh. I quickly explained to him how she'd done everything he'd asked. I also explained that as head coach and supposedly leader of the team he could not be that blind. I had to let him know he was allowing spoiled prima donnas to lead his team. And that a kid as smart and aware as Ashleigh would not follow someone that is wrong.

"You showed her that you did not care about her," I told him. He did not agree and walked away. That conversation left me with much disrespect for the coach and strained our relationship, as well as Ashleigh's relationship with him. Through all of the drama, Ashleigh continued to play hard on the court. On two separate occasions during the season, she was selected by the coach as Parkview's girls representative for the Gwinnett Tip-Off Club. These were the best players of each team for that particular month. The locker room issues continued and affected the team's play on the court. Because he failed to address those issues, team chemistry worsened, and the losses added up. Parkview failed to make the state playoffs.

During the off-season Ashleigh played club ball, took several AP classes and driver's education courses, and ran track. There were several days when she did not get home until 9 p.m. to start her homework. Some nights she would not complete her homework until 2 a.m. She'd wake up at 6:30 a.m. to be at school by 7:15 a.m. Her grades were better during this semester than any other. She played in an Adidas Showcase, a Nike Showcase, and a Tennessee Tech Showcase that summer. NCAA Division II college coaches were calling and writing her. Some of the schools were West Georgia, Southern Polytechnic, Mount Olive College in North Carolina, Reinhardt University, and Illinois Institute of Technology in Chicago.

She began her senior year at Parkview as the only senior on the team. All of the other seniors decided not to play for the coach. Other parents were outraged, but Sonja and I had already dealt with him. No one else would step up when we were having problems with him. The other parents finally went to the school's athletic director. We held a forum to talk about some issues. Coach could not emotionally handle the questions and tried to walk out—nothing really came out of it. Ashleigh did not allow the experience with the coach and other individuals keep her from pursuing the passion she had for the game of basketball, and we supported her. She had an average senior season basketball wise, but enjoyed a super year academically. She was selected as a 2007 National Achievement Finalist; was awarded one of the monetary scholarships that led to Hampton University offering her a 4-year, tuition-paid scholarship; and she graduated from Parkview with honors.

Ashleigh wanted to major in architecture and play college basketball. She called the coach at Hampton University. At the encouragement of a friend who played at Temple University where Dawn Staley (former Olympian and WNBA star) was head coach, she also called their assistant coach. Both schools have very good architecture programs and both coaches said they would allow her to walk on. We visited Hampton University and spoke with the coaches. At the time they were very encouraging and laid out their plan for walk-ons. Ashleigh enjoyed the visit so much she decided to attend Hampton.

She arrived at Hampton and prepared for a try-out with the basketball team. The coach brought the walk-ons in the gym for a shoot around only to tell them he would not be taking walk-ons. Ashleigh called us crying and devastated. I knew then she would not be staying at Hampton. She completed her freshman year and vowed not to return to Hampton. As soon as she returned home for the summer she called several coaches in the area. After speaking with the coaches at Georgia College and State University in Milledgeville, GA, they invited her to walk on. Ashleigh made the team, where she was voted as co-captain by her teammates. That's remarkable because at the time she did not play much. Through all of the adversity, her faith, integrity, and character held strong. She played at Georgia College for 3 years.

MALLORY

Mallory began her career as a percussionist, finally getting more music to play and fulfilling the need to express herself creatively through music in school. Even now at the university level, she performs in the marching band with passion. She took 2 years of dance through her high school and became a founding member and cocaptain of the high school's first step team. As she explained what was happening at school, we were most proud of the initiative she took to confidently present the proposal for the new performing organization to the principal of her school:

> Well, we first decided we wanted to start a step team at Parkview when we saw other schools had teams. We wanted to participate in an activity that demonstrated how proud we are of our culture. After talking to older students to see if they would enjoy having a step team at the school, Tomi, Morgan, and I didn't really know who we needed to talk to exactly, so administration seemed like the most obvious first step. They told us that we would have to start a petition and take that petition to the school board, who would then decide if we could have the team. In actuality, all we needed was a faculty sponsor. And I happened to find this out after talking to my Black dance teacher, who then happily decided to become our sponsor of the first Parkview step team.

One or both of us attended literally all of these performances and videotaped many of them.

FAITH, FAMILY, AND PARENTING

Our children's affection for each other has always been obvious. We insisted our children learn to share and care for each other, telling them that nothing except God is more important than family. We worked with them daily to help them develop caring, unselfish personalities. We made sure they knew that there were others in the world that had needs. The most important role we play in our children's development is as their greatest fans, describing to our children just how brilliant their performances are and displaying our pride in them and the pride that they have brought to our family.

Our children can be described as early starters, curious, confident, resourceful, and highly intelligent. As parents, we recognized early that our children needed resources and exposure to academic, cultural, and creative experiences in order to fully develop their potential. We both knew that we could provide our children with experiences our parents did not have the opportunity or resources to provide. We paid for ballet and gymnastics classes and piano lessons for our girls as long as they were interested. For our annual vacations, we drove everywhere in a family minivan or SUV. We helped mentor, coach, or provide resources for the groups and activities in which our children were involved.

One of the most important things we did for our daughters was to enroll them in the Duke Talent Identification Program, through which our daughters were able to take the SAT as seventh graders. This allowed them to begin to become familiar with the test that would later determine their fate during the college admissions process. Through parent networking, we found out about The Princeton Review's offer of free SAT practice test sessions and score reports. Having a network of like-minded parents was invaluable, as we shared academic and scholarship opportunities. More than that, we felt that other African American parents in our school community were experiencing the same challenges that we faced while ensuring that our children took advantage of every opportunity for advancement and recognition and that they were not denied these opportunities. It was important for us to let our children know that they were loved, that they were part of a family who put God first, and that we believed in their individual ability to achieve success in each endeavor.

Because we accepted no less than their best effort in school and gave specific praise for demonstrated creativity or work well done, our children knew our expectations for achievement. We set the bar high in our expectations for our children's academic performance, explaining clearly how they were to take responsibility for their learning while in class and take the initiative for strengthening their understanding by studying outside of class. When they reported test or project grades, I would ask them to describe how they had performed compared to other students on the same task. I wanted them to begin to make these comparisons on their own, and develop a competitive spirit. It was important to both of us that our children personally believed that they were as good as or better than their White peers, not as a human beings, but because of their effort and attitude. I wanted them to possess blazing internal motivation and undying hunger for learning that could only be satisfied by multiple successes.

We expected them to bring home A's and accepted B's only if we knew that a course was difficult and that they had made every effort to earn an A. We rewarded report card grades by taking them out for dinner to celebrate.

One of the best ways that we supported our children is by purchasing digital tools including a high-performing desktop computer, color printer, and digital cameras. We made the effort to learn how to use the technology in order to be able to help with project completion. These tools are necessary for gifted children to maintain high levels of challenge, skill development, and engagement. Digital projects provide alternative methods for African American gifted children to demonstrate their cognitive ability and creativity.

Gifted African American children face the deficit thinking of their teachers and often their gifted peers of other cultures. We made sure to meet their teachers each year and convey our expectations for our children's academic performance. I made sure teachers knew that I was a fellow educator that would support their efforts to provide the best learning environment. We encouraged our children's friendships with students who also excelled in school through socializing and by hosting study groups. Most importantly, we discussed the state of relations between cultures in America, highlighting attitudes that they must be aware of and prepared to confront. If they felt that they were being treated unfairly by a teacher, they were to let us know, so that we could address the concern directly by meeting with the teacher. If they were having a conflict with a classmate, we taught them to tell the person directly how they felt and to try and resolve the problem, but that they were not to let anyone push them around. We had to be constantly engaged in discussion with our children to remain aware of what they were experiencing daily academically and in their social development.

What I found most difficult about being a parent to three gifted children was maintaining a balance between advising, guiding, and insisting that they approach a task or obstacle my way, and allowing them the freedom to analyze, think through, and take responsibility for how they handled a situation. I fear that I may have denied my children the opportunity to demonstrate their flexibility and creativity many times as I foresaw possible obstacles, pitfalls, and time-consuming approaches. I wonder if my children would have learned a lot more to take with them into adulthood if I had allowed them to work things out for themselves.

QUESTIONS FOR REFLECTION

1. What are the most important or crucial ways parents can support their gifted African American children in the K–12 grades?

2. Even though Tory engaged and participated in AP classes, extracurricular activities, and enrichment programs throughout his K–12 experiences, he still was not successful in college. What experiences and challenges did Tory encounter in college that led to his decision to drop out of college?

3. Gifted African American students are often asked to perform at higher levels than their White peers to demonstrate their ability, as was the case for Mallory and Ashleigh. What impact does this have upon these students? What impact does this have upon the parents of gifted African American students?

4. What are ways parents can provide support when more than one sibling is found to be gifted?

THE OUTCOME

Tory, the acrobat, is currently studying avionics. Ashleigh graduated this year with a degree in exercise science with plans to earn a doctorate degree in physical therapy or pursue a career in teaching and coaching. Mallory will soon earn a degree in sport and entertainment management with plans to become an attorney in the entertainment field. Our children are now all pursuing their career goals with our continued support and guidance. They receive both not always graciously, but always knowing that we will be there for them if they need us.

CHAPTER 26

SHE'S BEEN HERE BEFORE

by Sabreen U. Jai

BACKGROUND

"She's been here before," my mother would exclaim after my daughter would say or do something extraordinary for a child at that particular age. And although I would never say it aloud, I would always ponder, "She does that all of the time, but what makes that special?" Now that I have my own grandbabies, I realize that *everything* they do is special and extraordinary. That's what makes them *grand!* But I still find myself asking the question, "When do I know that it's a gift? When do I know that it really is special?"

Over the years, I have heard that exclamation so many times by my own relatives about the children of our family tree by people in passing, and by parents of my students. And I've come to understand that often this statement is made when children respond with uncommon understanding or knowledge about something. They offer explanations and ask questions about things that appeal to those who are far more advanced in years. I have observed many times during a lesson or read-aloud that some students may exhibit unconcern or disinterest, but during discussion, they demonstrate uncanny understanding—understanding that generated from engagement and making relationships along the way. Obviously, had I reacted on my misperception or misinterpretation, the effects could have had long-standing negative implications.

THE STORY

RECOGNIZING GIFTEDNESS

I learned a lot about my daughter from asking the gifted instructor at my school about characteristics of gifted children and from my own reading and investigation. But I believe this knowledge should be readily available to teachers and parents alike. Specifically, all teachers should be educated about giftedness, if not certified, at least to the point of recognizing gifted attributes of students based on unbiased objective data. Otherwise, identification of giftedness in children, or adults for that matter, is completely dependent on subjectivity or culturally insensitive assessment tools and oftentimes culturally unfamiliar and/or insensitive teachers. My mother, along with many other elders whom I've been blessed to know, was not an educator by profession, but she indubitably could recognize innate gifts.

Just as home involvement is critical to a child's academic achievement, valuing the insight, intelligence, and contribution of familial relations and home environment should be fundamental for classroom practice. Associating what my mother saw in my daughter early on and what I eventually came to realize about my daughter's talents could have not only saved me a lot of heartache, but could have positioned her to have her giftedness assessed much earlier in school.

RECOGNIZING GIFTEDNESS IN MY DAUGHTER

As a parent, my receptivity to the possibility of giftedness came through my youngest daughter, Naaka. I never even considered Naaka as having gifted qualities because, first of all, she seriously lacked organizational skills. I was forever getting on to her about keeping her room clean or washing her clothes and even about combing her hair. These attributes did not qualify her as a gifted child in my estimation. I was under the impression that giftedness included being extroverted, expressive, and people oriented. Compared to my other children, Naaka was always a homebody. She would much rather stay inside and doodle and watch movies as opposed to being outside riding a bike, playing with dolls, or just hanging out with friends.

When she was 6 years old, Naaka became particularly fond of the movie, *My Girl*—so fond, as a matter of fact, she didn't want to watch anything else for what seems like a year! Not *Barney*, not *Sesame Street*, not even *Land Before Time*. And even if she did watch these shows more appropriate to her age, she soon popped in the video, *My Girl*, gathered her art bag that her Aunt Ba-Ba had bought her, and began to doodle. *My Girl* was about a little girl about 11 years old whose mother had died in childbirth and whose father was a mortician. She is pretty much a loner until she befriends a little boy who ultimately becomes her best friend. One day, while they are out playing, the little boy is attacked by bees and dies soon after. The plot centers around how the little girl deals with despondency while coming to terms with her grief and pain.

My husband bought the movie, and we watched it on our family movie night. Watching and critiquing movies was the uninterrupted time that our family treasured. We all liked the movie, but Naaka watched it over and over and over again. She always doodled, so it was not uncommon to see her drawing while watching the movie. One day, she brought me a drawing of the little boy in the coffin and the little girl bending over to kiss him. She was 6 years old! You know what my momma said—"She's been here before!" Had we known the signs of giftedness, we possibly could have encouraged her school to test her as soon as first grade. But we didn't know—we didn't have a clue that gifted traits often include disorganization, affinity for the nuances of learning as opposed to play, and boredom with the mundane and ordinary of daily rituals. What we did know was that she was a deep thinker and definitely had a love of art and a gift of bringing it to life. Little did I know, my baby Naaka was to be my orientation seminar to giftedness.

Naaka, for instance, was accepted in our county's high school of the arts, in great part based on her own initiative. She had to have a portfolio consisting of three drawings and/or paintings to present at her interview at the school. She had been asking me to get her art supplies to create her artwork and for whatever reason, I had not done that and her interview was in a few days. She had not reminded me, and it had totally slipped my mind. As I was passing the front door, I saw Naaka on the front porch painting. I asked her what she was working on and she told me that she was working on her portfolio pieces. Surprised, I replied, "Oh my God, your supplies!" She said calmly, "That's okay, Ma. I'm almost done now." "How?" I asked. She explained that she looked in the garage and found some red spray paint, then got cocoa, catsup, cottage cheese, and mustard from the kitchen, and created her colors. She had a beautiful self-portrait, still-life, and abstract. I am convinced that her ingenuity and resourcefulness played a great part in her getting into the school.

While at the school, however, she encountered the biases and culturally unresponsive curriculum indicative of the American educational system. I had to intervene a few times to ensure that *history* also included *her*-story. On one occasion, when I was concerned about the C's she kept bringing home in her AP History class, I asked her why didn't she get clarification during discussion in class. She told me they didn't have discussions—the teacher taught and they had to recall what she taught in their journals. If they recorded incorrectly, their grades suffered. I e-mailed the teacher and she wrote me back and stated, "I don't have the luxury of discussion" because, as she assessed, her "classroom time was limited." I was appalled, but, after conferences with her, the principal, and Naaka, she revised her instructional practices. She retired the following year.

RECOGNIZING NAAKA'S SELF-ADVOCACY

During her junior and senior years, Naaka auditioned and received several major roles in plays like *Mikado, Damn Yankees*, and *The Pajama Game*. Although I wondered out loud when were they going to present a production that at least incorporated the culture of many of the students of color, she was humbled and ecstatic about getting the parts and had no problem with the Eurocentric nature of the productions. Let me point out here that my daughter is quick to defend artistic expression from racial depictions and stereotypes. She would often tell me, "Ma, this is really not a racial situation. You're just too narrow." She believes that true artists see the world beyond color.

Obviously, though, some of my concern was projected despite Naaka's idealism, and she approached her artistic director about a more diverse performance. She said she asked if they could do something to incorporate a more modern time with parts specifically written for people of color or diverse cultural and sexual orientations. She said that she mentioned productions like *Hairspray, Rent,* and *Westside Story*. She was told that they couldn't do those because, according to the director, there are not enough racial demographics in the student body to reflect those depicted in the musical. When she countered that the play could serve as a learning experience and that make-up artists could take care of the rest, she said, "He flat out refused and said we couldn't do it—PERIOD!" She said she was surprised to see his forceful reaction.

On another occasion, she asked him if they could perform a current production of something like *Dreamgirls* and he retorted, "It's not part of the curriculum," essentially closing all doors of conversation. She was disappointed, but the event served as an eye-opener, inspiring her continued advocacy for equality and change. When I read this chapter proposal to her for her review, she offered this very appropriate quote from Albert Einstein to me, "Everybody is a genius, but if you judge a fish by its ability to climb a tree, it will live its whole life believing that it is stupid." The quote was so amazingly apropos, I couldn't help but think, "Yes, she's been here before."

QUESTIONS FOR REFLECTION

1. What might possibly have been one negative consequence on Naaka's education if her giftedness had not been discovered and recognized by her family? What seems to have been the most valuable effect of Naaka being recognized as a Black gifted female?

2. Naaka's gift manifested itself in her gifted artistic abilities, her understanding beyond her years, her deep thinking, and other characteristics. Her story indicates an IQ test was not administered in her early years of schooling and may not have ever been. Is IQ testing helpful and in what way?

3. Naaka had a mother, father, grandmother, and other extended family who were greatly interested in her success whether she was gifted or not. How can persons working in the community, non-profit tutoring organizations, churches, and other groups help to recognize gifted attributes in a child they are mentoring?

4. As Naaka's mother wrote, had she reacted to her misinterpretation of her students' disinterest during read-aloud time, there could have been long-term negative implications for children like Naaka. What might teachers or school administrators implement, especially in the Title I schools, to help recognize gifted students like Naaka?

5. In what ways do you think the busyness of families, whether valid or not, will have a negative effect on children not living up to their full potential? What can teachers we do cultivate relations with families who bring educational priorities to the forefront that empower children like Naaka to live up to their full potential?

THE OUTCOME

A very gifted artist, Naaka graduated with one honor from high school and no offers for scholarships. Undaunted, she pursued her own scholarships online and is now entering her senior year at Savannah College of Art and Design (SCAD) with a 3.7 GPA. I'm very proud of her tenacity, resilience, and determination to not be defined.

SECTION VII

GIFTED BLACK STUDENTS' PERSPECTIVES ON THE VILLAGE

CHAPTER 27

GO 'HEAD BABY, LET THE LORD USE YOU

by Shawn Adams

BACKGROUND

As an administrator at a small Christian university, I value the power of the mind and the complexity it presents to us as learners, leaders, and educators. Reflecting my own personal development as a leader and learner, I can see how significant a holistic approach to student development can be. There are so many factors that contribute to the effective development of students beyond the academic focus of the three R's—reading, writing, and arithmetic. For me, the arts promoted a discipline and commitment that impacted my total development as both a student and an artist.

The Black church was one of the institutions that fostered my development and created a haven for my growth and identification as a gifted learner. I was raised in an era where the school, church, community, and family were all closely connected. My skills as a communicator, leader, and even as a musician began when I was a member of the children's choir and children's ministry at Golden Gate Missionary Baptist Church in Dallas, TX. The activities that I participated in ranged from drama, where I once had the unfortunate opportunity of playing the role of Satan, to singing songs like "I Don't Know Why

Jesus Loves Me" by Andraé Crouch. Being able to perform before supportive parents and community created an inner confidence that flowed from the church house and into the classroom.

GROWING UP WITH MUSIC

This journey started well before I got to Golden Gate. My grandmother was an avid pianist who was self-taught and played by ear. Because she loved music, my grandmother invested in my mother's musical development as a classical pianist and vocalist. My family was deeply rooted in the church, so using and developing our gifts in the church was expected. As an adult, my mother was the youth choir director, so naturally all of her children were musical. Before I became a teenager, my instrument of choice was my voice. I sang frequently in the church. The church was the place where my first instrument was developed, especially because the music instruction in school was minimal; I do not recall our school having music as an elective, so all of my initial musical development took place in church.

When I was about 7 years old, my mother got a job promotion, and we moved from Lubbock, TX, to Arlington, TX. Upon our arrival, we were not really connected to any musical entity. Although we became members of a church, the musical opportunities were not readily available to me as they were when I was in Lubbock. It was not until we moved to Dallas a year later that I got plugged into church and school environments that allowed me to develop musically. Although my elementary school experiences are scattered, I remember that in Dallas, the school offered music electives, so I recall learning the basics of piano. I learned how to play a song, and even performed in a Broadway-type musical during the Christmas season.

In church, I was a member of the children's choir. We were tasked with singing a repertoire of songs every second Sunday of the month. Church provided a consistent haven for musical development. It was a part of my identity, so I was not bothered by weekly practices and monthly renditions. As a matter of fact, I enjoyed it. However, while I was able to minister at church and perform sporadically in elementary school, there was no integration between the two. However, that all changed when puberty forced my main instrument to change from voice to the B-flat trumpet in middle school.

TRUMPETEERING IN BAND

In middle school, I recall that my academic development and confidence was significantly impacted by the support and influence of my middle school band director, Cornell Thomas. The confidence that I lacked in much of the traditional academic coursework was strengthened as I began to master music, specifically playing the trumpet, an instrument I picked up in the sixth grade. As many brass instrumentalists can confirm, there is great difficulty creating a viable sound with consistent quality. I remember as if it was yesterday going to musical contests in Dallas, TX. I was in sixth grade, and I competed with other middle school trumpet players from across the city. I performed and received some very harsh marks regarding my abilities as a trumpet player. But during my eighth-grade year, it was different. After 2 years of struggle, I played a song that I really liked, "Trumpet Voluntary" by Jeremiah Clarke. The performance received the highest marks of the competition, and at that seminal moment, I developed a passion for music and a confidence that I did not have before. At that point, I also began to teach myself basic piano chords.

Up until this point, I had a verbal lisp. However, this did not prevent me from public speaking at church when the opportunity was "forced" upon me. My lisp also did not stop me from singing in youth choir. Incidentally, one of the byproducts of mastering trumpet was overcoming the lisp that I had developed as a child. My lisp became a thing of the past, and playing the trumpet made my speaking voice better. In addition, skillfully playing the trumpet required me to develop abilities of elocution that would become very important, not only as a performer musically, but also as a public speaker, both in the classroom and even later in the pulpit.

FROM BELOVED BRASS TO POISED PIANIST

Upon entrance to high school, the connection between church and school continued as my high school band director, Mr. Douglas Baskin, became a mentor to me. Mr. B. (the name we used for him) also served as minister of music at one of the local Baptist churches in Dallas and the influence of his work in the church filtered into our work at the high school. I was exposed to all types of musical genres as my love and appreciation for music continued to grow. I learned and played music ranging from gospel artists like The Winans to the rock band Chicago, and, of course, R&B stars like Michael Jackson and Prince. Within this spectrum of great music, Mr. B made sure that I was not only exposed to various types of music, but also to the theory involved in musical composition. Under his tutelage, I learned how to score contemporary and popular gospel and R&B songs for our marching and jazz bands to perform. This also influenced my development as a piano player because this was the instrument used to score the songs. Eventually, Mr. B., along with my peers, began to request that I accompany them as a pianist, not a trumpet player. Interestingly, I was never given the opportunity to play the piano at my home church, although I had developed a strong repertoire in case the opportunity ever arose.

Connecting my environments of church and school, it is significant to say that my high school band director was not the only public school teacher involved in developing the musical talent of youth in the local church. One of the most indelible influences in my life and to countless others during that time in Dallas was our church musical director, Mr. Michael Terrell. Michael, as we affectionately called him, also served as choral director for the well-known Booker T. Washington High School for the Performing and Visual Arts in Dallas, TX. Legendary talents like Erykah Badu and Roy Hargrove hail from this school. Michael's work exposed young inner city youth who would otherwise not be interested in music to a vast range of musical genres including Negro anthems, spirituals, and classical oratorios like Handel's "Messiah."

It was under the direction of Michael that I played the trumpet at church. I was able to utilize my musical gifts beyond singing in the youth choir. Although this was great in and of itself, I began to play the trumpet as an accompanist on several occasions. The confidence that I gained as an accompanist in church broadened my horizon outside of the church walls. My development as a church musician was more specifically recognized when I served as pianist for the University of Texas Gospel Choir. I was afforded the privilege to travel across the state to perform at various churches and competitions.

THE FAITH FACTOR

What are the ingredients that cause great talent to come out of the church over and over again? It is my opinion that a "faith factor" is present. There is an unseen ingredient that fosters and accelerates the potential gifts and abilities that many times lie dormant within a person. The King James Bible defines faith in Hebrews 11:1 as the "substance of things hoped for, the evidence of things unseen." This substance and evidence manifests within a community of believers when a supportive and nurturing environment create the opportunity for something supernatural to trigger the flowering of great talent and expressions of God's creative gifts. It is also my experience and belief that many of the greatest gifts and talents of generations past and present have never been seen by masses, only in church because of the unresolved tension between secular and sacred contexts for the use of those gifts.

Although I am not widely known like Whitney Houston or Beyoncé, my testimony and story of development is one that thousands of others share. My development to do what I do today is because the Black church was and still is a place where young people are placed in the hands of their Creator and given the opportunity to allow His grace of creativity to flower and stimulate in each of us, the beautiful portrait and gift He intended in the first place.

QUESTIONS FOR REFLECTION

1. How are musical talents identified and nurtured in schools and in your community?
2. Are Black children more likely to enroll and participate in programs for music and the arts over traditional academically oriented programs for talent development? Explain.
3. Do schools and faith-based organizations in Black communities have partnerships that support musical talent or talent development in areas? Why or why not?
4. What is the role of faith in developing talent among Black students in school?
5. In what ways can educators create partnerships with leaders in faith-based organizations to support development of talent in music and the arts?

THE OUTCOME

The experiences enumerated within this narrative have provided three specific descriptors concerning my current work that include the words *capacity*, *commitment*, and *compass*. Capacity refers to the developmental experiences associated with becoming a leader in both educational and Christian settings. As a local church pastor and university vice-president, I utilize the leadership gifts of communication, creativity, and team building gleaned from my local church and school experiences. I am also able to navigate freely between these two environments with a great degree of comfort. My past experiences have also impacted my personal commitment to leverage the resources that both institutions provide as places where youth can freely develop what God places within them. God has given every person a gift. It is our charge as spiritual and educational leaders to aid people in the discovery and development of that gift. This is my commitment and is the compass that guides the direction of my work. I am grateful for all of the teachers and mentors both named and unnamed on whose shoulders I now stand.

CHAPTER 28

KNOWING EVERYTHING BUT "ONE"

A NARRATIVE OF AN ACADEMICALLY GIFTED AFRICAN AMERICAN MALE

by Fred A. Bonner II, Petra A. Robinson,
Dave A. Louis, David A. Byrd, and Shailen Singh

BACKGROUND

With my roots firmly planted in rural East Texas, I, Fred, can reflect and pinpoint ways in which my journey was shaped by my life and experiences in that close-knit, hard-working community. Among the Piney Woods of East Texas, the approximately 1,500 citizens (60% White and 40% Black) of Jefferson, TX, attended the only option for elementary school (grades K–3), middle school (grades 4–6), junior high (grades 7–8) and high school (grades 9–12) the town offered. Although I lived in a small town, I grew up extremely proud of my home in the Ark-La-Tex, so named because the three states, Arkansas, Louisiana, and Texas, met in that small corner of the region.

The socioeconomic status for the majority of the population was mostly homogeneous; everyone but a few was of a working middle-class background. In this mostly blue-collar town, people worked for International Paper or Lone Star Steel. Some men were pulpwood workers and harvested trees for the paper factory, and some worked for the railroad. Although there was, in fact, a small group of people from lower socioeconomic backgrounds, there were even fewer families who were considered rich—a term typically reserved for the banker or pharmacist in our community.

Today, as I reflect on my history and contextualize it in the broader African American community, some might say I enjoyed an upper-middle-class experience. In retrospect, I had it as good as it would get, my parents were white-collar workers, a term in my community that typically referred to people who had a good education and were employed as teachers and preachers. My father was the assistant principal at the high school and my mother was a health and science teacher and, although they insisted on higher education as part of my journey, overall the values of the community, which were probably equally divided, promoted college education, getting a job right after high school, or entry into the military.

My hometown, which I still hold dear to my heart, helped to shape me, my educational experiences, and my overall life journey. The small size of the community and the absence of the fancy distractions of city life did not block me or prevent my peers from achieving amazing feats. I credit our success largely in part to teachers who were entirely committed to our learning and success. To date, I attribute my writing ability to lessons I learned in my junior year of high school. I honor the experiences I had in my small town and treasure the way in which they helped steer me through my life to where I stand today.

THE STORY

The theater serves as an appropriate metaphor in highlighting significant stages or acts in my development as African American gifted male. The acts occurred along parallel lines within interlocking circles—in angles and vectors and across trajectories that have sloped in steep upward, and at times downward, paths.

As I have grown as an academician and become enmeshed in critical race and social justice literature, steeped in the agency and reflective powers of pedagogues who embrace counter narratives aimed at dismantling hegemony, I now understand "who I am" and "what I represent." It is in three acts that I will explore and unpack my sojourn as an African American male who happens to be gifted or, as sometimes coded, high achieving. An ever-present theme across these acts is the impact that members of my immediate family have exacted on cultivating my potential and influencing who I am.

ACT I: LESSONS IN LIVING— THE FORMATIVE YEARS

One of the most influential characters in my life was a little brown-skinned lady who would immediately inform you, during your initial encounter, of her first and middle initial as well as last name. These informational tidbits were always supported by what she perceived to be another important identity marker, her town of residence. "I am Mrs. C. O. Northcutt from Linden, TX, the county seat of Cass County," she would proclaim. The C. O. stood for Colee Ophelia, and she was, among many important things, my grandmother. Mrs. C. O. Northcutt was a graduate of Bishop College, one of the original historically Black colleges and universities (HBCU) in the state of Texas.

Although she prided herself on sharing with new initiates her full name and place of residence, it was the nickname family and friends bestowed upon her that has had the most lasting and enduring impact. "Momma Cutt" is what we called her, and the lessons in living that she shared have consistently served as the bedrock of my being. As an academically precocious child, I was quick to share with anyone who would listen what I thought to be critical facts and lessons that I learned on my own and in school. People in my community would often comment on how surprised they were that at such an early age I seemed to develop communication and reading skills that were beyond the reach of normative preschool development.

To be the central focus in so many adult spaces, and to command the attention of "big people" who found my academic abilities not only interesting, but also cute, was seductive. Right after one of my many "one-kid show" performances, it happened. Momma Cutt sat me on her lap and said in a loving yet stern voice, "You know everything but one and I know that one . . ." Somehow this statement failed to compute; it didn't register in the well-advanced-beyond-kids-your-age brain that the adoring crowds seemed to appreciate. What was Momma Cutt trying to tell me, and why couldn't I use those same skills that had catapulted me beyond my peers to figure it out? She could tell by the quizzical look on my face that she had outsmarted the "smarty pants" 4-year-old. On the surface of this experience, it would appear that crafting an argument or presenting a conundrum to trip up a child who, regardless of keen intellectual ability, would be no match for a college-educated adult is silly. There was, however, a deeper purpose in her actions. "Yes," she said. "You know everything but one, and I know that." She smiled at me and then grabbed both of my cheeks and pulled me close in order to kiss my forehead. Being the curious child that I was, I followed with a question, "Momma Cutt, what's one?" She looked at me, smiled, and said, "That's for me to know and for you to find out."

The purpose of this lesson was to reveal to me very early on that it was okay to be a quick study, intelligent, sharp, smart, and popular (and all of the many wonderful things that people tended to say about me); however, it was also important that you be smart enough to know the limits of your knowledge, smart enough to know that no man—or in this instance, little child—could know everything. Even into my adolescence and young adulthood, well after completing my doctoral studies, I would still ask her, "What is one?" And, to her last days here with me on Earth, she would offer the same reply: "Well if I told you that, you would be as smart as me."

ACT II: NAVIGATING THE MIDDLE PASSAGE

The extant literature in my area of research—academically gifted African American male college students—is resolute in its message regarding the importance of family in promoting success for this population. What Momma Cutt started in the early years of my life was definitely continued and supported throughout my adolescence by her daughter, my mother, Dorothy Arline Jackson-Bonner. Because she had been an only child, my mother was determined to have more than one child—"at least three" was the story she consistently told herself. After completing both undergraduate and graduate school at Prairie View A&M University, another HBCU in the state of Texas, she embarked on a career and a marriage that would forever add to her title the labels teacher, wife, and mother.

Not only was my mother an exceptional student (valedictorian of her high school graduating class), but she was also a tenacious athlete. Often people would comment on the athletic prowess she possessed during her high school heydays. A common refrain was, "Boy, your mother was something else on the basketball court and the track—she was super smart too!" Even before the days of Title IX, my mother was creating a space as a woman in sports. At the same time she was crafting a model for Black women to follow that underscored the importance of being a good academic and athlete. This model she carried forth, going on to lead numerous championship basketball, volleyball, and girl's track teams in both segregated and integrated school settings.

What has become obvious to me over the years is that my mother, who she has become, is the sum total of all of her life experiences. She has become the mother to countless students and athletes, legions of women and men who continue to speak to the important role she played in their lives. Also, she has become the representation of that strong tower standing firm on a foundation of values aimed at promoting integrity and love. Although myriad stories exist attesting to my mother's presence and strength in supporting my giftedness, it is one story in particular that I find emblematic of the role that my mother, and all too often other African American mothers, played with high-achieving sons.

"Yes, I insist that you find him a seat!" These were the words that a composed, yet annoyed, Dorothy Bonner spoke to the coordinator of the Jefferson High School graduation ceremony. As a matter of tradition, students ranking in the top 10% of the graduating class were allowed to participate in the honors day convocation and graduation ceremony. Students ranked in the top 5% served in various capacities at the actual graduation ceremony such as valedictory and salutatory addresses, the pledge, invocation, and school alma mater. Students ranked in the 6%–10% range carried out the duties associated with the honors day convocation festivities. In the small East Texas town from which I hail, the top 10% of students was roughly 10 students. This particular year, two students tied for the fifth-place class ranking—a White, female student and myself. I didn't think much about the tie and the implications of what it meant on graduation night when our teacher and graduation coordinator said, "Well, Bonner, given the tie, I have decided that you will play a part in the honors day ceremony, and she will sit on the field graduation night." The 17-year-old brain that was taxed by 13 years of school, the last being filled with advanced English, mathematics, and science courses just to remain competitive said, "Okay!"

At home that night my mother, in typical fashion, inquired about my day and quizzed me on the latest graduation plans. In *typical* teen fashion, economizing my use of words, I said, "It's all good, we met about the Cancun trip, and I'm gonna get with Mrs. Jones to find out what I am supposed to do for honors day." As I was about to head out of the room to find some activity to keep me occupied for the rest of the evening, I was met with a "Wait a minute—whoa! What's this about honors day? You are going to be on the field." I could tell by her raised eyebrow and elevated tone that what I said in response was going to heal the land or lead to a valley of dry bones.

"Well, Carla and I tied for number five so she decided that she will sit on the field graduation night," I said.

"What, you have got to be joking—there is no way in the world that you will not be sitting on the field graduation night—who made this decision?"

I said to her, "It's no big deal, Momma, I don't care."

Her response? "Well I care . . . and it would seem to me that if you tied for this class ranking then they could find something for both of you to do."

My father, who was also the assistant principal at the high school attempted to chime in, "Well Jack (my mother's nickname—a shortened version of her maiden name Jackson), if he . . ."

"Stop, you stop right there I say," she exclaimed before he could say, in the vernacular of the Black church, "a mumbling word."

Just as this whirlwind began that night, it swiftly ended. My mother's last words to my father and I were "I'll handle it!" Like the literature has reported on the important role that both parents play, but particularly the mother's role, Dorothy was on a mission to "save her son." Before the end of school the next day, I was pulled out of one of my classes by Mrs. Jones who told me, "Bonner, I have a part for you to play on graduation night. The two of you, since you tied 'fair and square,' will be on the field."

"Okay Mrs. Jones, cool . . ." I responded. I returned to class but was unable to think about anything but my mother—what did Dorothy do? Say? Would my friends find out that my mommy came to fight my battles? Waiting for the bell to ring was like an eternity; I had to get to her to find out what she had done. I didn't have too far a journey since my mother was a teacher in the same school. I entered her room, eyes wide and mouth slightly snarled, ready to tell her how she had "messed up my reputation" by fighting with Mrs. Jones.

"Momma, what did you say to Mrs. Jones? She pulled me out of class. I told you that the graduation stuff was not a big deal and that I didn't want you to say anything about it."

She turned to me and said, "Your mother is a Christian and a professional—I only had to say to her 'this is my child and as a mother of a Black child, you understand what I mean when I say to you 'Find him a seat!'" This experience truly revealed my mother's willingness to fight for me. If she was willing to fight for me, I knew that I had to be willing to fight for myself.

ACT III: COMING INTO MY OWN

Such a bond and power exists between father and son, especially the bond that Black boys have with their fathers. First, I must acknowledge the fact that I was lucky—no, blessed—to have my father in my life. From my birth to his death, this wonderfully strong African American man was the "block" and I was the proverbial "chip" that longed to be a star in his eyes. Fred Arthur Bonner, Sr. was a graduate of both Paul Quinn College and Prairie View A&M University in Texas.

Many people remember my dad for his coaching abilities that led to numerous championships in football and basketball. Central High School in Jefferson, TX, the "colored school" that served as the crucible for African American children who were placed in "separate but equal" educational facilities in the Jim Crow South, was where his career began. Beyond his coaching skills, folks also remember my dad, Coach Bonner, for his care and compassion for his students, players, and other people. He went on to become the first African American athletic director in East Texas—a feat that he accomplished in integrated schools that was just as remarkable as his cultivation of winning teams.

Although my dad passed away in 1993, his legacy lives on. I am frequently affirmed by an unanticipated "Coach Bonner moment"! For example, after completing a presentation at the Texas Association of School Boards (TASB) Summer Leadership Institute in Fort Worth, TX, during the summer of 2009, I was approached by a woman who had been sitting in the audience during my session. "I have a question for you—is your father's name also Fred Bonner?"

"Yes," I replied.

"Well the reason I ask is that I am completing some research on African Americans who have been instrumental in sports in the East

Texas region and just finished reading about your dad! He was the first Black athletic director in East Texas!"

You could have bowled me over with a feather—here I was finishing up a presentation on African American male underrepresentation in Texas gifted programs and "up shows my dad"! I thanked her for doing her research and asked if I could get a final copy of the work via e-mail. "Absolutely," she said. This was but one example of the "Coach Bonner" moments that I continue to experience. What each of these moments speaks to me is this: "You must honor the legacy of this great man—honor him by crafting a life for yourself in which people will also want to speak blessings when they say your name."

Perhaps the most vivid memory I have of my dad affirming my academic accomplishments happened on a visit we made together to look at a particular graduate school. The drive to Waco, TX, was quite exciting, with my dad sharing vivid stories of his experiences living in the town as an undergraduate of Paul Quinn College (which was originally located in Waco before it moved to Dallas in 1990). He talked of how proud he was of my accomplishments and of me—acceptance to graduate school at Baylor University was, as he reported, "a major milestone." After our day of campus tours and meetings, as well as a quick lunch in the student center and jaunt across town to visit one of his friends who managed a large chain furniture store, we ended back where we started, in front of the student union. "I just want to run in and buy a T-shirt, Dad. I'll be right back," I said. "Take your time, I will just wait out here," he responded.

I zipped into the Baylor Bookstore, and when I returned, I found my dad standing, silent, in an almost eerily calm repose. He was looking into the bear pit—the Baylor mascot is the bear and the institution actually maintains a bear pit with one or more live bears on campus.

"Are you okay?" I asked.

"Yes," he said. "I was just standing here thinking about what this moment means."

Baffled, I asked, "What do you mean?"

He replied, "Well, son, you know I attended Paul Quinn and back in the day, the only time we [Black people] were allowed to step foot on this campus was to work. I worked as a waiter and busboy here for several formal banquets and events."

Where was he going with this story? I thought. Clearly he was moved, and I was fixated on his every word wondering what the denouement to this story would be. He continued, "The only time we were allowed to see the bears was on a short break in between bussing tables and serving food . . . and now, my son is about to attend graduate school here—God is good!"

QUESTIONS FOR REFLECTION

1. In what ways can the families of academically gifted African American males be more effectively included in the schooling experiences of their sons?

2. What experiences both within and outside of the classroom are key contributors to African American male success in school when they are "coming into their own"?

3. How can we address historical remnants of segregated minds and deficit thinking regarding African American students' access to institutions where their parents or grandparents were only allowed on campus to work?

THE OUTCOME

My family basked in my accomplishments as I earned a bachelor's degree in chemistry from the University of North Texas, a master's degree in curriculum and instruction from Baylor University, and my doctorate from the University of Arkansas-Fayetteville. For my dissertation research, I received the American Association for Higher Education Black Caucus Dissertation Award and, from the University of Arkansas, the Educational Leadership, Counseling, and Foundation's

Dissertation of the Year Award. Seeing me work hard and be acknowledged for such major achievements in my undergraduate and graduate school experience brought has my family pride and hope for the future of the next generation of Black leaders. Their pride continues to inspire me today.

RESOURCES

Bonner, F. A., II. (2010). *Gifted African American male college students.* Santa Barbara, CA: Praeger.

CHAPTER 29

CONVERSATIONS WITH DAD

by Bantu D. Gross

BACKGROUND

A name has been said to allow others to take a look into your life and gain a perspective of who you are. Some people possess common names, while others, like myself, have distinctive and unique names. As a child and throughout my adolescence, explaining to people what my name meant and where it came from became a point of tension at times, because I would either get teased or weird looks. This burden I felt from answering questions surrounding my name got so annoying that one day I decided I was going to adopt a new name. One of the reasons I considered a name change occurred during the first day of my freshman year in high school.

The high school I attended was Saint Augustine, a historically Black all-male Catholic high school in New Orleans, LA. St. Augustine has a reputation of being a school that produces some of the best and brightest young Black males in the United States because of its long-standing history and use of a paddle. It was here that my parents felt I would transform from a boy and into a man. During my first day in Civics class our instructor, who also served as a football coach, began to read the roll aloud and marked students present as they responded.

Then my name was announced "Bantu Gross." I timidly responded "here," and then what occurred would shape my first year. Upon hearing my response and taking a glance at me, our instructor inquired, "How did you get a name like that?" Before I could respond, he said, "What, did you play football, basketball, and was in the band too?" The class erupted and no one could contain themselves. As my classmates laughed and stared at me, I did my best to laugh along with the joke and seem undisturbed, but that was far from the truth. I just sat there in amazement thinking, *Wow! I didn't even have a chance to establish myself yet and am already getting mocked on the first day, but even worse, I have to deal with this for the next 4 years*!

As I look back on that first day in high school, I find my instructor's joke hilarious and think nothing of it now, but back then I struggled with accepting my name. I remember thinking to myself, *Why did my parents name me Bantu, why not a more common American name like Mike, Steve, or David?* Surely, they don't have to go through this, because they have regular names—Ernest and Vicky. I could have been Ernest Charles Gross, III, but no, I'm Bantu. This type of dialogue went on in my mind for years until I began a quest to educate myself on my name and ask my father why he chose Bantu and what it meant.

When I was about 12 years old, I had a conversation with my dad, and he explained to me that he found my name in a book he once read as a little boy. In the story, a boy named Bantu overcame peer pressure and became a leader in his village. In this book, Bantu means "spiritual warrior." However, through dialogues with friends from Kenya, Ghana, and Nigeria, I have come to learn that Bantu also means "people" and is a well-respected tribe throughout Africa. I prefer the meaning my father intended—spiritual warrior. My father told me that he loved what this character stood for and decided then that when he had a son he would name him Bantu. Once I heard there was a story behind my name and what it meant, I began to reconsider the name change. Learning about the history of my name and my father's rationale for naming me Bantu instilled in me a sense of pride and helped me ignore the insults. Soon I would come to embrace my name and didn't mind educating people on what my name means, no matter how silly they looked when they questioned its origins.

THE STORY

Through talks with my dad, not only was I able to learn about what my name means, but I also learned about many life lessons such as commitment, hard work, and the value of an education. Born and raised in New Orleans, LA, I am the middle child of my parent's three children. According to the Adlerian theory, it is said that I am a likely candidate for the "middle-child complex" and in some instances this was true. You see, I have an older sister, the only girl, and a younger brother, the baby. Because of my placement in this triumvirate, I tended to get lost in the shuffle at times, but not for long.

ON FIRE

One way that I remained relevant and garnered the attention of my parents was through academics and my behavior in school. For most of my time in school, I could be considered an underachiever and a class clown. It was a common occurrence for me to get involved in some sort of mischief in school, and I think my parents came to expect it of me at some point. I believe that my unruly behavior in school was not a cry for my parent's attention, but rather me just trying to spice things up at school.

During one of my misguided attempts to spice things up at school and without a clear plan or any gasoline, I set out to burn my elementary school down. I am still not sure what was going on in my head that day, but for some reason I thought a school made of brick and mortar could be burned down with a single match. My unsuccessful attempt at burning down my elementary school began in the boy's restroom. Alone in the restroom and equipped with a box of matches I came across the day before, I struck the first match. Marveling at the tiny flame of the match, I held it next to the brick wall and waited for the brick go ablaze, but nothing happened. In fact, the only thing that did happen was that I burned my fingertips several times. After numerous attempts to set the school on fire, I retreated back to my classroom with scorched fingertips.

Despite my best efforts to hide the box of matches in my pocket, they were discovered by my teacher. Following a series of questions where my teacher was able to find out what I was up to, my parents were called and a parent-teacher conference was set up. Somehow I was able to avoid expulsion or a suspension. In retrospect, maybe I should have received some sort of disciplinarian action, because from then on I worked harder at not getting caught.

CONVERSATIONS AS THERAPY

My inability to perform satisfactorily in school led to me having many heated discussions with my father about grades and behavior. The main reasons I performed so poorly in school was because I considered school boring and a waste of time. Operating with this type of mindset, I never really immersed myself in academics unless something piqued my interest. Because of this mindset, I became a regular in summer school from the fourth grade all the way up to my junior year in high school. So while my peers enjoyed their summer break, I continued taking classes.

After a while, being in summer school became a harsh reality for me. I dreaded the end of the school year, because I knew my parents would either receive a phone call from a teacher or my report card would reflect my inability to produce passing grades. Because my father was invested in me receiving good grades, whenever he learned I was not performing up to my potential we would have a talk. Typically, the conversations were one sided, with him talking and me listening. After my dad finished explaining to me the importance of an education, he would slip back into his counselor role.

As a social worker in the New Orleans public school system, my father was very familiar with troublesome children and knew how to help families solve problems. So whenever I became somewhat of a nuisance in school, my father had an idea on how to remedy my problematic behaviors. His preferred choice of correcting me was through conversation. At the time, that's what these discussions felt like, conversations, but due to his training as a counselor, I may have actually been receiving therapy.

GRIEVING LOSS, BEING LIGHT

Another motivating factor for me, as if I needed more, were my peers. Many of the peers I grew up with in my childhood neighborhood have died, been imprisoned, or still live there and are involved in the same thing they were doing when I left, the drug game. Even some of the little kids that I tried to help mentor still live there and aren't doing much better than when I left them.

During a recent trip back to my old neighborhood, I learned that one of these younger guys was gunned down in his car by a friend while his baby boy sat in the backseat. Learning about the incident hurts because we were all friends and knowing that one of them was murdered by a friend because of drugs is disheartening. Having a story such as this hit so close to home helps me better understand the condition some of my brothers are in and encourages me to think of ways to be a light for my community and to achieve my full potential.

DAD MODELING, LISTENING, WAITING, EDUCATING

Witnessing the accomplishments of my father was vital to my success. As the eldest of six children and the son of college-educated parents, my father learned at a young age the importance of an education. During his academic career, my father has earned a bachelor's degree and a master's degree in social work. Currently, my father is still married to my mother and is employed as a social worker at an elementary school in Zachary, LA.

As a child, like most boys, I admired my father and wanted to follow in his footsteps. I can recall wanting to be with my father wherever he went and always trying to learn from him. One of the ways that my father and I would spend time together was when he ran errands—or as he would call them, "runs." Whenever I saw my dad gathering his things to make a run, I would insist he let me tag along. During these rides my dad, or "Butch," as we would call him, listened to my dreams, paid attention, and offered advice when appropriate. As a matter of fact, it was during one of these runs that I learned about the different level of degrees one could achieve.

We were on our way to a grocery store, and I asked my dad, "What's the highest degree you can get and which one you got?" I laugh to myself now as I think back to that day and realize how innocent I was and how I eagerly anticipated a response from my father. Seizing every opportunity he could to teach, my father began explaining to me the different degrees and how far one could go with a particular degree. I was awestruck following the conversation and considered the idea of attaining every degree from an associate degree to a doctorate. The conversation we had that day stuck with me and became the driving force behind my obtaining an associate's, bachelor's, and master's degrees. Now, I am in pursuit of a doctoral degree and have every intention of continuing my education until it is obtained.

Making runs with my dad was not the only way I could spend time with him; sometimes, I would join him in the living room while he watched television. These moments occurred when he arrived home after work. On occasion I was apprehensive to join him, because I knew he would ask if I did my homework, which for the most part I did not like doing. I knew that if I went in there before completing my homework, then he would send me out and follow up with me later to see if I finished my assignments. However, when my homework was complete, I would join him as he watched his favorite television shows.

As I sat with my dad, he would begin asking me about my day and how I was doing in school. One of my father's favorite questions for me was, "What kind of grades you got?" For the most part I knew this question was coming, because one of the major tenets my father wanted to instill in me was the value of an education. I did not particularly like these conversations, because I was not a great student at the time. Despite my frequent poor performance in school, my father would continue to push and encourage me to do my best. On some nights, he would have me grab my homework and begin to go over it with me, making sure I understood the major concepts and having me repeat it aloud. These were not always the best of times, but I learned the material and knew my father cared.

AT HOME WITH DAD SHAPING MY FUTURE

By making time to be there for me, my father showed that he valued me and wanted to see me succeed. I believe another reason my father consistently stressed the value of an education and spent time with me is because of the neighborhood in which we lived. Our neighborhood had a mixture of middle-income and low-income families. The home we lived in was located directly across the street from the neighborhood park, where all of the *action* occurred. At one time, the park was a nice place to visit, but then graffiti started appearing, streetlights were being broken, and parts of the playground were shut down because they were now crime scenes.

I can recall peering out of my bedroom window one night and watching police make every Black man in our neighborhood, or so it seemed, lie down flat on the basketball courts like they were on a slave ship, patting everyone down and looking for drugs and weapons. At times, it was scary living in this neighborhood due to the acts of violence that would occur, but I survived largely because I earned the respect of my peers.

The guys in my neighborhood knew I went to private school and respected that—they never tried to pressure me into joining a gang, to sell drugs, or to use drugs. One of the few benefits of living in this neighborhood was that I got to see what I did not want to be. Watching grown men live with their mothers, drink 40s, and smoke blunts provided me with enough information to know that a quality education could take me to the places that I wanted to go.

My father spent the majority of my formative years stressing the importance of education. So when the time came for me to enroll into high school, my parents wanted to make sure I went to one of the better high schools in the city—St. Augustine. Although my father was not able to make all of the parent-teacher meetings because of scheduling conflicts, he made sure I stayed on task. One way he would follow my academic progress was through "checking in" regularly with me. This routine would be as simple as having a conversation about what I was doing in school. It was through these conversations and reviewing school reports that my father was able to keep up with my grades.

Because my father spent most of his time counseling in schools, he knew when report cards or progress reports were being sent home. Equipped with such information, he would arrive home looking for my grades. I usually hated this time because my grades were rarely exceptional and I knew was going to get into trouble for having poor grades. Some of these conversations I have intentionally forgotten because I hated them so much. However, as I look back on that time in my life, I believe what caused me to struggle in school was that I never got interested in school until college.

FOLLOWING DAD AND FAILING

Upon graduation from high school I attempted to follow in my father's footsteps by enrolling in his alma mater, Xavier University, Louisiana (XULA). When I finally graduated from high school, I saw college as an opportunity to redeem myself from the poor performances I displayed in school up until this point. By enrolling at XULA, I was attempting to make my father proud of me and prove to him that I was a scholar. Unfortunately, I was unable to make a successful transition to college and subsequently was dismissed from XULA for poor grades following my first year.

A major reason I was unsuccessful at XULA was because I never connected with students who could push me and provide me with academic support. Not having friends I could lean on when I was experiencing difficulties with certain aspects of college life and academics hurt. I never felt comfortable on the campus and, as a result, my grades suffered. This was a major setback for me. I felt like a failure and was confused as to how this could have happened to me. I feared that I would end up like peers in my neighborhood, but then I decided I would continue to press on and begrudgingly enrolled in Delgado Community College (DCC).

MAKING MY OWN WAY

At DCC, I began to truly appreciate education, because now I was financially responsible for paying my own tuition and I wanted to redeem myself. The smaller campus and classroom size allowed me to connect with students who shared similar interests and helped me feel welcomed. In addition to the smaller classrooms and campus, being able to interact with teachers who seemed to care about my success ignited a passion in me to improve my grade point average.

What was interesting about this time is that my father never showed any disappointment in me. When I informed my dad of my dismissal from XULA and that I enrolled at DCC, he went into counselor mode and proceeded to give me words of advice and allowed me to begin making decisions about my education. Once I was able to correct the missteps I made while at XULA, my grades began to rise at DCC and I made the Dean's List twice. I finally began to feel like I was going to make good on the promise I made to myself when I was a young boy. Everything was going well—I was a semester away from graduating with an associate's degree, and I had already begun contemplating where I would receive my bachelor's degree. Then, Hurricane Katrina altered my plans.

Because of the devastation Hurricane Katrina caused, New Orleans for all intents and purpose was closed. Now what was I going to do? At this stage in my life, my father was not as hands-on, which meant I had to figure out how I was going to continue furthering my education on my own. So, in an effort to become the first male in my family, other than my father, with a college degree, I enrolled at Louisiana State University (LSU). While at LSU, I began to experience similar difficulties as those I had while at Xavier University. My grades began to falter, and I was not able to find a strong support network, because most of my family and friends were scattered throughout Louisiana and surrounding areas. Being away from my hometown for the first time and without a strong network, I struggled to find myself and lost focus at times due to the stress I was experiencing.

CATASTROPHE, RECONNECTING WITH GOD, AND FINDING MYSELF

Most of the stress I was experiencing was due to a lack of guidance, because my father and I were not talking as frequently. The disconnect my father and I were experiencing occurred in large part due to our separation as a result of Hurricane Katrina and because I was maturing as an individual. Due to the effects of Katrina, I experienced financial and emotional difficulties. In an effort to find help that did not involve drugs or alcohol, I began going to church regularly.

I consider this a huge turning point in my life, because by attending this church, I began developing a relationship with the pastor (which continues to this day) that helped shape the way I view and live life. Locating a church home, meeting new people, and reconnecting with God helped me find a new support network. Up until I was 18 years old, I was a practicing Catholic, but when I began college I no longer followed the practices. Even though I no longer practiced Catholicism, I tried to maintain a relationship with the God through prayer. So when I met this pastor and realized that I needed help following Katrina to achieve my goals, I accepted Jesus as my Lord and Savior. Although my pastor was not my biological father, he helped me through this difficult stretch of life until I was able to reconnect with my father. When my father and I finally did reconnect, I anticipated him being upset with my new faith because I grew up Catholic, but I did not experience any resistance from him, just acceptance. I took this as sign that my father was allowing me to grow as man.

Several months later, residents were able to return to New Orleans, and I was able to reenroll at Delgado and complete my final semester, graduating with an associate's degree in business management-marketing. Shortly after graduating from Delgado, I enrolled into Southern University of Baton Rouge (SUBR) and pursued a bachelor's degree in psychology.

It was at this stage of my life that my relationship with my father began to change. My father was more closely involved in my education while I was in elementary and high school, but when I entered college I began to notice him taking a step back. When I noticed this, I realized he was allowing me to come into myself, but still interested in my educational attainment. My father would show his interest by checking in from time to time and inquiring about how school was going and seemed to be more relaxed than when I was younger. I can recall times when I was younger and my father would check in on my progress in school and it was not so relaxed because I was not living up to my potential. But now, I believe my father sees that I finally got the message he was trying to teach me.

QUESTIONS FOR REFLECTION

1. How can positive stories about African American fathers encourage other African American fathers to play an active role in their child's education?

2. What changes are needed in the African American community to encourage African American fathers to be active in their child's education?

3. Reflecting on the current state of African American fatherhood, what has contributed to the perception that African American men are comfortable neglecting their role as fathers?

THE OUTCOME

Currently, I am in the second year of my doctoral program in the Recreation and Leisure Studies program at The University of Georgia. I am confident that I will successfully complete all of the necessary requirements, because of the lessons my father has instilled in me. Much can be said for individuals who grow up with a positive father figure in their lives. I am one of the fortunate African American males who can attest to having a father who played a significant role in their education. Thanks, Dad.

CHAPTER 30

YOUNG, GIFTED, AND AFRICAN AMERICAN IN IOWA

by Asabi Dean

BACKGROUND

Ask any number of parents, and they will tell you that they desire that their children do better than they in academic, social, and occupational areas of life. In hopes for this, many parents find themselves evaluating their own upbringing and determining what would've given them greater opportunities in life. These desires cause many parents to raise their children with their future outcomes in mind. This is the case with Alonzo.

Alonzo Thomas's parents started focusing on his education very early on. They also began to educate Alonzo on his ability to do and be anything he wanted. As a result of their hard work and focus, Alonzo excelled once he was enrolled in school and eventually was identified as a gifted learner. Alonzo's parents (Mr. and Mrs. Thomas) were elated at his well-deserved gifted identification and expected his educational journey to be smooth and fraught with high points. However, the reality of their son's journey left them in shock.

Alonzo was born in a hospital on the south side of Chicago to married parents. Mr. Thomas was educated in the Chicago Public School System until his sophomore year of high school; he completed his junior and senior year in a private high school. Mrs. Thomas was educated in Chicago's public school system throughout her K–12 academic career. She experienced difficulty in learning and understanding mathematical concepts and principles and struggled with math and science throughout high school. She distinctly recalled being told by her trigonometry teacher that she "wasn't very good at trig, but since she was such nice girl, she would be given a C in the class." Although the teacher's generosity helped Mrs. Thomas graduate from high school, she became very discouraged about her future in college. She worried and feared that no teacher could teach her math at a higher level, and this concern remained in the forefront of her mind when Alonzo began school for the first time.

Mr. Thomas was quite strong in the science, technology, engineering, and math (STEM) areas while in school and succeeded in earning his master's degree in engineering and becoming an engineer. A conversation with Mrs. Thomas shed light on Mr. Thomas's belief about his son's potential: If his son was given the proper values, preparation, and support at home, then he would excel in any school system regardless of the condition of that school system.

ALONZO'S EARLY YEARS

As soon as they found out they were pregnant, Mr. and Mrs. Thomas began to research the best way to raise their son in a world where (they felt) African American boys were often misunderstood, undervalued, overlooked, and stereotyped to their detriment. Once Alonzo was born, his parents put all of their efforts and attention into him—the types of toys he would play with, the types of foods that he would eat, and so forth. However, they did not place a huge emphasis on their marriage and, as a result, Mr. and Mrs. Thomas divorced when Alonzo was 2.

When Alonzo was 3, his mother enrolled him in a homeschool where 12 students ranging from 3–15 years of age in preschool through 10th grade were educated. The one-room school was located in the basement of a large home. Alonzo was being taught three languages (Spanish, French, and Swahili) and beginning mathematical concepts, as well as reading, at the age of 3. He soared in this environment and came home excited to complete the work given to him by his teacher, Mrs. Jones, and her assistant, Ms. Meea.

However, as time progressed, Ms. Thomas noticed that her son's excitement about school had waned, and he was quiet and withdrawn when he came home from school. When she asked Alonzo how school was going, he would only respond with "It was okay." But after more probing, she found out that an older, larger child was bullying him and after discussing the situation with Mrs. Jones, she decided to withdraw him from school. Alonzo was only 4 years old.

After researching surrounding schools, Ms. Thomas found a free African-centered elementary charter school in Chicago. She begged the principal to consider taking Alonzo into the school despite the fact that he was too young to officially enter kindergarten. She shared with the principal that her son was too advanced to go into the preschool. The school administration held the belief that every child thrived best with his or her own peer group. Therefore, school policy did not allow Alonzo to skip a grade. But the school had an accelerated curriculum that would allow him to progress through his lessons at his own rate. The school also provided a healthy, vegetarian, and fresh-food diet and prohibited students from bringing food with animal byproducts or refined sugars. Ms. Thomas decided that this school was the best fit especially because she and her son practiced the same diet at home. Also, because the school was free, it was something that she could afford.

ELEMENTARY SCHOOL

As Ms. Thomas expected, Alonzo excelled to the head of the class in kindergarten and was awarded highest honors for his model behavior. The kindergarten teacher, Mama Kendra, was very impressed with his desire to pick up garbage around the classroom, his ability to follow directions, and how he would fold his hands and wait for the next instruction when he completed his work ahead of the other students. This type of behavior continued in the first and second grades where the teachers (Mama Sheena and Mama Bridgette) would tell Alonzo's mother that he was truly a gifted learner, although he had never been tested.

When Alonzo was in the second grade, the school implemented a "walk" system. This system allowed students who mastered grade-level concepts to be walked by a teacher to the next grade's class for math and reading. Alonzo was immediately chosen to take part in the process. Unfortunately, before the end of the first semester, the principal ended the walk system.

Because the walk system was halted, Alonzo's second-grade teachers implemented a program within their classroom for the students *they* identified as gifted learners. The teachers decided to seat the children in three rows according to their abilities (unbeknownst to the children). The last row consisted of children identified as "gifted or accelerated learners," the middle row consisted of children identified as "working at level," and the first row consisted of children identified as "slower learners." After the teachers presented the lesson and the third-row students completed their assignments, the teachers would allow the third-row students to help their classmates located on the first row. If time permitted, they were able to assist their classmates on the second row, too.

The row system remained in place for the rest of Alonzo's second-grade year, and Ms. Thomas felt that the arrangement allowed Alonzo to remain grounded in his abilities. He spent time helping his classmates who had a difficult time understanding the same materials he swept through. Most of all, the accelerated learners weren't bored in the class while they waited for time to pass. All of the students bonded with their classmates and the accelerated learners became peers tutors who were able to teach their peers using their own understanding of materials. As an added bonus, the teachers found that the same mentoring system transferred to the playground.

GIFTED—AT LAST

When Alonzo was in the third grade he tested in the 97th percentile (overall) and was finally, and officially, identified as a gifted learner. Ms. Thomas was told that she would now be eligible for services that would assist with building on his academic abilities. Ms. Thomas immediately looked into schools for gifted learners within their city and quickly became aware that the number of children identified as gifted learners outweighed the city's capacity to serve this population. As a result, the city developed a program that would allow a chosen few qualified students with the highest scores (within the identified gifted population) to be given the meager services available for this population in the city of Chicago.

The score that would be used to determine eligibility for the services provided in Chicago was derived from a test administered by the city of Chicago to children identified as gifted. Based on the score, children would qualify to receive gifted services on a particular level. This test had to be taken despite the fact that all of the children had already taken and scored in some of the highest percentiles in the nation based on their standardized test scores. To add insult to injury, the children had to report to testing centers, located outside of their immediate community, on a Saturday morning by 8 a.m. Failure to do so would cause the children to forfeit their opportunity to take the test.

Ms. Thomas made sure that her son made it to the test site. Alonzo took the test and although he did well, others scored higher than he, so he wasn't offered Chicago's top-tiered gifted services. Instead, his mother was offered the opportunity to enroll him in a classical school that was attended by gifted learners only. The school was located within a low-income community, and many parents complained about their children being bullied inside and outside of the school. After visiting the school, Alonzo and Ms. Thomas decided that the school did not offer as much as the school in which he was already enrolled, so they decided to remain at the African-centered charter school.

However, Ms. Thomas was interested in the top-tiered "gifted learning centers," so she decided to visit one of the six centers located around the city. She visited a center on the south side of Chicago. It was located in a predominantly Caucasian community. She also noticed that the teachers and the students were predominantly Caucasian. Ms. Thomas realized that not one of the gifted learning centers was located in a predominantly African American community and she remembered that most of the test administrators were also Caucasian. She wondered if this was only a coincidence, but she kicked out the thought and went back to her side of town to pick Alonzo up from school.

During his next benchmark year (fifth grade), Alonzo tested in the 97th percentile again and was again offered services for gifted learners; however, his mom simply filed the information away because she was well aware that they would more than likely still not be offered any better outcome than where they were. It was as though the offer was simply a sham; a procedure that had to be done, but didn't actually benefit most gifted children in the end.

Ms. Thomas did go to bookstores and teacher supply stores in her community and purchased workbooks at the level she knew her son was capable of working and put together a curriculum that she felt would challenge her son and promote use of his higher order thinking skills. She feared he would lose these skills if he was not required to use them regularly. Ms. Thomas also enrolled Alonzo in music school, where he would be further challenged to learn to read music and play an instrument (the music school had a scholarship program that allowed the child to attend for $9 a week and would even loan instruments to the children if they couldn't purchase one).

Every night after he completed his homework, Alonzo would also complete the workbook pages assigned by Ms. Thomas as well as practice reading his music and playing his instrument. There were times when Alonzo had school assignments that he had already completed in his home curriculum. He would complete it again in such a short time that the teachers felt compelled to inquire how this was possible, and Alonzo told them about his mom's home curriculum. His teacher met with his mother and warned her about pushing Alonzo too hard. But Ms. Thomas was confident and aware of how much was enough and how much was too much.

MIDDLE SCHOOL EXPERIENCES

Alonzo continued to attend the charter school until the end of his fifth-grade year when he and his mother moved to Iowa so Ms. Thomas could pursue her doctoral degree. Moving to Iowa City, IA, was quite a culture shock for Alonzo and his mom. Chicago was highly diverse and their community was majority African American, while Iowa City was not nearly as diverse and they now resided in a predominantly White community. There, Alonzo had to attend a school that had a majority of Caucasian students and teachers, which was the exact opposite of the school from which he came.

While interviewing for her doctoral program, Ms. Thomas was excited to hear that one of the top gifted centers in the nation existed on the campus of The University of Iowa. Because she had a son who was already identified as gifted, she felt that he would be a perfect candidate for their program. However, once she arrived in town and attempted to enroll him in the center for their specialized weekend and summer curriculum, she was informed that first the Iowa City Community School District would have to identify him as gifted or he would have to be subjected to more independent tests to be enrolled as a gifted learner. Given the amount of work that was already on her plate with the move and her own program, Ms. Thomas decided the school's identification was the best way to go about this process and she would enroll Alonzo in the gifted center afterward.

When Ms. Thomas called to inquire about enrolling Alonzo in school, she was asked if she was African American. When she responded yes, she was asked if she would be in need of low-income housing. She asked the clerk what this had to do with school enrollment and she was told that the community surrounding the school didn't have low-income housing and he wouldn't be eligible for that school if she didn't reside in that community. The clerk offered to provide Ms. Thomas with the number of the school within the low-income community that was on the opposite side of town. This was a shocking experience to Ms. Thomas and reminded her of how her son was shut out of the gifted programming in Chicago. Ms. Thomas refused the number and went about enrolling Alonzo in that school.

REGAINING GIFTEDNESS

Ms. Thomas did inform Mrs. Nelson (the principal), Mr. Donaldson (the vice principal), and the school clerk that Alonzo was identified as gifted in Chicago and was promptly told that until Alonzo was tested in Iowa, he would not be identified as such in their schools. Mrs. Nelson also shared that most children who came from Chicago Public Schools to the Iowa City Community School District tend to struggle with the curriculum. Ms. Nelson then informed Ms. Thomas that Alonzo would be placed in his appropriate grade based on his age (as she stated was Iowa's policy), meaning that Alonzo would be forced to repeat the fifth grade because he was the age of students in that grade in Iowa. At that point, Ms. Thomas decided enough was enough and informed Ms. Nelson that Alonzo wasn't going to repeat a grade due to their policy, given that she had records that showed that he had just finished the fifth grade in Chicago. A small battle ensued, but the school conceded to him being enrolled in the sixth grade, without a gifted status.

The school administrators were convinced that Alonzo wouldn't test as gifted in their schools (although he was tested using the Iowa Tests of Basic Skills, or ITBS, in Chicago), while Ms. Thomas was content to simply wait and see. When Ms. Thomas visited Alonzo's new teacher, Mrs. Spackler, she informed Ms. Thomas that the children in this school system were tested three times a year on the ITBS and that the first test was coming up soon in September. When the scores came back in October, Alonzo scored in the 85th percentile and Mrs. Spackler promptly informed her that his score was not within the gifted range.

Ms. Thomas was stunned because her son had never scored below the 97th percentile in all of his years. Ms. Thomas thought that it might have been the move and the adjustment to the new community and new routine. Moreover, she did not have time to work with him on her own curriculum given the amount of work that came with her new doctoral program. Ms. Thomas decided to ignore the test results and continue to support and encourage Alonzo's talents and wait until he was tested again in January when she hoped he would be better adjusted.

As time progressed, something happened that made her decide to make even more changes. One day, Alonzo came home and informed his mom that he was no longer gifted. Ms. Thomas asked Alonzo to tell her more about this revelation of his, and he went on to tell her that his teacher, Mrs. Spackler, told him that he was average and he worked on the same level as most other students, so he was not gifted. Ms. Thomas wondered how this conversation came about, but she knew that Alonzo *was* likely to share his learning abilities with his teachers and that this was probably how the subject came up.

Ms. Thomas asked Alonzo how Mrs. Spackler reacted to his work when he handed it in to her and he shrugged his shoulders and said, "I don't know, regular, I guess." He also told his mother that he remembered when he turned in his art with reading project Mrs. Spackler told him that it was good, however, it wasn't his best, and maybe next time he could do several things to make it better. Alonzo went on to tell his mother that when another student (Jack) handed in his art with reading project Mrs. Spackler exclaimed in a louder voice how much time and effort must have gone into his work because it was done very, very well. Alonzo told Ms. Thomas that he didn't think Jack's work was that awesome.

Ms. Thomas made an appointment to meet with Ms. Spackler and Mr. Donaldson (the vice principal who happened to teach two of Alonzo's classes) and informed them that she wanted to conduct an experiment of sorts and would need their full cooperation. After hearing Ms. Thomas out, both teachers agreed. Ms. Thomas asked that both teachers refrain from discussing Alonzo's graded work with him until after he was tested again in January. Between October and January, Ms. Thomas requested that all graded materials be put into a sealed envelope and sent home to her with her name on the front. Ms. Thomas asked that they try and simply teach her son without any discussion of how well he was doing on his assignments and exams. Ms. Thomas shared that she would do the encouraging and discussions of his grades during the experiment. Ms. Spackler and Mr. Donaldson agreed, and the meeting was adjourned.

Ms. Thomas used information from Carter G. Woodson's book, *The Mis-Education of the Negro,* to explain to Alonzo how some people will tell you that your work and your abilities are where *they believe* they should be as opposed to where they are or truly can be, and Ms. Thomas took the time to help her son understand what this meant. For the next several months, Ms. Thomas only gave Alonzo very positive responses to his graded work and spoke to him about his abilities as she had always done. In January, Alonzo was tested again, and when the scores came back, Mrs. Spackler and Mr. Donaldson asked if Ms. Thomas could come in and meet with them to receive the scores. Ms. Thomas agreed. When she arrived at the meeting, she was given Alonzo's scores and a packet of information about gifted and talented students that included his invitation to enroll in the gifted center on The University of Iowa's campus. Whew! She was so relieved.

Mrs. Spackler and Mr. Donaldson were interested in what Ms. Thomas had done during the experimental period of time where they were asked to not discuss Alonzo's grades and work with him. Ms.

Thomas informed them that she spoke to her son and promoted him for the better, while she believed they were doing the opposite. She also shared with them that she believed that from the first day her son had arrived in the school district, the teachers had had doubts about her son's abilities to do well or to ever be identified as a gifted learner.

Ms. Thomas explained that when Alonzo came home and told her that he had received negative verbal and nonverbal messages and when he tested in a percentile in which he had never tested, she was sure that the messages were affecting her son's beliefs about himself and being transferred to his test scores or maybe even other areas of his life. Finally, she told them that this was why she wanted to cut them out of the process completely. True to what she believed, Alonzo rebounded to where he always was once he was tested for the second time within that same school year.

Mrs. Spackler and Mr. Donaldson told Ms. Thomas that they never meant to deliberately do any harm to Alonzo. Ms. Thomas acknowledged that this could be and most likely was a truly subconscious act; however, it played out in a very real way in her son. Ms. Thomas immediately enrolled Alonzo in the gifted center's weekend and summer courses, where he was able to meet and work alongside students who were like him. The gifted center's curriculum was taught by college professors who challenged Alonzo, and he would often return home excited about trying to understand his engineering and advanced science problems. Alonzo stayed on campus for weeks at a time and never once complained about taking classes during parts of the summer or over the weekends.

QUESTIONS FOR REFLECTION

1. Alonzo was identified as a gifted student early in his educational experience, and the bumpy road to being educated at the appropriate level started just as early. How can educators help to smooth out the road and process for gifted African American children identified in school with similar circumstances such as Alonzo?

2. In African American communities, few gifted educational programs are available and those that do exist usually cannot take very many children. Alonzo's teachers attempted to remedy his school's situation. How can teachers in regular classrooms work with identified gifted learners who must remain in heterogeneously grouped classroom environments?

3. Single-parent female-led households are becoming a norm in our society. Ms. Thomas is a single mother who knew her son could do better if he was challenged. She had access to resources that helped her and eventually got her son into an educational program that would challenge and strengthen his talents. How can we help single mothers who have limited access to resources for their children? For themselves?

THE OUTCOME

Alonzo stayed at that school for the entire year (until it was time for him to attend junior high school at a different school) and the issue of his giftedness never came up again. Alonzo tested at the gifted level in junior high school each year and is now taking engineering classes at his high school in Iowa City.

PATHWAYS UPLIFTING GIFTEDNESS IN BLACKS

CHAPTER 31

THE IMPACT OF A SINGLE "TEST"

THRIVING AS A BLACK GIFTED FEMALE FROM A SINGLE-PARENT FAMILY

by Cheryl Fields-Smith and Cherranda Smith

BACKGROUND

"Momma, I tested the White people and they failed." These words were spoken to me by my daughter, Cherranda, one day when she came home from school in the seventh grade. Unsure of how to interpret such a pronouncement, I wondered why and how she was testing her classmates and how she was interpreting their so-called failure. Six years later, Cherranda and I reflect on this event as a pivotal moment in her journey as a Black gifted female in a predominantly White institution (PWI).

Cherranda wrote an essay in which she refers to herself as an outlier, because statistics suggest, given her race and her single-parent family status, she would be unlikely to excel as she had in high school. Conversely, Gladwell (2008) suggested that successful people are not outliers when we consider the alignment of timing, opportunities, and heritage found within their biographies. He writes that outliers maybe:

appear at first blush to lie outside ordinary experience. But they don't. They are products of history and community, of opportunity and legacy. Their success is not exceptional or mysterious. It is grounded in a web of advantages and inheritances, some deserved, some not, some earned, some just plain lucky—but all critical to making them who they are. The outlier, in the end, is not an outlier at all. (p. 285)

Although Gladwell perceives time and opportunity as either earned or by chance, we believe that many of the experiences Cherranda has been afforded have been due to divine intervention, her ability to embrace her racial identity and cultural legacy, and her ability to accept her giftedness. We have chosen to present these themes in chronological order because they are deeply entangled within Cherranda's journey.

CHERRANDA'S STORY

THE ROAD TO GIFTEDNESS

Cherranda's journey began in a Connecticut suburb where I was teaching elementary school. By the time she turned 6 months old, I was divorced. We lived in a two-family home owned by my parents, which enabled me to pay the expense of a high-quality preschool. Two White teachers, who created an environment in which Cherranda recalls feeling genuinely loved, owned her private preschool. The setting was predominantly White, but Cherranda never felt less than or different from any other child in the school. For kindergarten, Cherranda attended the school where I taught. Her teacher and assistant teacher were both Black, but the majority of her classmates were White. Like preschool, her kindergarten classroom was vibrant and provided a good balance of challenging, but meaningful activities. However, in retrospect, these wonderfully effective environments masked issues of race for Cherranda. For her first-grade year, we moved to metro Atlanta as I pursued a doctorate at Emory University. Cherranda's first-grade year would be in a predominantly Black setting; this Southern context revealed her developing racial identity.

Sitting in a restaurant in a Black Atlanta community, 6-year-old Cherranda observed with amazement, "Mommy, everyone in here is Black, the waiters are Black, the customers are Black. Everyone is Black." This signaled a need to be more forthcoming regarding issues of race. From birth, she had been immersed in diverse settings. Families in our eclectic Connecticut neighborhood claimed their ethnic identities (i.e., Polish, Greek, Italian, Dominican, and African Americans) more so than their racial (i.e., White, Black) identities. Cherranda's dolls even represented a variety of racial backgrounds. But in the South, our community became predominantly Black, and this had a profound effect on Cherranda. In retrospect, Cherranda came to realize that there were a lot more Black people on the Earth than she had thought.

Cherranda refers to her elementary school as an HBCU (historically Black college or university), but, in reality, had we lived in the community just 5 years earlier, the school would have been predominantly White (teachers and students). We moved into the community after of a mass exodus of White families. Coincidently, or by divine intervention, the newly evolved Black community provided Cherranda with support and inspiration to excel. It was here that Cherranda was identified as gifted. Moreover, her teachers contributed tremendously toward Cherranda's awareness of her cultural legacy.

Cherranda's elementary school teachers were all of African American descent and they used culturally relevant instructional strategies to maintain student interest and to inspire them. For example, teachers used popular music rhythms to help students remember facts, because they believed if students could memorize rap lyrics, then they could recall academic facts if placed to the familiar rhythms. Cherranda's fourth-grade teacher, who was gifted education certified, taught about slavery unconventionally. She had the students lay in the floor the way slaves were packed into ships. The teacher's intent was to simulate the slave ship experience to increase the students' understanding. She knew her students well enough to know that this class would respond with appreciation rather than feeling offended. The relationship of high expectations, mutual trust, and caring between the teacher and students also supported the students' response to this learning experience. Lessons like these fostered Cherranda's understanding of what African Americans have had to endure, provided her with a sense of purpose, and created a desire to know more about her people. Simultaneously, I was learning new perspectives on Black history in my studies. Segregated Black schools were not inferior as I had been taught in the past, in fact, research had documented a legacy of fervor in the pursuit of education (Siddle Walker, 1996). For our Black ancestors, freedom equaled learning to read, write, and count.

Another edifying moment came during a third-grade lesson on fractions. Instead of using worksheets, the teacher had students create surveys about themselves, graph the responses, and then use the information to create word problems. One of the questions inquired about whether the children lived with one or both parents. The results of this lesson excited Cherranda because not only had she learned fractions, but she also discovered that 18 out of 24 students in her class lived with only one parent, which meant that more than half of her classmates lived with their moms; thus, our household was not so unusual.

In this culturally affirming environment, Cherranda received the gifted label well. She enjoyed being pulled out for "Discovery," the in-school enrichment program; to her, being gifted meant doing "extra cool stuff." Many gifted students lived in our 100% Black neighborhood, which also most likely circumvented the ridicule gifted or otherwise studious Black students reportedly experience from their peers (Ogbu, 2004).

We both graduated in May 2004, which meant middle school would require another move. Getting Cherranda's gifted label to transfer to her new school was a challenge even though we were in the same state. Then, we discovered that gifted education in middle school would be nothing like gifted education in elementary school. After receiving packets of critical thinking questions, which gifted students would complete independently, Cherranda began to question the value of being gifted. Initially, I thought this was because of the lack of interaction until they could hire a gifted teacher. This leads us to that pivotal moment when Cherranda tested her White gifted colleagues.

THE "TEST"

As a reminder, Cherranda came home from seventh grade one day proclaiming that she had tested her White classmates and they had failed. I listened carefully as she explained the way she had set up her White classmates by asking them for an answer she already knew.

Explaining the significance of the "test," Cherranda states,

The gifted title formally ushered me into the White academic culture in middle school; however, the social White culture was not automatic. I began the process of entering the White social culture, but was unsure about betraying my own race. My elementary school exposed me to advanced science experiences through a weekend enrichment program where I dissected various animals including pig fetuses and frogs under the direction of a university professor. So repeating the same experiments in seventh grade provided the perfect time to test whether the White social culture would accept me. I tested two White girls next to me by asking for help on a portion of the dissection that I secretly knew how to do. I was evaluating the girls' capacity to help a potential member of the same social group. They failed. They only gave muffled responses and vague excuses. Then, I knew that I could not depend on these girls for academic collaboration or a vital friendship. They had excluded me from their academic circle, I'm assuming on the premise of my race. I felt separated from the group, unwelcome, and less than, because I was Black. Their actions toward me took me back to the documentaries we watched in class where Blacks were called derogatory names and spat on. Their unwillingness to help me was the saliva, and their muffled excuses of why they couldn't help me despite the fact we shared several conversations outside of class was the N-word that sent me running back to my people.

AFTER THE TEST

In the years following her test, Cherranda continued to thrive academically, but there were battles to be fought socially. Pressure from Black peers' ridicule of her focus on her studies and even her relatively light skin tone increased, but began to subside toward the end of ninth grade. In reflection, we believe that her motivation and determination became somewhat cemented by the test. She knew who she was as a gifted Black female. Her faith and ability to embrace her cultural legacy and her giftedness became her foundation. During this time Cherranda began expressing her feelings through poetry and Spoken Word. Much of her work provides details of what she values and captures her emotions at a particular point in time. An example of Cherranda's poetry written after the test follows to demonstrate Cherranda's struggles as a gifted Black female and her sources of empowerment.

Light-Skinned Mentality
January 17, 2009

When will I be admitted to the Sistah Soulja club? Or am I too light?
Second-guessing myself when I lift up that fist.
If one more person asks me if I'm mixed, I will recite this!
Does my lightness offend you?
Do my curls and sun-kissed skin appall you?
When some look at me they suffocate with jealousy and turn blue.
I just walk on and swing my hips, like I was born to do.
"Why don't you straighten your hair?"
"Who in your family is White?"
"Do you get perms?"

"Can your hair be activated?"
Does my skin give permission for me to be interrogated?
"You half a sistah."
"Your heritage is like a twister."
Let me tell you something sister . . .
Your ancestor was underneath mister, just like mine.
Don't you think I get tired of saying what I am all the time?

The hours I spent attempting to straighten my mane of mistakes.
The damage I did to my precious crown clumping on gel on top of grease on top of mousse on top of water trying to lay down the fuzzy imperfections.
Let me make a correction.
They are not mistakes, they are me.
When your great-great was set free,
So was some of me.
When I recited "looms but the horror of the shade."
When I made the grades
All I heard were grunts
"Girlfriend trying to be White."
Why can't you be happy for me?
Happy that I'm breaking the stigmas?
The stereotypes, and labels.
But y'all label me, like some of me wasn't swinging up on that tree.
Sure some of me was watching the scene.
But don't act like you ain't got no cousin who don't need afro-sheen.

Call me a half-breed, like I might be a dog, a mutt
I couldn't care less of how you see me but . . .
Let me just say young King or Queen
Just 'cause I'm light don't mean that none me didn't scream.

My sun-burned nose don't mean that I don't know what Dark
and Lovely is
'Cause believe me sister girl
Some days even I need a fix.

Just because right now I am who I am
Doesn't mean that at one point I wasn't proud to be
Don't fret sister girl, 'cause one day we'll both be set free from
this Light Skinned Mentality.

QUESTIONS FOR REFLECTION

1. What factors enable our Black children like Cherranda to avoid
   getting stuck in the victim role when faced with discrimination?
2. After more than 10 years after the passing of No Child Left
   Behind, why don't teachers have the professional freedom to
   implement culturally relevant instructional practices such as the
   ones used by Cherranda's elementary school teachers?
3. If Cherranda were to visit your classroom, what would you want
   her to share with your gifted students? With you?

THE OUTCOME

Today, Cherranda thrives as a student attending one of the nation's
most prestigious predominantly White institutions with an undergraduate admission rate of less than 10%. Early in her college choice process, Howard University and Spelman College, historically Black colleges and universities, were at the top of her list. In April of her senior
year of high school, she received an invitation to an extended weekend
as part of a Duke University recruitment of Black students. She stayed
in a dorm with Black females in their freshman year. She attended

classes and met Black students from all over the world who would be choosing among the most elite schools. In the end, Cherranda turned down a 4-year scholarship from a historically Black college and university to attend Duke based in part to the extended immersion into campus life, from a Black perspective, which enabled her to experience the bond she thought could only exist at a HBCU.

Thinking about her decision to attend Duke instead of a HBCU, Cherranda states,

> I get frustrated by the reoccurring looks questioning how I got here, but I'm glad I came. Being around these interactions pull me closer to my Black community. I have a family within a family. God has provided a strong support system of students and faculty here. At an HBCU, I would not be exposed to the negative perspective of myself as much, but nor would I have access to the many opportunities this PWI has to offer. I am able to meet extraordinary Black people who had similar high school experiences. This happens at HBCUs all the time, but the difference is that we (Black students at PWI) consciously decided to have this experience in order to build a firmer foundation for our aspirations. Not to discredit HBCUs at all, because I am missing A LOT by being here. However, when you look at someone who is premed, the connections available at Duke and other PWIs are impeccable. Personally, I wanted and needed to go to a school where changing my mind about majors would not discredit my degree. In other words, I needed to be able to change my major and still be at a skill with a renowned, top, or credible department. Also, I wanted to go to a school where interdisciplinary studies were not looked as rare cases. These two factors are not always available at HBCUs.

Within her first semester at Duke, Cherranda has assumed the role of chaplain for the gospel choir and dance team. An ordained minister, she is preparing to preach a sermon on Duke's campus for an ongoing, midweek Christian worship service she helped to initiate. She applied to become part of a woman's leadership program along with 145 of her classmates; only 18 were chosen, and Cherranda is among them. Finally, as I write this, Cherranda is among the many Black students who are protesting a research paper written by Duke professors questioning the validity of affirmative action. This protest has led to a meeting with the university's president, and they are not done yet. All of this within the first 4 months on Duke University's campus! Divine intervention, affirmation of her cultural legacy and racial identity, and embracing her giftedness have brought her to this point.

REFERENCES

Gladwell, M. (2008). *Outliers: The story of success*. New York, NY: Back Bay Books.

Ogbu, J. (2004). Collective identity and the burden of "acting White" in Black history, community, and education. *Urban Review, 36,* 1–35.

Siddle Walker, V. (1996). *Their highest potential: An African American school community in the segregated south*. Chapel Hill: University of North Carolina Press.

CHAPTER 32

PUT A LITTLE PAINT WHERE IT AIN'T

THE UNWELCOMED INFUSION OF HIP-HOP IN SCHOOLS

by J. Sean Callahan

BACKGROUND

At the time when hip-hop was labeled the new social pathogen by White folks and Black folks from the Civil Rights generation, I was enraptured by its beats, creativity and audacity, and rhymes. This chapter has several contexts, but only one background—a chord that stretches through 27 years of my life: hip-hop. The stories in this chapter take place in desegregated schools amid the segregated mindsets of the predominantly White student and teacher population. These stories were written to document my experiences coloring outside the lines and consequences of putting a little paint where it ain't.

THE STORY

AT WORK IN WHEREHOUSE MUSIC

At the now defunct music store, this guy asks me to direct him to the rap and hip-hop section of the store. I walk over to the section with him.

> **Sean:** You lookin' for anything specific?
> **Customer:** *(scanning the rows of CDs)* Yeah. I'm lookin' for some ol' school. Something without a lot of cursin' it, somethin' like Run-DMC.
> **Sean:** *(No big deal,* I think to myself, *there are plenty of 30-something-year-old White guys who like and grew up listening to Run-DMC. But he really trips me out.)*
> **Customer:** It's for my son. He's doing a report for school on Run-DMC.
> **Sean:** What grade is he in? *(My left eyebrow begins to raise.)*
> **Customer:** Fifth.
> **Sean:** Okay, "King of Rock." *(I hand him a Run-DMC CD. He nods his head in approval, and we both make our way to the register.)*

This 2-minute interaction changed the entire course of study of my doctoral program. It got me thinking about two things in particular: (1) my own memories as a fifth grader, and (2) the first time I tried to bring hip-hop to the classroom.

MUSIC INTERESTS IN FIFTH GRADE

As long as I can remember, I've always been interested in music. I was in the school band from the fifth grade until I graduated from high school, so if I wasn't playing an instrument to make music, I was listening to it. I liked listening to all sorts of music—jazz, reggae (I had an older cousin who turned me on to Bob Marley when I was about 10. What I could make of it blew my mind.), classical, blues, and the gospel songs that my grandfolks played. With phrases I didn't quite understand, I watched the singer's voice carve and crease their mahogany faces with triumph and travail. Music has always played an important part in my life.

HIP-HOP IN HIGH SCHOOL

The first time I tried to bring hip-hop to the classroom was in the 10th grade at a school where the Black-to-White student ratio was about 30/70 with an overwhelming percentage of White teachers. Like any other 15-year-old, I was very impressionable and desperately seeking an identity within the stratum of high school society. When efforts to find myself failed, I found solace in the music I listened to. Hip-hop music etched images of Africa and proud, intelligent Black people. The lyrics and music of artists like Public Enemy, KRS-One, Eric B. & Rakim, MC Lyte, X-Clan, Intelligent Hoodlum, and Poor Righteous Teachers not only talked about the serenity and nonviolence of Martin Luther King, Jr., they also invoked names like Malcolm X, Marcus Garvey, Sojourner Truth, Bob Marley, Nat Turner, and groups like the Black Panthers—Black people who fought back. They fought back with fiery words and seemed ready and willing to defend what they believed in. Through hip-hop, I was filled with information and struck with hunger to know more about Black folks. I was tired of watching that same weak-ass PBS Eyes on the Prize rotation they played in school every Black History Month. I was tired of watching *Roots* and having to hear White kids snicker under the cover of the dim blue light from the television.

Term papers and school go hand-in-hand. So when it came time to select topics/people for a social studies term paper, instinctively, I looked for Black people. *Sojourner Truth, Harriet Tubman, MLK, Jr., the Civil Rights Movement . . . We didn't even get that far. We never covered the Civil Rights Movement!* I read and thought to myself, scanning the teacher-generated list for something or someone that escaped February's expected exhumation.

I asked permission to do my paper on the Black Panthers. The teacher said he didn't know much about them, but it would be okay if I chose them for a topic. After searching the school and public library for references, I managed to garner three books between both libraries. Two of which were the same book. Didn't matter. I was hungry. I read through each book synthesizing them into (what I thought to be) 7 pages of literary genius. After turning in the paper and waiting anxiously for a week and half, I received my grade. On the last page of the paper scrawled in red ink was an encircled C. The only comments throughout the entire paper read: "This is not a research paper. This is propaganda." Once again it seemed hip-hop and the lessons it taught me had no place in the classroom.

Unfortunately, this was not the only occasion in which teachers (knowingly or unknowingly) sabotaged my motivation to learn, nor was I the only student targeted for such attention. Many students who began to identify with hip-hop came under fire. Our style of dress, language, and interests were scrutinized while our role models and inspirations went unacknowledged.

HIP-HOP AT HOME

Hip-hop was therapeutic in a number of ways for me and my brother, James. For example, James had a horrible stutter when he was younger. It was so bad, in fact, that in the third grade, he made himself sick enough to go to the hospital for 3 days. He hated school. The teachers and his classmates thought he was dumb because he wasn't able to speak without stuttering. But I knew better; my brother was smart—smarter than me. He was cunning, charismatic, and exceedingly willful.

By the time James was in fourth grade, he was skipping school. He would make himself a fried bologna sandwich, walk halfway down the hill, double back, and then hide in the storage space under the house until he heard my mom leave for work. At that time, the school would make "robo-calls" to your house if you were absent. But as long as you were able to answer the phone when they called, everything was gravy. This plan worked for a long time before he was caught.

Before they divorced, my parents sent James and me to a private Christian school that guaranteed that we would be reading by the age of 3. They delivered on their promise. In public school, however, James was retained twice before he reached the fifth grade. By the ninth grade, he dropped out, left home, and started rapping. Yeah, he became a rapper. It was the craziest thing. When James was on the "mic," I never heard him stutter, not once. At age 16, James and his group released a full-length album. They toured regionally, and he performed in clubs that he was too young to get into otherwise. James's charm, creativity, and hardheadedness were channeled into the art of rapping. He had learned techniques for breath control and cadence—integral skills of the craft. My mom, my baby sister, and I saw James perform once; they left shortly after one of the dancers started grinding on the microphone stand.

With all of the confidence of a 17-year-old who had rocked crowds and made grown women shake their behinds, James returned to school, joined the basketball team, and enrolled in college prep classes. Interestingly enough, the basketball coach was also the world history teacher who gave me a C on my paper about the Black Panthers. Things were going well up until James began having trouble in the coach's class and his reputation as an MC caught up with him. He became ineligible to play. James asked the coach for help in the class, but because he wasn't "shootin' the rock" (playing basketball), the coach had no help for him. Disheartened and discouraged, James dropped out (again).

"Unless these White folks can get something out of you, they ain't got nuthin' for you," James told me one day.

So what does my and James's story have to do with hip-hop and stories of Black students in predominantly White schools? Well, I'll tell you. Hip-hop did what the school wasn't able to do. My brother had seen speech therapists from the time he entered public school until the fifth grade and his impediment saw little improvement. He was

16 before I ever heard him speak without it. This is not to say that his therapists were inept, not at all. But they couldn't teach him not to stutter. For him, hip-hop forged a path toward confidence. He took that hard-earned confidence to school with him, but it seemed that his brand of self-assuredness was unrecognizable and misinterpreted in the classroom. Without support and acknowledgement from teachers in predominantly White schools, the lessons and knowledge gifted and talented Black students learn from hip-hop can easily be misunderstood and lead to disengagement and distrust of teachers.

DOING SOMETHING WITH HIP-HOP

Let's go back to that day at Wherehouse. My shift ended, and while walking home I'm thinking about these incidences. And truth be told, I was gettin' mad. For all of the acts of emotional and educational sabotage endured by the Black folks I went to school with, for all of the mocked intentions, for the White kid doing his report on Run-DMC, somebody had to do something. Too many bright kids were falling or being pushed through the cracks. Like the old heads say, "You can either talk about it or be about it." I decided to *be about it* and this is what I decided to do. I started thinking of ways hip-hop culture could be used to engage and motivate students to read, think critically and creatively, and sharpen their research and writing skills. I wanted to provide opportunities to study how history and culture shape who we are. And I wanted to do it in a way that allowed (and sometimes forced) students to recognize their gifts and potential and develop them into spectacular performances of passion and intellect.

BEGINNING GRADUATE SCHOOL

I moved to Athens, GA, in the summer of 2000. By January of 2001, I began to notice the flyers advertising hip-hop shows at some of the bars and venues in the downtown area. As a country boy from rural Northwest Georgia who had been listening to hip-hop since 1984, the fact that I had only seen two live shows in my life made this a good opportunity to meet new people, feed the Loas, and, hopefully, hear some dope music. But as an expectant father with two jobs and no car, I didn't have the time, energy, or money to engage in the scene. I had to somehow prove to the gatekeepers that I was ready for graduate school; reassure my girlfriend, who was 5 months pregnant at the time, that I still thought she was pretty; and convince her parents that I wasn't selling herb to make ends meet. For the time being, leisure and ceremony would be confined to our small, drafty apartment. Thankfully, the flyers continued to appear and the events they listed became more varied and frequent—open mic night on Wednesday, freestyle battle on Thursday, live shows backed by a live band on Saturday. There always seemed to be something happening.

On the bus ride home from the obstetrician's office, I was telling my girlfriend, Nikki, about a freestyle battle, titled "King of the Ring," being held on campus that night and about my experience.

> **Nikki:** (*Cupping her hands over her mouth to perform an airy beat box*) I didn't know you could rap. Go ahead, bust a rhyme.
> **Sean:** Girl, you know I can't rap. I'd probably pee on myself before anything came out of my mouth. I'm just going to watch. (*I watched Nikki grip the stair rail to steady herself as she giggled.*)

At the lecture hall, I took a seat. A few minutes later, I was approached by young man who was short in stature, with baggy fatigues, and a dark-colored baseball cap with the bill turned backward and angled rakishly. His dreadlocks rested comfortably around his neck and shoulders.

> **M-Dos:** What's up, brotha? You wanna be a judge? We need another person.
> **Sean:** Cool, I'm Sean.

Surprised and flattered, I hesitantly agreed, praying that they wouldn't ask me to display my nonexistent rhyme skills as a badge of legitimacy. Looking down, trying not to trip and tumble down the steps, I reached the judges table. We exchanged the soul shake at which point I inquired the whereabouts of the men's restroom.

ZIGGY

The airbrakes on the city transit bus squeaked and whooshed as it came to a stop in front of the Memorial Hall bus stop. I stepped off and headed toward the university library. Walking past the psychology building, I heard a voice from the top of the staircase overlooking the bus stop.

"Zi-i-i-g-gy!" he called. I could hear the smirk in his squeal. Trying to ignore him, I cursed, then prayed, and pressed on. Again, he drawled, "Heeey, Zi-i-g-g-y!" Now, I know doggone well that I don't look anything like Ziggy Marley. Sure, we are both Black men with dreadlocks and scruffy beards, but I'm at least 5 or 6 inches taller than Ziggy. This guy was mocking me. His arrogance invaded my nostrils like the stench of the river that meandered around the sprawling campus and through the small, rural, university town. I looked up, but didn't need to see him to deduce that my assailant was more than likely a young White male between the ages of 18 and 22, a typical undergraduate at this large, public, research university. And no, this is not a grand indictment of all White folks who attend this university, nor am I implying that every person who has insulted me by calling me a name has been White. But when one considers that of the more than 34,000 students who attend this university, more than 75% identify as White, I felt fairly certain about my assumptions.

I wish I could say this kind of thing didn't happen often, but I can't. It occurs entirely too much to be taken as flattery. My name is not Ziggy or Bob. And I'm not Jamaican. However, given the fact that I haven't shaved since 1998 and my hair drapes past my waist, I can understand how my appearance might evoke thoughts and images of Rastafarians and reggae music. But who I am, what I am, and what

I strive to be is much more than cool hair, an exotic accent, and an embodied soundtrack for smoking overpriced marijuana. As long as blood, breath, and spirit circulate, it is completely within my rights and capacity to offer something spectacular without having to become a spectacle. And if this young man was unable or unwilling to appreciate my efforts, then that should be his problem. I have my own fears to conquer; I don't need to be reminded of his. After this incident, I had had enough and to decrease the likelihood of something like this happening again, I used a portion of my graduate assistantship stipend to buy a 256MB mp3 player. With music in my ears, I imagined it easier to deal with the forays of disrespect and ignorance.

With my newly purchased mp3 player, a cheap pair of earphones, a Black wool/poly knit toboggan that I "borrowed" from my girlfriend and a massive collection of hip-hop music, I created a social prophylactic to defend myself against any incursions of bigotry and ill-formed curiosity as I walked around campus and the downtown area. OutKast's Aquemini was the first CD that I downloaded onto that player that became like Afro-American Express for me—I never left home without that little blue box. I mumbled the lyrics of the song to myself, tucking a few errant locks under my black hat. The ritual of twisting and tucking my hair into this hat prepared and protected me. The music worked like a talisman set to hand drums and synthesizers warding off haints (spirits) sent to cause tension and disease.

Listening to hip-hop was more than a simple act of disengaging from my surroundings. The lyrics were scriptures and provided insight for successfully sustaining multiple identities, traversing treacherous sociocultural landscapes, and developing individuality and self-awareness. The artists' music, like much of the hip-hop I listen to, spoke to my experiences as a Black person and doctoral student on this campus—moving between and through multiple worlds, challenging conventions, and devising tactics aimed toward "finessing the struggle" (Flowers, 2001, p. 2). When I thought about that particular experience, I wondered how other Black students on campus made sense of similar encounters. What kind of stories might they relate? Had they too created ritual practices to protect themselves from stressful situations? Did hip-hop play a part in their rituals as well?

QUESTIONS FOR REFLECTION

1. What are the experiences of other young unidentified gifted Black students who engage with hip-hop?

2. What can teachers do in the classroom to allow gifted Black students to use hip-hop? Even further, what can teachers do to allow all students to engage whatever genre of music and culture that might be their passion?

3. Because it is not solely the teacher's responsibility to make room for or introduce passion areas into the learning environment, what can students do to bring music and cultural passions to the classroom?

4. Considering that Black students are underrepresented in gifted programs, what type of resiliency (e.g., strategies, techniques, and crosscultural knowledge) is necessary for them to thrive?

5. What habits of mind do gifted students develop as a result of their engagement with hip-hop?

THE OUTCOME

James currently works as a driver in the trucking industry. He earned his GED and briefly attended a small university in Northwest Georgia. As a hobby, he continues to record and produce music in a DIY studio in his garage. M-Dos currently works a sanitation worker. He still hosts hip-hop and networking events in his spare time.

REFERENCES

Flowers, A. R. (2001). *Mojo rising: Confessions of a 21st century conjureman.* New York, NY: Wanganegresse Press.

CHAPTER 33

"BACK IN THE DAY, MAN, I WISH SOMEONE WOULD HAVE TOLD ME LIKE IT REALLY IS"

LIBERATORY EDUCATION FOR GIFTED AFRICAN AMERICANS

by Eric M. Bridges

BACKGROUND

During the 1970s in DeKalb County, GA, many African American students participated in a busing program known as Majority to Minority. The intention of this program was to integrate the segregated schools of the county. Many African American students from the southern area of the county were bused to predominantly White schools in northern DeKalb County. White students from the predominantly White schools in the northern area of the county could opt to attend the predominantly African American schools in South DeKalb County. Very few White students participated in this option.

MY STORY

WHAT IS EDUCATION?

In African American folk language, the phrases "going to school" and "getting an education" are synonymous. When African Americans are educated in American schools, they are not taught to question how their lives have been affected by White supremacy. African Americans are expected to accept an education that teaches them nothing about themselves as historic beings. African Americans learn that we were slaves, Abraham Lincoln freed us, and we prayed for the benevolence of a country to live up to its creed that all men are created equal. Many times as an adult, I wonder how different my life and the lives of millions of African Americans would be if we were taught that we came from vibrant and cultured African civilizations and that the enslavement of our people by Europeans and others was the most barbaric event in the history of mankind. And, even though Africans were enslaved, we orchestrated rebellions to free ourselves from our bondage and the horrendous things done to us, maintaining our humanity and a faith in the divine that is testimony to our spiritual resilience. If I had been taught these things, I think my sojourn through the "Hells of America" would have been a lot easier. Maybe my matriculation through the American educational system would have really demonstrated that this country truly believed in democracy—by providing a culturally relevant education that taught me the truth about this country and millions of people who came to these shores on not so happy terms.

As a scholar, I have explored the ways education can be taught to young people to give them an accurate depiction of history while giving them the tools that they will need to thrive in a multicultural society. Recently, I have discovered that for me as an educator, I need to look at the education I received in the public schools of DeKalb County, GA. Although I am not a famous person, I imagine that the education that I received had some rays of light that allowed me to become an associate professor of psychology at a small, metropolitan university in Atlanta. As a teacher, scholar, and part-time activist, I felt an autobiographical account was necessary to see if I received an education or my teachers provided me with an education that I could designate as liberatory—an education that gives you the skills necessary to be successful in a global world community while simultaneously teaching them about their heritage.

This is a walk down memory lane to see if my parents and teachers prepared me to be a change agent and to see if there are things I can teach gifted, young African Americans that will enable them to continue the struggle for human freedom.

BACK IN THE DAY

I came from a Southern, working-class background. I was raised in a two-parent household in Decatur, GA. My dad worked nights at General Motors and my mother worked in the insurance field. There was this expectation that I should do well in school so I could attend college, so I did well in school. I was basically quiet, studious, and introverted. Not introverted in the sense of being shy, but, as my mother tells it, I had to always be mentally engaged because I was a child about which my elders would say, "an idle mind is the devil's workshop," and I would get in trouble if I didn't have a book or some project to work on. I was considered a devious child.

I remember being labeled as gifted in the third grade. I took the necessary IQ test (I can't recall the name of the test) and after taking the test, three other children and I participated in a gifted pull-out class. My mother never told me my IQ (she thought that telling me would make me arrogant). But I liked feeling special because I had big plans. I wanted to be an astronaut, a doctor, and an astrophysicist. My mother would ask me what I wanted to be when I grew up, and I told her these three professions. I knew early on that I wanted to leave planet Earth because Black people caught much hell here, and I didn't want anything to do with it. I had decided I would explore the cosmos with other smart Black people and create a new society, one where people were powerful, spiritually enlightened (of course, at the age of 6, I knew what enlightened meant), and were really cool. This was my dream, and I figured that a gifted Black boy could have dreams, especially because dreaming kept me from devilment, as my mother would say. Although I wasn't monetarily rich as a child, my world was culturally rich, colorful, and quite fun. I had my family (extended and nuclear) and even though I was sneaky, I always knew that my family loved me. I knew I was supported. Although I wanted to leave planet Earth, my mother would always remind be to never forget where I came from and that I should help other Black people, who have endured so much here in America. My mother taught me what I call "grounding lessons." One that really resonates with me even to this day was when my mother asked me, "What do you call Black men with a lot of money or Black men who have Ph.D.s?" I said I didn't know and she promptly told me the answer, "a nigger, and always know that this is how many White people will see you even if you achieve all your goals." Some people may find this teaching technique problematic, but it has saved me from much psychological distress and depression. I would latter learn that many Black children received this same lesson.

The lessons I received in elementary school never felt like I was being prepared to rule the world I would travel to, or this one, for that matter. However, I always looked forward to my gifted classes because I was allowed to be inquisitive and creative. But I never learned anything about Black people or any other non-White people. I don't know if I had the intellectual sophistication to think along the lines of culturally relevant education and the fact that I was not receiving this type of education. I wish I could say that I learned about Nat Turner, Malcolm X, Fannie Lou Hamer, Marcus Garvey, and Harriet Tubman, but I didn't. Now looking back, I would love for every child to receive an education that is inclusive of everyone's heritage and culture, because if I had been educated in this way, I would have had a very different pride in myself and my people. I would not have tried to emulate Whites in the way they acted and I would not have thought that Whites must be better than Black people.

I came home one day and told my mother that my gifted education teacher, who was a tall, blonde, upper-middle-class White woman, said that I would receive a better education if I attended a high school on the north side of the county, which happened to be predominantly White. My mother stated emphatically that her tax dollars supported the neighborhood high school, which was 99.99% African American. The suggestion made by the White gifted education teacher was one of many that she made that had a connotation that anything African American was inferior and anything White was superior. I never remember this teacher teaching me anything about African American history and culture, yet she knew I was interested in history and culture. She was clueless on truly educating me so I could really contribute to my African American community. She made sure I was exposed to American history, sans African American history. I knew more about Edgar Allan Poe, Jack London, and Atlanta Braves baseball (racist tomahawk chop and all) than I knew about Langston Hughes and Tommie Smith and John Carlos of the 1968 Mexico Olympics. I mentioned Atlanta Braves baseball because I remember her taking me to the games, even though I disliked baseball. My parents never really had the time for outings like this because they were too busy working to put a roof over my head and food on the table for my brother and me. In her own paternalistic way, maybe my White gifted education teacher thought she was "doing right by me" as the special African American child from the "Deck." She never really knew how I felt. I felt like a project or, worse, someone who needed fixing.

It was not until I got to the predominantly African American high school in my neighborhood that I received my first exposure to African American history and culture. More importantly, my teachers, especially my African American gifted education teacher, Ms. Smith, told me and my peers what to expect from the majority White American society. She told us what my mother told me, that regardless of my achievements, I would still be viewed as an inferior person, a nigger. However, the way White Americans may have viewed me was not my problem, it was theirs. My teachers told me to have pride in myself and my peoples' history, because we were resilient, strong, and survivors.

Most importantly, Ms. Smith told me to get as much education as I could and come back and help my community so we could end racism and injustice. In my Advanced Placement English classes, we read Toni Morrison and Langston Hughes. But it was those personal and "real talk" lessons I received that helped me navigate a hostile and racist society. One particular instance stands out in my mind. My 12th-grade Advanced Placement teacher, Ms. Moore, went down the class roll and called everyone's name. As she called our names, she would say either Black or White. So the event went like this: "Eric Marcell Bridges, Black; T. N., White; K.W., Black (initials used instead of full names). I asked Ms. Moore why she did this, and she told us that White people could label us as Black or White by our names, and colleges and employers could discriminate against us even though they had not seen us. I know my White gifted education teacher would not have given me this valuable lesson.

TEACH THEM WELL AND LET THEM LEAD THE WAY

If I had to put a label on the type of education I received, I would say it was progressively liberatory. I had been labeled as gifted early on, but my nascent gifted training in the school system did not prepare me to question societal inequities. It was my family and my gifted high school teachers who gave me a sense of who I was as a budding African man. When I conceptualize liberatory education, I now do so with different lenses. I now view liberatory education as a reciprocal process between communities, families, and schools that are culturally and historically linked to educate gifted young people to continue the struggle for human freedom and dignity while allowing them to explore the richness of who they are as individuals.

QUESTION FOR REFLECTION

1. How do we teach, nurture, and love gifted African American youth so that they can create a better and more just society?

THE OUTCOME

I eventually received my Ph.D. in educational psychology from The University of Georgia. I am passionate about liberation psychology, given my experiences growing up in the deep South as an African American male. I work with my students to critically analyze the aspects of society that disempower them so they can strategically empower themselves to affect change.

RESOURCES

Freire, P. (2007). *Pedagogy of the oppressed.* New York, NY: The Continuum International Publishing Group.

Kunjufu, J. (1985). *Countering the conspiracy to destroy Black boys.* Chicago, IL: African American Images.

Noguera, P. A. (2009). *The trouble with Black boys . . . And other reflections on race, equity, and the future of public education.* New York, NY: Jossey-Bass.

Shujaa, M. J. (1998). Education and schooling: You can have one without the other. In M. J. Schujaa (Ed.), *Too much schooling, too little education: A paradox of Black life in White societies* (pp. 13–36). Trenton, NJ: Africa World Press.

AFTERWORD

UNDERSTAND WITH YOUR HEART AND ADVOCATE FOR GIFTED BLACK STUDENTS AND ADULTS

The age at which one comes to understand that he or she is intellectually, academically, and/or creatively "different" varies by each individual, but when one is cognitively advanced and very perceptive and introspective, this realization often occurs rather early. Since the age of 4 or 5, I began to know what it is like to be gifted *and* Black. As an early adolescent in middle school (then called junior high school), I learned what it is like to be gifted *and* Black *and* female. While attending an expensive, elite, private, extensively White high school for girls (upon receiving an academic scholarship), I further learned what it is like to be gifted *and* Black *and* female *and* low income. At that time and even later in college and social settings, these four realities frequently collided, seldom blending into a harmonious whole. As I have poured my soul out elsewhere in the preface of *Reversing Underachievement Among Gifted Black Students* (2011), I am (erroneously) frequently viewed as an anomaly—too smart and ambitious to be Black, too independent and assertive to be a female, and too optimistic and efficacious to be poor!

As a mother, grandmother, aunt, educational psychologist, and counselor, I found the personal entries in this book to be authentic, as well as gut-wrenching and all too real. Reading these entries took me down memory lane—I recalled my experiences as a gifted Black student and adult and *read with my heart* to empathize with others. I frowned and smiled, I cried and laughed, I cringed and rejoiced, and I prayed for change!

In three concise, powerful words captured in the book's title, Grantham, Trotman Scott, Harmon, and the many contributors have captured the spirit of the complex and varied experiences—and voices—of gifted and talented Blacks from all walks of life who are and indeed can be *young, triumphant,* and *Black.* For far too long, their voices and stories have been silenced, untold, ignored, and discounted by educators and decision makers.

This qualitative work, which captures the experiences and shares the voices of real people, is priceless and unique! Less than a handful of books share the voices and lived experiences of gifted Black students and adults. *Nowhere* will readers find such a comprehensive qualitative collection on gifted Black students and adults than in this compilation. Age, gender, income, educational level, geographic region, and special education needs are addressed in multiple ways.

Several concerns and needed changes come to mind when I reflect on these heartfelt autobiographical accounts and biographical stories of gifted Blacks, most of whom are resilient and most of whom are succeeding despite roadblocks and gatekeepers: (a) the power of deficit thinking (low and negative expectations) primarily from educators, but also from families, friends, and classmates; (b) the tragedies associated with biased and unfair measures, especially tests; (c) the biases and inequities of subjective educator nomination forms and checklists; (d) the inequities of colorblind/culture-blind policies and procedures, especially when underrepresentation is obvious, pervasive, and long-term; and (e) the discriminatory outcomes of social capital and White privilege rarely experienced by racially, culturally, and economically marginalized groups, who then find themselves lacking the capital and power to take advantage of benefits set aside for the status quo.

Many of the stories in this book—from childhood to adulthood—enlighten and remind us that education is not yet (but can and ought to be) the *greatest* equalizer per Horace Mann. These real stories and voices also remind us that families, friends, mentors, role models, and communities gravely matter. As advocates and proponents, they promote and increase resilience—surviving and thriving—so that gifted Blacks of all ages and backgrounds can be triumphant.

The collection of voices reminds us that underrepresentation among Blacks is stubborn, pervasive, and entrenched. They also encourage readers to believe that change is possible. As of 2009, Black students are underrepresented in gifted education classes by almost 50%—this totals some 500,000 Black students in public schools who have been denied their right to an appropriate, equitable, and biased-free general education, gifted education, and special education. And, sadly, the numbers increase when Advanced Placement, Honors, International Baccalaureate, and higher education enrollments are added. Clearly, a mind is a terrible thing to waste *and* erase.

The Black students and adults in this compilation rightfully complain and vent, and then offer suggestions for change, either directly or indirectly. For indirect instances, this is where reading with one's heart matters. Confusion, frustration, and pain, followed by their internal resolve and strategies to be triumphant promise to inform educators and families of what is necessary to improve the outcomes for Black students who are gifted, even if not formally or officially identified as such. These chapters on gifted Black students and young adults clearly cannot speak on behalf of all Blacks, but I found their stories to be quite representative. In one source, rarely will one learn about gifted Blacks who have special education needs, who inform us that gender differences matters, who remind us that family structure matters, who remind us that context is important. Differences aside, the coeditors have done a superb job of demonstrating the resilience of Blacks, more of whom can be triumphant. When they are, we will all be victorious.

Donna Y. Ford, Ph.D.
Professor of Education and
Human Development
Vanderbilt University

ABOUT THE EDITORS

Tarek C. Grantham, Ph.D., is an associate professor in the Department of Educational Psychology at the University of Georgia. He teaches in the educational psychology degree program, primarily in the diversity and equity strand in the gifted and creative education emphasis area. He has developed and taught courses to address recruitment and retention of underrepresented groups, such as Multicultural Gifted and Talented Education, Retention of Ethnic Minorities in Advanced Programs, Gifted and Advanced Black Students in School, Creativity and Equity, and Action Research. He has served as Program Coordinator for the GCE on-campus and online graduate programs. Dr. Grantham's research addresses the problem of underrepresentation among minority students, particularly Black males, in advanced programs. He guest edited a special issue for *Roeper Review* entitled "Underrepresentation Among Ethnically Diverse Students in Gifted Education," and he coedited *Gifted and Advanced Black Students in School: An Anthology of Critical Works.*

Dr. Grantham has consulted with university programs, schools, community groups, and parents on issues of underrepresentation and underachievement among culturally different students enrolled in advanced programs. Dr. Grantham has served as a board member on the Education Commission and on the Diversity and Equity Committee for the National Association for Gifted Children. He was elected as a board member for the Council for Exceptional Children, Talented and Gifted Division, and he co-chairs its Parent, Community, and Diversity Committee. He is a member of the American Education Research Association and has served as a conference program coordinator for the Social Contexts in Education Division. Dr. Grantham has served on the editorial review boards of top-tier educational journals such as *Gifted Child Quarterly, Exceptional Children, Journal of Negro Education,* and *Urban Education.* He has been awarded the 2012 Mary M. Frasier Excellence and Equity Award by the Georgia Association for Gifted Children for outstanding achievement in practices that promote equitable identification procedures and/or provision of high-quality services to gifted students from underrepresented groups. He is the fortunate husband of a wonderful wife, Dr. Kimberly D. Grantham, and the proud father of three children: Kurali, Copeland, and Jovi.

Michelle Frazier Trotman Scott, Ph.D., is an assistant professor at the University of West Georgia. She teaches in the area of special education within the Department of Clinical and Professional Studies. Michelle earned her doctorate degree in Applied Behavior Analysis with an emphasis on special, gifted, and urban education and her master's degree and bachelor's degree in education from The Ohio State University.

Dr. Frazier Trotman Scott's research interests include the achievement gap, special education overrepresentation, gifted education underrepresentation, creating culturally responsive classrooms, and increasing family involvement. She has conducted professional development workshops for urban school districts and has been invited to community dialogues with regard to educational practices and reform. Michelle has written and coauthored several articles and has made numerous presentations at professional conferences. She is the coeditor of the book *Gifted and Advanced Black Students in School: An Anthology of Critical Works.*

Michelle has reviewed for journals in several disciplines and is a member of multiple professional organizations. Michelle is married and is the mother of three daughters.

Deborah A. Harmon, Ph.D., is a professor of curriculum and instruction in the Department of Teacher Education at Eastern Michigan University. She is also Coordinator, Urban Education, Office of Urban, Community, and International Outreach in the College of Education at Eastern Michigan University. Dr. Harmon earned her doctoral degree in educational leadership and human resource development (1999) with a specialization in multicultural education, urban education, and gifted education and a bachelor's degree in psychology and child development (1975) from the University of Colorado. She is creator of the Minority Achievement, Retention and Success (MARS) program model and the Developing Resiliency and Education Achievement in Minority Students program. Dr. Harmon conducts research primarily in multicultural/urban education and gifted education. Specifically, her work focuses on: (a) recruiting and retaining culturally diverse students in gifted education and teacher education; (b) multicultural and urban education; (c) reducing the achievement gap; and (d) teacher preparation for urban education. She consults with school districts and educational and legal organizations in the areas of multicultural/urban education, reducing the achievement gap, and gifted education.

Dr. Harmon has authored and coauthored chapters and books including *Elementary Education: A Reference Book*, "The Underachievement of African American Males in K–12 Education" in *The State of African American Males in Michigan: A Courageous Conversation Monograph*, and "The Underachievement of African American Females in K–12 Education" in *Nurturing Our Future as African American Females: A Courageous Conversation*.

ABOUT THE AUTHORS

Shawn Adams serves as founder and lead pastor for Connection Point Church, a church plant in Atlanta, GA. He has served in both private and public K–12 education for more than 12 years and is presently the Vice-President for Student Life and Enrollment Management at Beulah Heights University in Atlanta. Shawn's educational background includes a bachelor's degree in business administration from The University of Texas at Austin and a master's degree from Oral Roberts University. He is currently completing his doctoral degree at Liberty University in Lynchburg, VA.

Fred A. Bonner II is Professor and the Samuel DeWitt Proctor Endowed Chair in Education at the Graduate School of Education at Rutgers University. Dr. Bonner's work has been featured both nationally and internationally; he has been the recipient of numerous awards, including the 2010 Extraordinary Service Award from the Texas A&M University College of Education and Human Development, and the 2010 Faculty Member of the Year, Texas A&M University Student Affairs Administration in Higher Education (SAAHE) Cohort. He has been elected to membership of several National Honor Societies and serves in different editorial capacities for top-tier journals.

Patrice S. Bounds is a doctoral candidate in the Counselor Education and Supervision program at The University of Iowa. She is an adjunct professor in the psychology department at Chicago State University and counselor education department at Argosy University, Chicago.

Eric M. Bridges is a graduate of The University of Georgia's educational psychology program with a specialization in gifted education. He was a student of Dr. Mary M. Frasier, who was an example of excellence and humanity. His research interests include liberation psychology, multicultural gifted education, and the healing connections between indigenous spirituality and psychology. Eric is associate professor of psychology at Clayton State University in Morrow, GA.

A graduate of Clark Atlanta University and The University of Alabama, **Samantha Elliott Briggs, Ph.D.**, has nearly 20 years experience in social justice education, sociology, and women's studies. A former elementary school teacher, Dr. Briggs currently works as an educational consultant and adjunct professor in Birmingham, AL. She also conducts program evaluations and is a curriculum writer with her own company, PEACE Consulting: Providing Equal Access to Children in Education. Dr. Briggs can be reached at sbriggs@consultingpeace.com.

Karen Harris Brown, Ph.D., CCC-SLP, is an associate professor at the University of West Georgia. Her current research interests center on professional efficacy and assessment practices when assessing the communication skills of K–12 students who are English language learners. Dr. Brown holds an ESOL endorsement and degrees in the fields of special education and speech-language pathology. A licensed and certified speech-language pathologist with 20 years of experience, Dr. Brown continues to work with individuals across the lifespan in a variety of school-based and clinical settings.

Dr. Rhonda M. Bryant is an associate professor in the Department of Counseling and Educational Leadership at Albany State University. She earned a Ph.D. in counselor education from the University of Virginia and has been a counselor educator for more than 10 years.

Dr. David A. Byrd is the Assistant Dean for Undergraduate Academic Affairs in the College of Education and Human Development at Texas A&M University. His research has included the transition issues faced by underrepresented community college transfers at predominantly White universities and providing a pathway for student athletes to enter the teaching profession. He has published in the *Journal of Negro Education* as well as other peer-reviewed scholarly publications. Dr. Byrd completed his Ph.D. in higher education administration from Texas A&M University and has taught courses in multicultural education and in professional leadership studies.

J. Sean Callahan is currently an assistant professor of psychology at Georgia Highlands College in Marietta, GA. His research explores student engagement in hip-hop culture and how it is used to navigate the social, cultural, political, and historical conditions impacting schools and communities.

Dr. Callahan's work contributes to educators' and parents' understanding of the educational value associated with practicing hip-hop.

Kristina Henry Collins is a doctoral student and instructor of record in the Department of Educational Psychology at The University of Georgia, where she also received her education specialist degree in educational psychology, specializing in gifted and creative education. She holds a bachelor's degree in electrical engineering technology from The University of Alabama and a master's degree in mathematics from Jacksonville State University with more than 18 years of educational teaching and leadership experience. She is currently the Executive Director and president of East Metro Alliance for Gifted Education (EMAGE), a regional affiliate of the Georgia Association for Gifted Children. Her research interests include fostering STEM identities in culturally diverse gifted students. Kristina is married to Maj. Tony Collins (USAFR) with two sons, Tony II and Ty.

Joseph N. Cooper is currently a Ph.D. candidate at The University of Georgia in the kinesiology department (Sport Management and Policy program) where he studies under Dr. Billy Hawkins. His research interests include sport, race, and education. His dissertation focuses on examining the impact of the institutional culture at a historically Black college or university on the college experiences of Black male student athletes.

Dawn L. Curry taught for 12 years in both private and public elementary schools. She has earned a master's degree in education with a specialization in reading and literacy. Ms. Curry is currently a doctoral student in the elementary education department at The University of Georgia. Her research focuses on gifted African American students and parental engagement. She is married to William and has three children, Timothy, Gabrielle, and Jacob.

Asabi A. Dean is a doctoral candidate in the Counselor Education and Supervision program at The University of Iowa. She is a single mom to an African American adolescent male who has been identified as gifted. Other research interests of hers include, but are not limited to, mental trauma, bullying in higher education, urban youth, and counselor training. Upon completion of her doctoral degree, Asabi plans to practice, teach, and conduct research at a university in the Midwest or East Coast area.

Jessica T. DeCuir-Gunby is an associate professor and program coordinator of educational psychology in the Department of Curriculum, Instruction, & Counselor Education at North Carolina State University in Raleigh, NC. Dr. DeCuir-Gunby earned her bachelor's degree with a double major in psychology and Spanish from Louisiana State University in 1998. She earned both her master's and doctoral degrees in educational psychology at The University of Georgia in 2000 and 2003, respectively. Her research and theoretical interests include race and racial identity development, critical race theory, mixed methods research, and emotions in education.

Cheryl Fields-Smith is currently serving as an associate professor in the Department of Elementary and Social Studies Education at The University of Georgia. She completed her doctorate in 2004 at Emory University under the direction of Dr. Vanessa Siddle Walker. Her research has focused primarily on family engagement of African American parents. Today Dr. Fields-Smith documents the phenomena of homeschooling among Black families.

An academic specialist for Macon County Public Schools in Tuskegee, AL, **Erinn Fears Floyd** has more than 19 years of combined experience as a K–12 gifted educator in rural school systems in Southeast Alabama. She has also served as a school improvement specialist and literacy coach, conducting training for teachers and other school personnel to improve students' academic achievement. As a gifted specialist, she has created and provided gifted programming for gifted students and trained teachers in the identification of gifted African American students. Dr. Floyd earned her Ph.D. from The University of Georgia. Her research interests include gifted African American students, diversity training for educators, and rural gifted education. Dr. Floyd is married to Christopher, and they have two children, Christopher, II (6), and Chloe (2).

Sonja L. Fox is a doctoral student studying gifted and creative education at The University of Georgia and for 27 years has taught K–8 students in regular and gifted instructional settings. She is currently a gifted program teacher in Duluth, GA. Ms. Fox received a bachelor's degree in liberal arts-history, from The University of Texas at Austin and a master's degree in educational administration and policy and a specialist degree in technology integration from The University of Georgia. Ms. Fox is committed to providing equitable learning and assessment opportunities and seamless integration of technology for high-potential culturally and linguistically disadvantaged students.

SaDohl K. Goldsmith earned her master's degree in counseling from Clark-Atlanta University and her doctorate in counselor education and supervision from The University of Iowa. She has worked in school, clinical, and community settings with multiple populations including adolescents, adult addicts, and geriatrics.

Ain A. Grooms is a doctoral candidate in the Educational Administration and Policy program at The University of Georgia. Her research interests include desegregation and integration, school choice, the achievement gap, and educational equity and adequacy. Ms. Grooms has worked extensively with high school students on issues related to the college admissions process and leadership development, and has also served as a founding administrator of a college preparatory charter high school in Boston.

Bantu D. Gross is currently a doctoral student in the recreation and leisure studies department at The University of Georgia. Bantu's research interests include resiliency in adolescents, leisure preferences, and the "acting White" phenomenon amongst African American youth. Bantu has obtained a master's degree in psychological counseling from Nicholls State University and a bachelor's degree in psychology from Southern University of Baton Rouge. While pursuing his master's degree Bantu began working as a child and adolescent counselor and leading substance abuse groups for at-risk African American adolescents.

Kiesa Ayana Harmon was identified as twice-exceptional in elementary school. She received services for twice-exceptionality throughout elementary and middle school and then moved to a state that did not offer gifted education programming. In high school, Kiesa took some AP courses. After graduating from college with a degree in event planning, she went back to school to become a radiology technician.

Shani Harmon received her bachelor's degree from Yale College and master's degree from Yale School of Forestry and Environmental Studies. She currently works in environmental policy for the federal government. She is also obtaining a law degree, with a focus on environmental law.

Billy Hawkins is a professor at The University of Georgia in the Department of Kinesiology where his teaching and research contributions are in the areas of sociology of sport and cultural studies, sport management, and sport for development. His recent book, *The New Plantation: Black Athletes, College Sports, and Predominantly White NCAA Institutions*, examines the role of Black male athletes as athletic laborers for these institutions. He is also coauthor of *Sport, Race, Activism, and Social Change: The Impact of Dr. Harry Edwards' Scholarship and Service*. He received his Ph.D. from The University of Iowa in sport and cultural studies, a master's degree in human performance from the University of Wisconsin at LaCrosse, and a bachelor's degree in business administration from Webber International University.

For the past 6 years, **Sabreen U. Jai, Ph.D.**, has served as the reading specialist at an elementary school in an Atlanta suburb. The school has recently received Title I designation. Her research interests focus on the persistence of the achievement gap, particularly the consistent and questionable postulation of the literacy incompetence of Black males. She is currently conducting action research with the goal of publicizing culturally responsive pedagogy by culturally represented participants both as students and teachers. She is the mother of five beautiful daughters, three very smart and industrious sons, and 16 precocious grandchildren.

Christopher Oliver Johnson is a doctoral student in the Educational Psychology Department at The University of Georgia. His research interests are motivation, racial identity, and gifted Black males. After he finishes his degree, he plans to become a professor, conducting research and teaching on diversity and equity issues.

Jaimon Jones is a doctoral student at The University of Georgia in the Gifted and Creative Education Program within the Department of Educational Psychology. His research focuses on diversity and equity through multicultural social studies curriculum for advanced learners. He also strives for equity in gifted education by serving on his school's gifted team, which identifies and services gifted and talented students.

Toni Jones is a professor and graduate coordinator in the Educational Media and Technology program area of the Department of Teacher Education at Eastern Michigan University. She has served as a member of the board of examiners for NCATE (soon to be CAEP) since 2003, and is a former ISTE board of director. Dr. Jones received her Ph.D. in instructional technology from Wayne State University and has a master's degree in instructional technology and a bachelor's degree in business education–secondary. Her research interests are in the effects of technology integration and professional development to support teaching, student learning, and parental involvement. She can be reached at tjones1@emich.edu.

Through internships, postdoctoral training, and independent private practice, **Samuel J. Maddox** has extensive experience working with families of children with a variety of developmental, behavioral, emotional, and academic difficulties. Dr. Maddox also provides school- and community-based services through consultation and program evaluation to promote positive growth in the individual and society as whole.

Renae D. Mayes is a doctoral candidate in the College of Education and Human Ecology at The Ohio State University. She is also a Gates Millennium Scholar and a Todd Anthony Bell Fellow. Her research interests include African American males, gifted and special education, and multicultural competence in K–12 schools.

James L. Moore III is a professor in the College of Education and Human Ecology at The Ohio State University. He is also an associate provost in the Office of Diversity and Inclusion, where he serves as the director of the Todd Anthony Bell National Resource Center on the African American Male. He has published nearly 90 publications, obtained nearly $7 million in grants and contracts, and given more than 150 scholarly presentations and lectured throughout the United States and other parts of the world.

Candice Norris-Brown is a professional school counselor in the DeKalb County School System in Georgia. Dr. Norris-Brown has 16 years of experience as a counselor and educator. She is a licensed professional counselor and nationally certified counselor.

Beryl Ann Otumfuor is a doctoral candidate in educational psychology at The University of Georgia. She received her master's degree in research, evaluation, measurement, and statistics from UGA. Her research interests are in spatial ability, mathematical knowledge, and underachievement among gifted minority students.

Delila Owens is an associate professor at Indiana Wesleyan University (IWU). Prior to joining IWU, she was an assistant professor and program coordinator for school counseling at Wayne State University in Detroit, MI. Her research interests and expertise include urban education, school and multicultural counseling and emotional/social development of Black girls/women.

Born in the Caribbean and raised as a Carribean-American, **Angie C. Roberts-Dixon, Ph.D.**, has had an ongoing in interest and commitment to the education of minority students for more than 20 years. She has worked with youth across the United States, from New York City to Walla Walla, WA. Dr. Roberts-Dixon has also examined issues of diversity in countries such as Guyana, Kenya, and Thailand. She believes that the key to having students embrace a multicultural perspective involves creating centers of learning where they can interact, form friendships, and grow through discovery.

Dwan V. Robinson is an assistant professor in the Patton College of Education at Ohio University. She is in the Department of Educational Studies in the Educational Administration program. Dr. Robinson earned her bachelor's degree from Oberlin College in government, her master's degree in public policy from the University of Chicago, and her Ph.D. from The Ohio State University in educational policy and leadership. Her research interests include school, family and community collaboration, educational opportunities for marginalized groups, and social justice in education.

Petra A. Robinson is a research associate in the Graduate School of Education at Rutgers University. She received a bachelor's degree and master's degree from Nova Southeastern University and completed her Ph.D. in educational administration and human resource development from Texas A&M University. Her research focuses on issues of race, class, color and gender, international adult learning and development, and on social justice in education across institutional contexts development. She can be reached by e-mail at petra.robinson@gse.rutgers.edu.

Valija C. Rose is an assistant professor of educational leadership and policy studies in the School of Education at Virginia Tech, where she teaches courses in quantitative research methods and educational policy. Her research focuses on Black students' access to educational opportunities, including honors and Advanced Placement courses and gifted programs.

Cherranda Smith was born in Stamford, CT, and raised in Georgia. She is a licensed minister and attends Duke University, where she is currently a sophomore. Cherranda plans on obtaining a Ph.D. in psychology and attending divinity school.

Jocelyn D. Taliaferro is associate professor and director of the graduate program in the Department of Social Work at North Carolina State University. Dr. Taliaferro earned her bachelor's degree in psychology with minors in African American studies and English from the University of Delaware and her master's degree from Howard University in Washington, DC. She returned to the University of Delaware to earn her Ph.D. in urban affairs and public policy. Dr. Taliaferro's teaching and research interests include African American student achievement, social policy, and lobbying and advocacy for operational citizenship.

Ursula Thomas is an assistant professor of early childhood education and Birth Through Age Five Program Coordinator at the University of West Georgia. Her research agenda includes issues of cultural mediation and its effects on instructional choices, the power of teacher educator research on diversity in the classroom, views of social justice in the early childhood classroom, and preservice teachers' disposition on professionalism and diversity in teacher preparation programs. Dr. Thomas can be contacted at uthomas@ westga.edu.

Robin Vann Lynch has worked in the field of teacher education since 2000 and currently serves as an affiliate faculty member with Drexel University's School of Education. She teaches campus-based and online courses in social and cultural foundations, diversity education, curriculum design, research and evaluation and assessment. As the principal consultant for RVL & Associates, Dr. Vann Lynch designs and facilitates professional development seminars and workshops on parent engagement, cultural proficiency, diversity and inclusion, and reflective teaching practices for classroom teachers and school administrators in both urban and suburban school settings. Her published work has appeared in *Educational Studies*, *Action in Teacher Education*; *The Journal of Reading Education*, and several edited volumes.

Gilman W. Whiting is an associate professor of African American and Diaspora Studies, creator of the Scholar Identity Model™; and chair of the Peabody Professional Institute's Achievement Gap Institute. Dr. Whiting has authored more than 40 articles and teaches courses at Vanderbilt University, Nashville, TN, on Black issues in education; Black masculinity; race, sport, and American culture; Blacks in the military; and research methods. His areas of interest and research include efficacy and motivation of underachieving students; developing scholar identities; educational equity; young Black fathers; health, fitness, and nutrition in the Black community; and special needs populations. Dr. Whiting consults with school districts nationally and internationally on various issues related to psychosocial behavior and motivation among students.

Sheneka M. Williams is an assistant professor in the College of Education at The University of Georgia. Her research focuses on education policy in general, and student assignment, school choice, and issues of equity and access specifically. Dr. Williams received her Ed.D. in educational leadership from Vanderbilt University's Peabody College of Education and Human Development in 2007.

CPSIA information can be obtained
at www.ICGtesting.com
Printed in the USA
LVHW06s2318010618
579354LV00004B/9/P